In Jewish Texas
a family memoir

In Jewish Texas
a family memoir

▶▶▶

by Stanley E. Ely

TEXAS CHRISTIAN UNIVERSITY PRESS • FORT WORTH

Library of Congress Cataloging - in - Publication Data

Ely, Stanley E.
     In Jewish Texas: A Family Memoir / by Stanley E. Ely.
     p.   cm.
     ISBN 0-87565-187-9 (alk. paper)
     1. Ely, Stanley E.   2. Jews – Texas – Dallas – Biography.   3. Gay men – Texas
     – Dallas – Biography.   4. Dallas (Tex.) – Biography.   5. New York (N.Y.) –
Biography. I. Title
     CT275.E425A3   1998
     976.4'2812063'092
     [B] – DC21   97-52961 CIP

Design/Margie Adkins Graphic Design

To those people who through their foibles, their affection
and rejection, provided the material for this story.

"There is nothing higher, or stronger, or sounder, or more useful afterwards in life, than some good memory from childhood, from the parental home. You hear a lot said about your education, yet some such beautiful, sacred memory, preserved from childhood, is perhaps the best education. If a man stores up many such memories to take into life, then he is saved for his whole life. And even if only one good memory remains with us in our hearts, that alone may serve some day for our salvation."

Alexei Karamazov, *The Brothers Karamazov*
Dostoevsky

▶▶▶

"This is earth, not heaven."

Despina, *Così fan tutte*
Mozart

Contents

Acknowledgments

After the hundredth person came forth with a doubt-filled squint and said, "You mean you're Jewish, and you're from Texas?" I realized it was time to more than smile "yes." Here's the outcome.

Many people have encouraged and aided me in this task. Charles Salzberg was my teacher at Writers Voice, the writing school attached to the West Side YMCA in Manhattan; he gave me not only a needed push but continuing and invaluable advice, and I thank him the most. Other writer and agent friends helped guide me through the choppy sea of publishing a first book. They include Matt Sartwell, William Novak, Felice Picano, Barney Karpfinger, and Susan Davis.

Tom Wilkinson, my sole non-Jewish Texas friend, labored through several versions of the text and offered plenty of encouragement and sound suggestions. My other old Dallas friend, Stanley Angrist, also read and helped correct part of the book. His wife Shirley discovered letters I had written to them forty years ago. Dallas friends and family appear frequently in these pages, but in a few cases the names of characters have been changed.

Thanks to my cousin Ann White, early days in Texas were opened up for me. My brother Jerome's friend, David Zesmer, provided helpful information on the parts relating to the two of them. A careful reading of early versions of the book came from my friend Dru Sherrod, of Pasadena.

Family members Paula Manaly, Elissa Ely, Marcia Ely and Arden Reed lent patient ears as I waded through this project. So did other valued friends who helped in various ways: Marilyn Ely Lieberman, Pauline Graivier, Rob

Copeland, Paul Thomas, Herb Reis, Bill Coffey, Murray Friedman, Arch Garland, Jeanette Doronzo, Bill Crawford, and Phyllis Goldman.

Without my mother's Houston friend, Rose Keeper, many small moments in my mother's early days would have been lost. Rose, by saving so many of my mother's letters, greatly enriched this book.

"Letters from Little Becky" was published in an earlier form in *Good Old Days* magazine. "Florence—A Near and Distant Loss" was published in an earlier form in *Christopher Street* magazine.

I guess that few Christian university presses would consider bringing out a book with both a Jewish and a gay theme. It was my luck to find one at TCU. Many thanks go to them, and especially to Judy Alter, their director and my editor.

To all these people, I'm grateful.

Stanley Ely
New York, New York
December 1997

Introduction

Back to Texas

"We're beginning our descent into D-FW," the pilot advises, "and the weather in Dallas is seventy-eight and severely sunny."

Traversing the skies from New York City, my six-foot frame has been confined to the side of a lady of pronounced dimensions, in the near-250-pound range. "Aah jus dun know how a fat person would eeever fit into one of these tiny chayurs!" announced the woman as she shimmied into the aisle seat. She settled in, I smiled and was sent hugging the window. Now, three-and-a-half hours later, debarking into a severely sunny Texas day sounds very nice.

I know what to expect: bluebonnets growing wild and lush along the sides of the road, bringing back that familiar refrain: "Beautiful, beautiful Texas, where the beautiful bluebonnets grow." Bumper stickers that caution enigmatically, "Don't Mess With Texas." Markers on the interstate that permit a return to sixty-five miles an hour travel sooner than any other state. Azaleas planted by the hedge instead of by the bush. A high-school stadium the size of that in many colleges, without an empty seat for most any Friday-night football game.

For me, it's a visit from my adopted state back to my birthplace, the land where almost a century ago, my mother's family, the Shapiros, emigrated from Russia, and my father's family, the Elys (more likely, Elyavitchs) arrived from Romania. They were two families who avoided Ellis Island and New York, the traditional destination for European Jews. Instead, they both headed to Houston, for a welcome from cousins already transplanted from the old country.

Years later, Jerome, my older brother, moved from Texas to Connecticut; my older sister, Florence, to Colorado. They both married and had children. I remained the unmarried, gay son, but soon followed their lead of breaking away from the South.

But not my parents. They gave no thought to deserting their new home. With the family name shortened, they built a Jewish nest, planting Texas roots, letting them spread.

Until I was seventeen, finished with high school and a year at Southern Methodist University, I was a full-time Texan, too. That makes more than forty years since I relocated north. Even so, when I return as I do this spring, I find myself telling friends that I'm going "home" for Passover.

A major effort over those years has gone into losing the Texas drawl. But on the plane I'm reminded by my neighbor's accent that, when I return below the Mason-Dixon line, things are bound to go smoother if I also return to the language and manners of the South. As the lady slowly unleashes herself from the seat, I practice with a slight bow of the head and a wish for her to "Have a good day, mayum."

▶▶▶

Jewish Texans—more numerous than most non-Texas Jews realize—manage to create an unusual merger of the ambition and independence of Jews with the bravado of Texans. They build houses of worship and country clubs splashier than their northern Jewish cousins or southern gentile neighbors. They establish residences for their senior citizens that become models for the rest of the country—at the end of their lives, my mother and three aunts lived in the same one in Dallas. If they're Jewish girls and marry fellows from out of state, they often don't move to their husband's hometown. They bring the husband back to live "in the right place"—Texas.

My father, who had to cross nothing less than an ocean to become a Texan, demonstrated his ambition and independence by passing up a lucrative partnership with his brothers and going to work for himself. That self-determination never included leaving Texas, however. "Henry leaves New York to the New Yorkers," my mother stated often and accurately.

Or take Uncle Morris, Mother's baby brother, now in his late eighties. He showed his ambition and independent streak by marrying a wonderful but, shh, gentile lady and furthermore increasing his capital with long periods of gambling. Yet his devotion to Dallas sports teams and nature is total. Gleefully, he escorts me out to the small patio behind his apartment. "Look, Stanley," he says, "red roses—yellow roses! Roses in October! That's Texas for you."

Well, okay, that is Texas.

▶▶▶

Rebecca, my mother, was the eldest of five children, and she and her little sisters Fannie and Pearl Shapiro fled with their mother from Minsk around the turn of the century. They went to catch up with my grandfather, who was among the priestly set and therefore had neither experience nor fondness for work. He had already left for Houston to join the cousins Leon, regrettably much poorer than he thought and hoped.

All of them were escaping the pogroms of eastern Europe where Jewish children and adults were systematically accused of and punished for crimes committed by others. Aunt Fannie, who died in the spring of 1996 at around age ninety-seven (they were never sure of exactly when they were born), remembered looking out the window of her grandparents' house in Minsk when she was five, seeing Russian soldiers at night moving trucks loaded with bodies of Jews they had murdered.

▶▶▶

Mother died in 1987, a dozen years after the death of my father. Jerome died an early death at age thirty-eight, in 1963. And Florence passed away in 1992, just before her seventieth birthday. That has left me the sole living member of our immediate family and one of the few in an extended family. It has made the Shearith Israel Jewish Cemetery an important destination when I go to Dallas.

During that spring visit following the airplane ride with the southern-sounding lady, I made my usual long drive back to the old part of town to visit my dead folks. It's a place I like, shady and solitary, where I can amble among the graves of my family and those of parents of friend after friend I knew when

I was young. At the top of a marble tablet is the name of Solomon (Shlomo) Ely, my father's father, for whom I was named. Solomon is inscribed as a founder of a Romanian congregation that later merged with Shearith Israel and inaugurated that cemetery. He's buried there, alongside his wife Esther (Bubbe Ely), and not far from the Shapiros, my other grandparents, plus Aunt Pearl and Aunt Fannie's first and second husbands, Arthur and Dave, and, recently, Aunt Fannie, too. Plus my own parents. To imagine all those people being so neighborly is a stretch, much as it is to reach the Shearith Israel Cemetery, located in what for Jews was their first Texas neighborhood but is now an old and shunned part of town.

I still see those people as I meander around the grounds. My mother's card-playing "girlfriends," my father's "shyster" competitors in the insurance business—they're there, too, more silent than it seems as if they should be. Until I left Dallas, I had only one non-Jewish friend, Tom Wilkinson, but of Jews there were plenty, and most of those at whose homes we gathered are now laid to rest in those grounds. Mr. and Mrs. J. looked like immigrants and never lost their Old World accents, but they made a fortune and presented their daughter Emily with a convertible for high-school graduation. There's Mr. T., my friend Jean's dad, who everyone thought was Mafia. Parties at Jean's were the only times we could rely on access to a liquor cabinet.

The decades between then and now have seen me go away and finish college, survive a couple of mandatory years in the army, gravitate to New York, take jobs in advertising and then teaching, reach six feet and replace trying to add pounds with trying not to. They've seen me hesitantly reverse the roles I played the first couple of decades of my life, emerging less Jewish and more gay.

As a 1940s adolescent, then teen-ager, I was a dependable if unenthusiastic bar mitzvah and confirmation student and then a fervent attendee at a parade of Jewish sweet-sixteen dances. To the world—and somehow, helplessly, even to myself—I played straight, even as, in the privacy of my bedroom, I sneaked looks at the muscle magazines I had wrapped up and brought home.

But if for me there was no internal gay liberation, there wasn't much external either. The 1940s were the all-time decade of conformity, when a teen-ager in my school risked being junked if seen in anything other than white socks and penny loafers. Life went better if you not only spoke like a Texan but thought and presented yourself like one.

In the selection of a hero, there was no competition between a high-school journalist and a football player whose masculine stance (and presumed heterosexuality) was a given. A boy who differed from others either tried faking the standard mold or courageously suffered the jabs that came his way. I was of the former sort. In that old crowd there must have been one or two others with the same affinities as me, but since I can't think of who they might have been, I conclude that they were fakers as well.

It wasn't total fakery, however. I clung to that Jewish group as a necessary prelude to the long process of shedding my denial and coming out as a gay man, an evolution that barely started until I was in my mid-twenties, and went on for years thereafter. Those teen-age parties worked for me because there was dancing but no sex—and there was acceptance.

But the process of change is about complete. As I walk around the cemetery and see the stone marking the graves of Mr. & Mrs. J, I remember that, growing up, my friends and I called them the older folks, or, as it's unflatteringly said in Yiddish, the alte kahkers (old shitters). Now—an unwelcome revelation—a young person could say the same about me. I approach the cemetery knowing I must delay no longer to make peace.

Armed with flowers, I give a brief greeting to Aunt Pearl and Aunt Fannie, women I greatly loved. But at the graves of my mother and father, the central players in my life, I schedule a long stop. First, I deliver to them news of their grandchildren, the offspring of Florence and Jerome, and now a quartet of great grandchildren. (They've stopped expecting news of my children, resigned to the idea that I didn't contribute any.) That done, I relax and impart whatever rises to the surface: anger, love, apologies, or all those. I mostly seek—even vocally ask for—a release from the tangled continuing feelings of affection and regret that they, my parents, evoke.

That requires attention. Giving it my best, I look up momentarily and discover that there's company. With a full face stare from the branch of a live oak tree, a red-headed bird is intruding on my visit. What an orchestra seat on mortality that fellow has had! Imagine the number of funerals he has attended right here, the private moments he's witnessed uninvited, the laughs he's gotten out of folks like me who were babies of a family and who have come to try facing the fact that they ceased to be kids long since.

After an hour or so, I run dry on news and even anger for Mother and Dad. "Well, I'll be back again," I tell them, and decide I must go. I follow tradition and leave a pebble on their stone. Then, heading toward the gate, with throat still tight, I turn back and see that the winged creature isn't the least moved. He simply chirps, lifts off for a ten-second circular trip, settles back on his branch and does a carefree reprise of his song.

In the plot where my parents are buried, a couple of unused spaces remain. They belong to our family and now, I suppose, to me; my father paid for them decades ago. Regardless of my mixed feelings about family or all the years away, one of those spots is where I've decided I want to end up. I'm not sure why, since there's no temptation to call that state home again. Not now and not soon, if I can help it, but one day. Back in severely sunny Dallas, where I started. Back next to my folks and the handsome white marble stone that marks their place.

And back with that bird.

"So," I say, with a skeptical glance at the red-head resting in the tree, "so long for a while. You'll be seeing me again."

XX

Part One

Getting Settled

1

Royal Flushes, Seven No-Trumps and a Lazy Father

If it had gotten to be ten or eleven at night and my grandmother wasn't home, my mother, still a teen-ager, would step in. "Mrs. Rabinowitz," she would plead on the phone, "it's eleven o'clock! It's time for Mama to be home. She's been up since six this morning!"

"Leave your mother alone, Becky," came Mrs. Rabinowitz's stern voice. "She's having a good time here. It's the only fun she gets. Anyway, she's winning, and we're not going to let her go away with so much money."

So my mother would have to shake her shoulders and wait until Grandma Lena returned home, not before midnight and not infrequently with a few dollars. Rarely, though, would the dollars add up to many, not from an evening's game of poker that she had played with other immigrant women in the second decade of this century in Dallas, Texas.

My grandmother and grandfather would never have signed on to the notion that card playing was fine only for the lower classes. I've heard of some Jewish people who thought so, but not the Shapiros. Not that they weren't part of the lower classes. But in those early days, cards offered the fastest distraction from the dulling poverty that enveloped Mother's family and their friends, all of whom just a few years before had gotten off boats from eastern Europe—setting foot on land in Galveston.

It was a good thing when Grandma did win at cards, because from his days in Russia Grandpa Max had no acquaintance with work. Why would he? He and all seven of his brothers were among the Jewish highborn whose duties were limited to studying the Talmud. He didn't see why that needed to change just because he had crossed an ocean into a new country. For the most part, it didn't.

My mother must have been right to worry about my grandmother's penchant for staying out late. Between that and housework, Grandma Lena wore herself out and died in January 1933 at age sixty-two, weeks after I was born. My Aunt Fannie, who was then thirty and recently died at past ninety-five, slept at the foot of her mother's bed until Grandma passed away.

Grandpa Max, a short man with glasses, little hair and a great fondness for pretty girls, lived on another six years after his wife. One day in October 1938, when I was six, I came in the house and my mother and her sisters were crowded in our little living room dressed in black because Grandpa had died. But the color of those clothes was a ruse. His children were above all relieved no longer to need excuses not to give him the money they earned, money they feared he would squander at cards.

It's evidently something that runs in our family, this affinity for card playing. After inheriting it from her parents, my mother tried to pass it on to my father, but he was less skillful than she. I always suspected he felt inferior to the Shapiros' penchant for and success at gambling. Still, as I was growing up, my parents spent dozens of Saturday nights hosting the Goodsteins or the Friedlands, who came to our house for gin rummy and cake served around midnight.

▶▶▶

Aunts Fannie and Pearl were good players too, but neither as accomplished as Morris, the youngest of the Shapiros. Once he had survived three years of military service in Alaska during World War II, Uncle Morris turned his talent with a deck of cards into a profession. The passion for cards even was transmitted down to Florence and Jerome, my sister and brother. Jerome was a good bridge player, Florence a better one. She used to attend tournaments and return with prizes. The last trip she took, shortly before her seventieth birthday, was to a bridge tournament in Las Vegas. She insisted on making the journey even though she was then an invalid, suffering from cancer and a stroke, needing to be accompanied by two helpers. The trip ended for Florence with a fatal heart attack just after her husband picked her up at the airport and she was entering her house.

My mother didn't go to tournaments, but until she was in her mid-eighties she played a regular game of bridge or canasta with her "girlfriends," all aged seventy and beyond. Those events didn't even wait until afternoon; they would begin at ten-thirty or eleven in the morning, as soon as breakfast coffee cups had been put away, and beware the scowls that greeted the woman who arrived late.

On and off over the years, I'd venture into the room where Mother and her friends were at cards. The silence and cold looks always startled me. Where was the atmosphere of fun and relaxation that I thought was supposed to be present? Still, that seriousness paid off. For decades, Mother set aside her winnings at cards, and later she distributed them to her grandchildren, Florence's and Jerome's kids, to be used for college. They added up to low four figures.

And me? While I was in college, I tried my hand at bridge, but only because it was the thing that pretentious college boys did in the 1950s, along with smoking and wearing V-neck cashmere sweaters. I quit bridge before smoking, an injudicious choice dictated by the fact that I was proficient at smoking but mediocre to poor at bridge and the only one in my family who was. I never concentrated enough to be good at it, and never took the game seriously, and, as it was said, "We all know that you CANNOT play bridge that way, Stanley!" I pretended that I didn't care, but in truth, I think I shared my father's sense of inferiority to the Shapiros.

Feeling different enough from the rest of the family without also being the perpetual dummy, I resigned from card playing right after college. The exceptions were the times, years later, when my mother was widowed and old, and going out at night had become difficult for her. If I was on a visit to Dallas, we might play gin rummy for diversion. Somewhere around nine or ten o'clock, the hour didn't make any difference, my mother would say: "Hmm, Stanley, how about some gin tonight?"

"You're not tired?" I'd ask.

"Tired? What's to be tired?"

.

"Okay," I'd respond, "but you shouldn't stay up too late."

My mother grinned. "I used to say that about my mother."

"And she paid you no attention."

"That's right."

"Like you're paying me no attention."

"Hmm."

"You know what happened to your mother!"

"My mother died pretty young. I'm already past eighty."

I'd go to the closet to take out the game table, thinking that Mother's memory for which cards had been played and which hadn't—those essential portals to good bridge that I never managed to breach—was as sharp as forty years earlier. I wasn't excited over what was about to happen.

"And don't you purposely let me win!" she'd command, as she went to the kitchen for a bowl of fruit.

Given the history of our card games, I'd look at her chagrined. "What, are you kidding?"

2

They Came with Candlesticks from Russia

Yes, they got off the boat in Galveston, not Ellis Island. And they stayed. But tell a Yankee that you grew up in Texas—and Jewish—and watch the eyes narrow and the head bob up and down with a cynical glare. "No, you're not, you're surely kidding. Are there Jews in Texas?" It's a refrain that feels as old as Hatikvah.

The speakers, the most provincial of all? New York Jews, of course.

There's a good tally of Jews living in Texas. A couple of pages of Goldbergs and Siegels fill the Dallas and Houston phone books, though few can claim family residence back to the years when the state got tossed from under the governance of one nation to another, as we used to (had to) study in school. Temples and synagogues are plentiful, but they're new and memorable mainly for their size and cost. A few years ago, a friend of mine entered the opulent new Temple Emanu-El building in North Dallas. "It may take me a while to learn just to worship God in here," he said.

What Texas Jews had in common with their northern brothers is that they all arrived fleeing the denial of citizenship or the pogroms of eastern Europe around the end of the last century, at a time when they stood a good chance of being tortured or shot for crimes they didn't commit.

Why did Russian or Romanian or Polish Jews head for Texas? Because some cousin or great uncle was already settled there and had written to offer a bed and oatmeal. Why had *they* come? Because big eastern cities like New York were being overrun with Jewish immigrants, causing them to disperse over the

United States. Many got shipped by boat to Galveston, though it wasn't an ideal choice. With the damp weather and poor housing there and in Houston, immigrants became easy targets for fevers and tuberculosis.

Grandpa Max and Grandma Lena were living in Minsk with their daughters Becky (my mother), Fannie and Pearl at that time, the turn of the century. Grandma's parents owned a prosperous grain store, which she ran even as she was raising three young girls. Presumably, Grandpa was at the schul examining commentaries on the scriptures.

Cousins of Grandpa—the Leons—had emigrated to Houston. News started to reach Minsk that everyone in America got rich. That fit fine with Grandpa's idea of life, so he packed up and left, by himself, to join the Houston cousins in luxury and get ready for the arrival of his wife and daughters. The Leons, wouldn't you know it, turned out to be less rich than Grandpa expected—poor, to put it plainly—but he didn't know that until he got there. He soon wrote for Grandma to come.

Meanwhile, life for Jews in Russia grew more dangerous. Aunt Fannie, a beautiful auburn-haired woman who survived a perilous beginning plus a chancy adulthood, yet didn't begin to show signs of aging until she was past eighty, remembered:

"After Papa left for America, Mama and Becky and Pearl and I lived in the attic of Mama's family's house in Minsk. While Mama worked in the grain store, Becky and I would go there to help with little chores, or to play. I remember the strong smells from that place—oats and barley heaped into big drums, fresh wheat that got chopped up for baking. It was like all the earth gathered inside.

"One Friday Becky and I went to the store—Pearl was there, too, in her crib. I must have been about six, Becky was about eight. We were playing and Mama was working behind the counter when some other women, friends of hers, hurried in looking worried. They started what seemed like a serious conversation. Suddenly, the women rushed out and Mama looked at Becky and me and told us to run home. 'Go fast,' she said. 'Take the baby, lock the door when you get there, and stay inside!' Becky and I ran out, frightened, with Pearl in our arms. I could see others closing up their stores and rushing home, too. Men on horseback started to come up.

"When we got home we jumped up on the stove, a tremendous iron thing where we'd go to keep warm. It had a flat top, big enough for two or three of us, and we'd sometimes sleep up there if it got really cold. Mama closed the store even earlier than usual for the Sabbath and came in looking pale. She didn't say anything, but after supper when we thought she was asleep, Becky and I tiptoed to the little attic windows and got on our stomachs to look down. There were soldiers marching through those narrow streets. We could see a sort of big flat bottom truck, and they were piling sacks on to it and carting them away.

"I can hear the clicking of those soldiers' heels even now. Becky and I were so scared that we held on to each other. Later, we found out that the sacks held the bodies of Jews they'd murdered."

That day was probably in the year 1900, just as Grandpa was writing for Grandma to join him in America. Even without his letter, Grandma knew she must leave, and quickly. Within a few days she had hired someone to run her parents' store and gotten ready for a long trip. In a bag she packed a few pieces of sturdy clothing for her and her three daughters. Grandma must have learned the Talmudic lesson that dictates Sabbath candles be lit in twos, and that if economy dictates a choice be made between the lighting of the candles and saying the blessing over the wine, one must favor lighting the candles. Wrapped among the garments she hid a pair of tall silver candlesticks that would be the sole connection to the world they were leaving.

"The worst part of our going away," Aunt Fannie said, "was that Mama had to say goodbye to her mama and papa. They were too old to come with us. I remember my grandmother; she was a darling little lady who wore a wig parted in the middle. She and my grandfather cried and nearly crushed me and Becky and Pearl when they kissed us goodbye. Of course, neither Mama nor any of us ever saw them again."

Grandma Lena bribed a driver who took her and my mother and Aunt Fannie and Pearl out from Minsk in a wagon, not very different from the one my mother and aunt had seen through the windows. "I imagine Mama must have paid a lot of money," said my aunt. "We traveled a very long time, covered under a blanket. Once in a while I would look out and see a moon shining above, and snow on the ground. It was beautiful."

The four of them reached Poland, then Germany, where they embarked on a boat from Hamburg. "We were on the bottom deck for what seemed like forever," recalled Aunt Fannie. "'How much longer, Mama?' I would ask. 'Not much—a little while still,' she'd say. I can see baby Pearl licking a jar of jelly she had between her legs. We looked up at the people on the top decks; they were so beautifully dressed and it looked so nice. But we didn't care because we were heading to America.

"The boat stopped in New York, but we didn't get off. Weeks after we started—though it seemed like months—Papa greeted us in Galveston. I remember being so glad to see him, though that was mostly because we had been seasick the whole way over!

"A Rabbi Cohen came to the boat with Papa. He used to meet the ships and help Jewish people get adjusted. He brought us bananas, something I'd never seen before. We were examined to be sure we didn't have lice or anything and then vaccinated before we could get off the ship. I still have the marks from those vaccinations."

With that, the Shapiros turned the page into America—Texas, more specifically, setting foot into a life as different from the one they left as if they had descended onto a new planet.

As a youngster growing up in Dallas, I craved facts about that first part of my mother's youth, and I questioned her constantly. "Tell me about your house in Minsk," I asked as I sat in the kitchen, smelling the simmering chicken soup, watching Mother start to lay out dishes and silver for Friday night dinner.

She looked sharply the other way. "I don't remember," she snapped, ladling gravy over a roast.

"I'll help you with the tablecloth," I offered, and with great care, helped her spread out the Friday night white linen cloth. "What about the grain store that your grandparents had?"

"My grandparents?" Mother hesitated and momentarily put down the cloth, as if the memory was pushing itself through. But it never did. "Don't remember," emerged a firm reply.

Or I would try a different approach. "Tell me a word in Russian, any word in Russian."

No response. Only hurried setting of the dining table and rushing into the bedroom to change into a nice dress for the Sabbath meal.

Those unfinished dialogues left me hungry. Only Aunt Fannie recaptured fragments of the early years, and how much memory can you ask of someone at age six? Aunt Pearl had been too young, and my mother, though she was older, remembered nothing.

Not until after Mother was gone did I learn about the life of Jews in Russia at the end of the nineteenth century. They were restricted to living in what was called "The Pale of Settlement," a large area of eastern Poland and western Russia. The Shapiros were lucky; they at least were in a comfortable big city and not a poor shtetl (ghetto). Furthermore, Jewish children usually were not allowed to attend Russian public schools. If Jews were so cut off from non-Jews, it's likely that Mother never learned to speak Russian, since at home her family spoke Yiddish. But she never told me that. For all her lively memory at card playing, she must have forgotten what she had no wish to recall—perhaps not even remembering what she had and hadn't learned in those early years.

She was part of a majority in that. A good number of my friends' parents came from a start similar to my mother's, but I don't remember that any of my friends were instructed in Russian or Polish or told about their parents' early lives. Even Yiddish, the tongue so familiar to that generation, used for private messages between parents, went largely untaught to their children. Among my parents' immigrant friends, there seemed to be a collective drive to leave behind as much as possible, especially as they became more involved in Texas life.

For a long time I felt cheated that I knew so little—practically nothing, in fact—of where Mother had come from. All the greater chagrin since for no apparent reason I developed a special affinity for Russian music and theatre and literature.

Finally, I had an obvious conclusion to face: if I really wanted to know any of the language, I could go and study it myself. If finding out more about the Russia of those days was important enough, there were plenty of books in which I could delve into it.

▶▶▶

Aside from what must have been an early formed habit of finishing a meal with a piece of crusty bread, those delicate candlesticks that Grandma Lena packed and that my mother inherited remained the single piece of evidence that Mother had ever been in Russia. Under Jewish tradition, the privilege of reciting the blessings over candles is assigned to the wife, as she is considered the foundation of the home, the peace bringer. All her adult life, Grandma's candlesticks held the candles that Mother lit every holiday and Sabbath evening. After Mother died, the candlesticks were received with love by Jerome's older daughter Elissa, who uses them every Friday night.

For me, those lacy objects have their own significance. To this day, it's easy for me to see my mother standing over them, eyes closed, making the circular motion with her hands as year after year, no matter the external events, she lighted Friday night candles with a gentle smile and a look of serenity.

Then there's the link that the candlesticks offer to Mother's family's life in Russia. How I'd love to have seen them holding candles that were lit on Sabbaths in the house in Minsk when she was a six- or seven-year-old or to have been there to climb up on the belly of that big iron stove in winter, to inhale the fragrance of barley and wheat from the downstairs lockers in the Shapiros' old grain store.

Though the candlesticks survive and continue to be used as they have been for decades, that store is surely gone long ago, just as are my great grandparents, the people who owned it.

3

Letters from Little Becky

Next to card playing stood friendships as the salvation for poor Jewish immigrants. They cost nothing but effort, and if you were lucky, you hit on someone who helped cushion your pathway into the new world.

No one drew a better hand on that than my mother. At ten, while still living in Houston, she met Rose Bumar, a Jewish girl of her age. Rose was of serious demeanor, with an intellectual bent and a plain but happy appearance. Neither Mother nor Rose was flighty; both felt a bit apart from the lifestyles of their peers, distanced at times even from their own families. With so much in common, they linked together in friendship.

My mother and Rose would have remained schoolmates, but Grandpa Max, disillusioned that Houston streets were paved with mere concrete and hearing an offer of help from another cousin in finding a job, withdrew his family and moved them north to Kansas City. Cooler air offered no antidote to laziness, and Kansas City proved as unprofitable as Houston. After a couple of years, Grandpa brought his wife and kids back to Texas, this time to Dallas. Mother and Rose Bumar started to write to each other, and without telling my mother, Rose began saving the letters Mother sent her.

In 1918, Rose married Joe Keeper, a jolly, slender, bespectacled accountant. They had a daughter, then two sons, and they remained in Houston. The fact that Mother moved away barely affected her friendship with Rose, which was carried along the rest of my mother's life by occasional visits to Houston but mostly by correspondence. If I saw Mother break into a broad smile when the mail arrived, I could be fairly certain that among the letters was an envelope with the strong, clear handwriting of her friend from Houston.

It was Rose who gave the most remarkable gift Mother ever got. Without telling her, Rose continued to store away the letters—many dozens of them—that Mother sent her over six decades. In 1983, Rose surprised her by sending them back all in one big bundle.

By then I was living in New York but happened to be on a visit in Dallas when the box arrived. I took it from the mailman and opened the package, postmarked from Houston. "Mother," I hollered, astonished, when envelopes with two- and three-cent stamps started to tumble out. "You will not believe what's here!"

"What's that?" she asked from another room.

"Letters," I replied. "Dozens and dozens of them."

"What letters?"

"Your letters—to Rose Keeper."

"I haven't written her in a long time."

"But you did in 1912!"

There was a strange pause and an amazed response. "1912?"

So many letters—the first ones in fading ink on thin paper, folded inside envelopes addressed to Rose's maiden name. "Let's read them," I urged, figuring they'd be a window back to those younger days my mother so liked to forget. "Don't you want to?"

Mother came into the room and looked at the collection of letters that covered the table. "Heavens!" she exclaimed. "She saved all these!"

My mother's sight by then was poor. "Well," she said, "if you want to, you read them. I'll listen."

We settled on the sofa in her den, and I began to read aloud letters that started when Mother had just returned to Texas from Kansas City, when she still signed her name, "Rebecca."

"Dear Rose," she wrote at age fifteen from Dallas. "Yesterday evening I had three roots of my teeth pulled. I dread a dentist worse than anything I know of. It makes me sick to know people are saying, 'If it wasn't for her teeth, she wouldn't be so bad looking.' I don't think anyone knows how miserable my teeth have made me."

A vain side of my mother that made me chuckle!

Work was the destiny in that era of young girls like my mother, but not every job was approved of. In 1913, when she was sixteen, Mother wrote that she was going to start the next week at the Southwest Telephone office as long distance operator. "I think the work will be interesting," she wrote, "only their wages are very low to begin with. The folks don't want me to remain long on account of the reputation the operators have."

The work didn't excuse Mother from duties at home. "It was still my job to make up the beds, sweep and dress the baby (Morris) in the mornings," she reports.

Mother adjusted to the telephone office and was proud of coming home alone on the streetcar late at night, after work. "I sometimes feel real brave to think I am not in the least bit afraid to be out so late, while some girls are afraid to leave the house after dark." But she adds, "I have very few real friends here. I don't think it's anyone's fault, for after all, most people don't have much use for telephone operators. Sometimes it amuses or hurts me to see how people look when they learn how late I stay out. I don't really care to know what all these dear people say behind my back."

"Our pay man has named me Smiley," she adds, "but that's because he only sees me on payday."

Teeth were one issue, Mother's height was another—something that she rued all her life. Being the eldest of her family, she apparently thought that she ought to also be the tallest. But she wasn't. "Everybody always outgrows me," she complains to Rose. "I keep hearing behind my back, 'Isn't she cute?' No wonder the word 'cute' gives me the creeps."

Love and its elusiveness are topics that fill many pages of the letters between Mother and Rose. "We are not the only girls who made mistakes," Mother declares. "All of them do sooner or later. No one can ever say they didn't do anything foolish in their youth."

I've always thought that a stream of Russian pessimism and darkness inhabited part of my mother's soul (as it does mine). At age seventeen, she tells

Rose that she hasn't met anyone whom she could call a man. "I'll be ashamed to confess how many times I have cried, quietly to myself—not for any boy especially, but many times for my dear girl friends . . . even for the boys, too. I've met such silly ones lately that I have been tempted to laugh in their faces."

"There are so few people in this world happy or contented," she adds. "And too much worrying isn't good for anyone, Rose. I love to watch the moon and the stars, though they often give me the blues." (It's true: many nights I saw Mother step outside on the porch to take a long, yearning look up at the sky.)

From the one-sided correspondence, I learned when Rose Bumar got engaged to Joe Keeper and how my mother fretted over her own chances. Marriage seemed to become less and less a likelihood. "I can't imagine myself mated," she tells Rose. "I don't think a single life will be very happy, but it's better than to marry the man that wasn't meant for that girl."

At age eighteen, of an unnamed male friend, she wrote, "Papa does not like him. You can't blame me for not caring what the public's opinion is—that, of course, means the Jewish people. Some might have been my 'friends' if I had money, swell clothes, and could devote my time to what they call their social affairs, but as I have none of those things I feel happier out of their company."

When I looked up from the letters, I could see her gently shaking her head, acknowledging that even then she enjoyed not caring what others thought. Brava!

In 1919 comes a profound change of mood. "I am the happiest and proudest girl there ever was," Mother exclaims, at age twenty-two. "For no other reason than that I am engaged to the dearest man. And, Rose, he has blond hair and blue eyes!" (It would have been superfluous to mention that he was Jewish.) "His hobby is hard study. He only comes to see me on Fridays and Sunday afternoon and evening. However, I don't feel slighted."

She didn't say that Henry, my future dad, was not silly like the others, but she could have. Our family album holds a copy of their engagement photo. In a large armchair, he sits stiffly in high collar and tie; she perches on the arm of the chair in a frock that must have cost a week's salary from the pay man. Dad appears stern, Mother looks meek in a way that fits her more as young letter writer than as the sturdy mother whom I, born twelve years later, ever knew her to be.

But that photo was later. Meanwhile, their engagement remained a secret. "It's almost killing me not to be able to wear my ring all the time," Mother writes to Rose. "I do wear it at night, when I'm sure no one is coming in to see us. It's hard for me to adjust my mind to these happenings. Last year I fully decided to be an old maid."

The album contains Mother's wedding portrait, from the year 1920. Anyone looking at that photo might sympathize with her plaintive cry about others outgrowing her. There Becky (née Rebecca) Shapiro, a tiny young woman, looks more like a girl playing wedding in a lacy wedding dress than a true bride.

It happened that my father's older brother, Sam, had already married, and also to a Becky, so with my parents' marriage there emerged two Becky Elys. My mother never surpassed five feet, but Aunt Becky was a regal lady of five foot eight, meticulously dressed, combed and made-up. Someone got the idea to call her "Big Becky" and my mother "Little Becky." The nicknames stuck, and forever after they were called by those names that unsurprisingly pleased only fifty percent of that duo.

It was nearly evening by the time I read even half the box of letters Rose had sent. I had the odd feeling that I enjoyed revisiting those days more than my mother did, since looking back was something she liked to avoid. The letters may not have thrown light on her life in Russia, but they didn't lack in surprises. What son imagines that his mother, then a widow of a fifty-five-year marriage, ever worried about being an old maid?

The letters were also the painting of a loving friendship. I realized how blessed was Mother to have found this person who in her eighties (and today past 100) wrote with a clear handwriting, called Mother on the phone, sounding like a young woman, read poetry in Yiddish, and managed to keep track of dozens of grand and great-grandchildren spread around all parts of the country. Not to mention, who guarded a friend's letters for six decades.

"You've had a beautiful friendship," I said.

Though I watched my mother shake her head in agreement, I could see that she looked tired. It must have been hard for her to comprehend how far back that friendship went, to realize how both she and Rose, grandmothers many times over, could ever have been so young.

She had grown uncharacteristically quiet. "So, what do you think?" I asked, finally, as darkness settled outside.

"I think," she said, "all that seems like a different lifetime."

4

On Forest Avenue They Loved Each Other but Not Grandpa

"Study without work leads to sin."
The Talmud

According to his children, the two most salient facts about Grandpa Max were his taste for young women and his distaste for work, both traits he seemed to share with his brothers.

Mother's cousin Ann, who knew Grandpa when she was a young girl, says that he wasn't alone in his affection for girls. "I ran when I saw any of them, Max or any one of his brothers," she says. "That could have been Max or Hyman or George, it didn't matter. They all had their hands out, ready to grab."

Cousin Ann, who had a couple of marriages and a good career in public relations when southern Jewish women didn't do either, took a dim view of the Shapiro brothers. "To them," she says, "wives were just there to keep house and earn a living. When Hyman was still in Russia, he served as tutor to two daughters of a wealthy engineer whose wife had died. There came a time when the engineer had to leave town, and he said to Hyman, 'Look, I can't leave you here with my two girls. You'll either have to quit or marry one of them.'

"'I'll marry one, then,' said Hyman.

"'Fine,' said the engineer. 'Which one do you want to marry?'

"'It doesn't matter,' Hyman responded. 'Either one.'"

Hearing that, it came as no surprise to learn that from Aunt Fannie's viewpoint, the worst thing about her papa, Grandpa Max, was that he liked women, "but he ignored Mama." "And she was such a pretty little lady," says my aunt, "someone who loved everybody. She'd read us the letters in Yiddish that came from her sisters who were still in Russia. 'You should live and be healthy,' they'd write. And then they'd list every one who should live and be healthy: Rivke (Becky), and Pearl, and me, and everyone. One by one, every one of us should live and be healthy! We laughed, we thought the letters were so funny. But Papa? He never laughed. Around us, he was sullen. He only smiled when he was away from his family.

"It was hard for me to understand how Mama and he had ever connected, and I once asked her. 'I was engaged to another man,' she said, 'but your papa came along and he just took charge of me. He was such a good dancer, and he was so good looking.'" (Even nearsighted, you'd find that photos of Grandpa show him to be an incontestably plain-looking man. If I were married to him, I'd go out in the evening to play cards, too. Though I might stop short of Grandma Lena's other passion, which was to accompany her women friends to the funerals of people they didn't know, just for a good cry.)

Aunt Fannie's analysis of her father politely omits the fact that, together with his brothers, he possessed a chronic disinclination toward earning a living. But it seems to me that it wasn't altogether his fault. The Torah stipulates that, to avoid formation of an intellectual aristocracy, Kohanim (priests) like Grandpa could own no property. Moses carried out the edict, and while Jews lived in the desert, the Kohanim were supported by taxes paid by others. These taxes continued even after the Jews settled in Israel.

So, maybe credit needs to be given to Grandpa Max for making at least a half-hearted effort to support his family. It seems that's all it was, though, especially to listen to his offspring. One day I came across a photo of Grandpa in his grocery store on Hall Street, looking quite responsible in shirt and tie, and I said to Aunt Rose, the youngest Shapiro daughter, "Look, how can you say that Grandpa never worked? Here he is, recorded forever, tending his own store on a nice street in Dallas."

"What you don't see," said Aunt Rose, in her sharp tone, "is that Papa was so nasty to his customers that if they once came in, they never came back.

'Don't touch that fruit!' he'd yell at them. 'Take your hand away!' Some businessman he was."

Aunt Rose's conclusion was that Grandpa claimed he had tried to run a business and proved he couldn't because the grocery store was a failure. Therefore, no one ought to expect him to provide for them. Which, probably out of exasperation, they finally didn't.

At that point, Grandpa was left to meeting with his synagogue buddies and at least intermittently concentrating on the Talmud. He practiced card playing, too, when he could get money from one of his children. When Aunt Fannie says that "he liked the women," she's saying (so I'm told) that his hand was known to periodically find itself under the skirts of young girls, not to exclude on occasion one of his own daughters.

But ask me about Grandpa, and you'll hear another tale. When I was three or four, while Mother was out playing bridge in the afternoon, Marietha, our nanny whom I adored, would take me over to Grandpa's house on Forest Avenue (credit for the purchase of which went, of course, to his wife and children). I'd put on the white boots that had been a present from him and that I longed without success not to outgrow. He and I would drink lemonade on the big front porch, where he'd put me on his knee and call me his little prince. Of his laziness and playing around I was ignorant.

That front porch was also where the Shapiros went to rock in a big swing and catch a breeze in the long Texas summers before air conditioning. Behind their house lay a big yard, populated with a live oak and a fig tree, one chicken and Frank, an unfriendly duck that, according to Aunt Fannie, used to follow Grandma around and bite anyone who tried to interrupt his travels. As for the trees, Texas live oaks reach such grandeur that they have streets named for them; put a fig tree next to one and, gnarled and gray, it pouts like an unloved sibling. "The fig tree wasn't pretty," recalls Aunt Fannie, "but it gave fruit that we preserved and ate during the winter."

Before Mother married, there were five Shapiro children crowded in that house, the one where (as she wrote her Houston friend) she had to make the beds and sweep each morning. They included Mother, Fannie and Pearl, plus

Rose and Morris, the two youngest who were born after the family had settled in America.

And Helen, a youthful, light-skinned black lady whom they hired to work in the house, someone Aunt Fannie characterized as being "hardly much poorer than we were."

Because my mother was so small, no one knew when they arrived in Dallas that she and Aunt Fannie were two or three years apart in age. The two of them enrolled together in the fourth grade. "I was furious," says Fannie, "because Becky got promoted right away. I figured that meant she was smarter." It hardly made much difference, though, since both of them and Pearl, not long thereafter, quit school and went to work. "We had to help take care of Rose and Morris, the babies," says Fannie. "Plus Papa, the third one."

The transforming event of the Shapiros' lives on Forest Avenue was the installation of a new streetcar line, one of the first in Dallas and the same one that my mother later bragged about taking home alone from her job at the phone company.

Like nothing else before it, the streetcar enlarged their world, allowing for easy trips downtown to the movies or to window shop and to Fair Park, the huge grounds that housed and still house the Texas State Fair in October. A streetcar ride became an event, portal to a wider universe, something to dress for and talk about to your friends. As my mother and her sisters were growing up, the streetcar also rendered their house on Forest Avenue more accessible to young men coming to court.

But like Dallas rest rooms or movie houses or even drinking fountains of those days, the streetcars were partitioned: white people were assigned to one part, black Americans to another. There was a big sign that divided the two sections. "Negroes," it said in bold letters, with an arrow pointing to the rear.

Grandma Lena never thought much of the idea. In her mind, black and Jewish families weren't very different, since it was the women who did the work in both. She believed that at least women should be able to sit where they wanted to, so if she and Helen rode the streetcar to town, they'd nonchalantly take seats together in the front. In fact, Helen adopted a look that invited no comment and sat there with or without Grandma.

When Grandpa died in 1938, all the women (Marietha, included) crowded together in our little living room on Grand Avenue. The significance of his death eluded me at age six, though what I did understand was that he would no longer be there on Forest Avenue, and I didn't foresee anyone else bringing me around a pair of white boots or calling me his little prince.

Mother offered me the choice of going to Grandpa's funeral or playing with Janice, a distant cousin of my age with whom I occasionally shared toys and a bath. Opting for the familiar over the unknown, I went to play at Janice's and later regretted that I had missed my only chance to see Grandpa buried.

▶▶▶

Eventually everyone emigrated from Forest Avenue and the Shapiros' old house was reconfigured into doctors' offices, the big front porch deemed expendable and removed. If you were to drive around there today, you'd find other differences from the street they knew. A funeral home with gospel singing sits across the way from their old house. Friedman's Drug Store, once on the other side of Forest Avenue, is long gone, its corner now occupied by a fast-food outlet. Buses have replaced the streetcar, just a memory along with the tracks that guided its journey into other parts of town.

Considering its current surroundings, the fig tree probably looks pretty good.

But the memory of those early days in Dallas lives fresh in the minds of the three last surviving Shapiro children, Fannie and Rose and Morris. Talk to them about it, and you realize that the most lasting impressions seem to be left either by the best of us or the worst. In their case, it was the latter, their father.

Aunt Rose looks as if she has to keep from spitting when Grandpa's name comes up. Aunt Fannie says, "Except for Becky, all of us kept away from Papa. Becky felt sorry for him because everyone else ignored him." (My mother, the toughest, may also have been the least affected by him, though cousin Ann says that Mother had such strength in her that she would never show any hurt.)

Aunt Fannie made a tantalizing statement. "Papa once did something to me that I never forgave, and after that I kept my distance from him."

For years I wanted but never dared to ask what that "something" he did to her was. Given his affection for pretty young girls like her and Cousin Ann, I suppose I could guess. "Me, they always called cute," Mother used to say, ruefully, "but no one ever called Fannie that. She was beautiful!" Despite her Russian birth, Fannie had a soft spoken, sometimes laconic southern manner that complemented a gentle voice, flawlessly smooth skin, soft brown eyes and hair. If Grandpa found her tempting, no wonder—though not her fault.

Uncle Morris has an especially descriptive way of expressing his feelings about his father, dead sixty years. "I go to Shearith Israel Cemetery and say Kaddish for Mama," he says, then adds, firmly, "but not for Papa!"

5

One Sister Surprises Everyone by Going Away

High school diplomas never hung on the walls for the three eldest Shapiro sisters. My mother and Aunt Fannie and Aunt Pearl all had to leave school and go to work.

Pearl was the most studious of the four sisters, the youngest one to have come from Russia, the one who introduced me to classical music and *The New Yorker*, the one who cared least for material things and seemed to be the least attached to her early Jewish upbringing. She was also the only one who never married. Short and pretty with dark eyes, Pearl had a round face and a smile that revealed a gentle but surprisingly determined nature.

Shortly after my mother started as a long distance operator at the phone company, Aunt Pearl got a job in the personnel department of A. Harris & Co. One of Dallas' largest department stores, it was located in a fine building at the corner of Main and Akard streets.

Even as a teen-ager, Pearl's tastes had been well honed, and in the personnel job at A. Harris' she would immediately discount any applicant who arrived for an interview chewing gum. The store managers took note of that kind of diligence, and within the next several years my aunt got promoted until she rose to become secretary to Mr. K., the store's president. There, for a decade, she underrated her value to him while also engaging in an unhappy, one-sided romance with him. Like most successful Dallas retail merchants, Mr. K. was Jewish. He also was a man long married, with no notion to change that.

Finally, Pearl knew she had to get away from her boss and the store, and to go one better, she decided to get away from Dallas. Against the urging of the other Shapiro sisters, by then all married and determined Texans, she bought an inexpensive used Ford and set out in the mid-1940s for the several day, couple-of-thousand-mile drive west to San Francisco. Without ever having been there, it was a city where, like so many others, Pearl thought she'd find contentment. She made the long trip alone except for occasionally stopping to give a ride to hitchiking soldiers for whom she felt sorry.

Though Uncle Morris, Aunt Rose and especially Aunt Fannie often visited her later, they never stopped worrying about Pearl's solitary life across the Golden Gate Bridge in Mill Valley. That's where she eventually settled in with a large black male cat who one day followed her home, jumped inside through an open window and decided to stay.

Aunt Pearl's house on Woodbine Drive, whose purchase Uncle Morris helped underwrite, was a simple one-story redwood structure with a large kitchen, a couple of bedrooms and a well-used fireplace in the living room. She furnished it with comfortable sofas and chairs and a collection of copper and brass cooking utensils and knickknacks acquired from visits to thrift shops or garage sales. Perched on the side of a hill, the house had a long back deck that looked over a drop-off and a forest of redwoods. To reach the place, the daring driver or energetic hiker had to approach along a steep, narrow, winding road. Even her driveway offered an adventure, as it took a sharp drop from the street down to the house and would get filled with mud whenever a heavy rain came. By those impediments, Pearl seemed unbothered.

The first time I visited her in Mill Valley was also the first time I saw California. It was in 1956, on my return from serving in the army in Korea. Though as small in stature as my mother and more soft-spoken, Pearl managed to get my name called on the loud speaker from among the thousands of soldiers lined up on a troop ship after we had docked at dawn in the harbor of San Francisco. Baffled by why I would be singled out and imagining only horrors, I stumbled down several decks and through a maze of corridors to find my tiny aunt standing sheepishly at the gate, holding cookies and mail for me. We looked at each other silently for a couple of minutes. She hadn't seen me in four or five years and didn't recognize me, I had gotten quite thin after a year and half overseas. To that I had added a complexion of ghostly white after a week's trip across the Pacific during which I was almost the whole time prone from a relentless case of seasickness. We both laughed and hugged when recognition set in.

I was discharged from the military at Fort Ord south of San Francisco and went back to spend a week with Aunt Pearl and the cat, whose only communication with me were hostile glances that he heaped my way until the day he saw me finally packing to leave. It was February, the rainy season, and we stored up food in case the driveway became impassible from the mud, which it did.

But before that, we toured the foreign neighborhoods of San Francisco and the gigantic redwoods of Muir Woods. I took a walk every morning on the tree-lined roads that led from Pearl's house down into the village. Like the rest of the family, I marveled at the nonchalance with which my aunt managed there by herself, something I had never before known a woman to do and a Jewish lady from Texas least of all. I met a few of Pearl's friends, interesting people, but I could see that she was essentially alone. Having fled an environment in which she felt the outsider, Pearl found serenity through an existence that confounded everyone else: living with unlocked doors and, for a sole companion, an animal who exited each night into the woods and returned ready for a nap at dawn. Much of that picture, including her devotion to the feline species, I realized, I stored away for emulation later on.

Pearl worked intermittently at secretarial jobs but none with the importance of the one she had left in Dallas. It seemed as if her spirit had been broken by that adventure at A. Harris. "There is no other family like ours," she often stated of her brother and sisters who helped support her.

Pearl's life with her cat continued until she was suddenly taken ill with cancer in the mid-1960s, a decade and a half after moving to Mill Valley. Friends of hers called Morris in Dallas to tell him that she had fallen a couple of times and that they were concerned about her. He and Fannie and Rose all rushed to California and, getting a bad prognosis from Pearl's doctor, insisted that she come back to Dallas for medical and family care. With great reluctance, she agreed to do so. They began gathering together her belongings and went looking for the cat, who had sensed trouble and vanished. Trapped after a couple of days when he reappeared hungry, he became a moody companion on the trip to Texas.

Pearl and the cat moved in with Aunt Rose and Uncle Herbert in Dallas. After a few months, the cancer in Pearl's brain grew so bad that she could no longer speak or attend to simple functions. At that point the doctors determined that their only hope would be a risky operation. They decided to go ahead with it, but since Pearl was unable to talk or ask anything about it, they reluctantly took her into surgery without telling her. She died during that operation, in 1966, when she was sixty-five. I was living in New York, and to my chagrin, my mother told me nothing of her death until after the funeral.

The cat survived Pearl by a couple of years, living principally in the alley or under the bed. He gave an occasional purr to Rose or Herbert only, as Uncle Herbert often said, because it was they who were feeding him.

After Pearl died, Morris and Fannie and Rose went back to Mill Valley to close up Pearl's house in that setting so idyllic that Aunt Fannie said it was painful for her to remember it. I was sad when I found out that her home was to be put on the market, since I held to some impractical fantasy of future visits as meaningful as the first one. Selling it, of course, was the only thing to do, since no one in the family wanted to live there, nor was anyone close enough to watch out for it.

When the house got sold, it was worth more than what Pearl had paid for it. The profits went to Uncle Morris, since it was he who had helped Pearl buy it. He distributed that money among several in the family, myself included. A few pieces of Aunt Pearl's ceramics and copper also came my way. They are small, inexpensive items I cherish more than many things of more value.

Though she cared little about Judaism and avoided long visits in Dallas, Pearl is buried in the Shearith Israel cemetery, not far from Grandpa Max and Grandma Lena, her parents, and next to a simple white stone ordered by Uncle Morris that says, "Beloved Sister." When I go to visit my parents' graves, I visit hers with some flowers as well. If she can hear, she knows I miss her.

6

Another Sister Just Gets a Surprise

Like her sister Pearl, Aunt Fannie also started working at A. Harris' as a teenager. "I was really just a messenger," she explained of her job as a cash girl. "They'd holler 'Cash,' and I'd come running." Young and pretty and friendly, Aunt Fannie made the ideal cash girl, and she loved working and meeting people at A. Harris'. But after a couple of years she decided what she really wanted to be was a legal secretary and later maybe a court reporter. To achieve that goal, she'd set funds aside every week until she had enough to enroll in the Manhattan School to study stenography. Even after leaving, she returned to A. Harris' whenever she could and used Pearl's discount to buy makeup and a pretty new outfit for work.

When Fannie completed her stenography course, her friend Sadie Gold arranged an appointment for her with James Bagby, a partner in the law firm of Bagby and Long. On a bright April day, while my mother went off to her job at the phone company and Pearl to hers at A. Harris', Fannie put on a new woolen dress and white gloves, kissed Grandma goodbye, averted an approving look from Grandpa, and paid the four cents for a ride to town on the Forest Avenue streetcar.

A beautiful receptionist ushered her into Mr. Bagby's office. "He looked frightening to me," Fannie recalled, "there in a wood paneled room in his navy blue pin-striped suit and gold watch and shiny black shoes." Bagby had hair that was thinning and gray along the sides.

"Miss Shapiro?" he asked her.

"Yes, sir."

"Do sit down, Miss Shapiro. Don't be nervous, now. Is this your first job?"

"Well, yes, except for little jobs at A. Harris and in my father's store."

"Oh," said Mr. Bagby, very friendly, "what sort of store does your father have?"

"Sir, he doesn't have it any more. It was a small grocery on Hall Street, not far from where we live, on Forest Avenue."

"So your father made his money and retired?"

She coughed. "I guess you could say so, sir."

"You can take steno and do typing, of course."

"Oh, yes. I brought my diploma from the Manhattan School to show you."

Mr. Bagby ignored the diploma and the difference in their religions. "Can you start work right away, Miss Shapiro?"

"Certainly," she said. "I'm ready any time."

After that, the room grew quiet and Aunt Fannie wondered if she had said something wrong. "Did you want me to take a test?" she asked.

"Let's plan for you to start tomorrow," Mr. Bagby told her, with quite a warm smile. He mentioned a modest salary, but more than what she had earned as a cash girl. "Just come in at nine."

Wearing another of her new A. Harris & Co. outfits, Aunt Fannie arrived early the next day and started to work—without taking any test. It seemed that she was the youngest girl there by a number of years. She worked diligently, and Mr. Bagby was very patient, but every time she'd sit down at the typewriter she'd try so hard not to make any mistakes that that's all she seemed to make. She even stayed late some days to practice, but it hardly got better.

Finally, after two or three months, Aunt Fannie went in one morning practically in tears. "Mr. Bagby," she said, "I'm really sorry, but I just don't think I'll ever get this right."

By that time he was calling her Fannie. "Why, Miss Fannie," he said, with a smile, "you've been doing just fine. Everyone here likes you. I like you!"

"But I keep making so many mistakes. It's not that I'm not trying!"

"We all make mistakes at first, dear Miss Fannie," said Mr. Bagby, stepping out from behind his desk. "You're so young. Don't worry. Don't be hard on yourself."

"Maybe I need to go back to school."

Mr. Bagby was quiet and gave my aunt a long look. "Don't think any more about it today," he said, finally. "I'll tell you what. How about if we just go buy a box of Barton's chocolates and some Dr. Pepper, and we'll drive out to White Rock to spend the day. It's Friday, anyway."

Aunt Fannie felt relieved at that, so she packed up her things and they set off in his convertible to that pretty lake at what was then the eastern edge of Dallas. They spread a blanket under a big live oak and opened the chocolates.

"I apologized again for my poor work," Fannie recalled, "but he wasn't listening to that. 'Why don't you just stretch out on this blanket, Miss Fannie?' he suggested."

"Oh, I'm just fine like this," she said, sitting up straight against the tree.

"But you look so uncomfortable that way. Perhaps you'd like to...rest your head on my lap."

"No, oh no, I wouldn't want to bother you like that," she replied, and tried to move the subject back to the office. But he kept on not listening and it wasn't long before Fannie realized that her stenography was not what Mr. Bagby had on his mind.

Fortunately for my aunt, clouds gathered and it started to look like rain. Their odd sort of picnic got cut short, and Mr. Bagby drove Aunt Fannie back home to Forest Avenue. They rode without talking, Fannie pretending to need protection from the wind in the convertible by wrapping her head inside a large scarf. "Thank you for the very nice afternoon, Mr. Bagby," she said formally, as she jumped out of the car in front of Grandpa's house.

"I was nervous all weekend about what I'd do on Monday morning," she says. "Of course I went in to work, sure that everyone in the office must have heard what happened at White Rock. Probably, though, no one did."

After that, Fannie stayed out of Mr. Bagby's way and she says he seemed to stay out of hers. When he needed to give dictation, he called Alma, the other secretary.

"Then something strange happened," my aunt recalled. "When they handed me something to type, it suddenly came out a little better. My typing improved—somewhat. I thought maybe I had a future with those gentiles at Bagby and Long, after all."

She pauses a moment and adds, with a wry smile, "On second thought, maybe not."

7

Under Pearl's Bed

As the cat lover and bachelor lady of the family, Aunt Pearl was the one I would have been closest to, had she not lived so far away in California. Then, too, she died relatively young. Still, she paved the way for my leaving Texas. Like me, she was a writer, and she penned funny dialogues with cats. After she died, I was happy to keep those papers. Unfortunately, I don't think they were read by anyone but me. Here, however, is a story from the early days in Dallas that I like to remember exactly the way she narrated it to me.

When Pearl was nine, Forest Avenue was like the streetcar, divided between white and black. White families lived on one block, black on the next block down. Grandma Lena knew a lot of black folks and wouldn't have cared if Fannie or Pearl played with their kids, but they mostly didn't. Grandpa paid no attention.

One quiet Sunday afternoon in July, all the Shapiros had gone out except Grandma Lena and Pearl. They had just finished the dishes, and Pearl was about to settle down with *Pride and Prejudice* when she and Grandma suddenly heard shouting from outside. "He's gonna kill me, he's gonna kill me!" screamed a voice.

Grandma ran into the living room and Pearl followed, and they saw a tall black man running down Forest Avenue. Grandma dashed out front to get a better look. It was John Davidson, a neighbor from the next block. "Hey, John, in here," Grandma hollered to him when he passed near their house. "Come in here."

John was an old man, but he raced panting up onto their front porch.

"Who's chasing you?" asked Grandma.

"Some white man," John said. "I don't even know him."

"Get inside," she ordered, having no idea what it was about. Grandma pushed John, trembling, into the living room. Aunt Pearl said that she suddenly didn't feel good, so she retreated to watch from behind the door to the hall.

"Quick," said Grandma to John, "go into Pearl's room. It's in the back and you can hide under her bed. It's the one near the window."

My room, thought Pearl! The room that Fannie and she shared. Suppose the man comes in, finds John and shoots him in the bedroom! Pearl thought of blurting that out to Grandma, but she wasn't the kind of person to complain to about something like that.

John followed Grandma down the hallway, and Pearl heard the door to her room close. Then she heard her mother telephone and explain to the police what had happened and tell them to come quickly.

After a couple of minutes, Pearl slowly retraced her steps into the living room to see if the white man might still be in the street. There wasn't anyone. All the neighbors who had been alerted to their front porches by John's screaming had retreated back inside and away from the heat.

Pearl collapsed on the sofa, where she could watch through the window. Soon a couple of police cars came cruising slowly up and down Forest Avenue. They may not have cared much about John Davidson, but they probably knew that if they hadn't come, Lena Shapiro would pester them until they did.

A July quiet took over. Pearl heard Grandma go toward the kitchen, rattle an ice tray and open the door to the bedroom. "Here's a cold Dr. Pepper," Pearl heard her say to John.

"Were you scared?" Grandma asked, coming into the living room and seeing Pearl peeking out under the shades.

"Me? Not a bit."

To prove her point, Pearl took her book and stretched out on the hardwood floor, just inside the front door, the coolest place in the house. Grandma brought the sewing that she did to earn extra money and turned some low music on the radio. "I'll sit here a while," she said, "where I can keep an eye on the street."

Pearl started planning how she'd tell the story to Fannie and Becky when they came home. How much she had participated in rescuing and hiding John would need to depend on whether or not Grandma was within earshot. For now, a breeze rocked the curtains and sifted in the front door, and with the book open over her face, she dozed off.

"What'd you do this afternoon?" Fannie asked, shaking her awake.

"Wait till I tell you!" Pearl said, quickly alert. The chance to keep her older sister in suspense came rarely. "Come on—to our room."

They started down the hall and passed Grandma and Grandpa's bedroom. The door was open, and Grandma was napping. Safe.

"Well," said Pearl, "I saved John Davidson, the old Negro man from the next block."

Fannie looked doubtful. "Saved him from what?"

"From probably getting killed."

The two sisters were at the door to their room when Pearl remembered that John Davidson had been told to hide under her bed. She didn't know how long she had been asleep. How could she convince Fannie that she had hidden him there if she was afraid to look?

"Go in the room," Pearl said, suddenly. "Go on." She gave a little push.

Fannie looked at her and shook her head. "Why?" she asked. "Why are you so nervous?"

"Why would I be nervous? Just look under my bed and see if anyone—anything's—there."

"What, are you crazy?"

"Please," Pearl begged. "Just go on and look."

Fannie marched into their room while Pearl waited in the hall, looking the other way. Then she heard the springs on the bed creak. "Not on the bed," Pearl yelled. "Under it."

A long moment elapsed, then Fannie reappeared. "Well?"

"Yes," said her sister, smiling. "My blue scarf, the one you borrowed. It was under the bed."

"Just that?"

"Uh, huh."

"Good," said Pearl.

She and Fannie went in the room and closed the door.

At dinner, the rest of the family was back home and Grandma told the story about John Davidson, including the part about Pearl hiding behind the door to the hall. "After a while I figured it was safe to tell him to leave," explained Grandma. "Pearl never heard him go out—she was fast asleep," she added, grinning.

Becky grinned, too. Grandpa glanced up from his plate. Fannie shot darts out of her eyes at her sister.

The story of Grandma's rescue got quickly around the neighborhood and furthered her reputation as odd. Helen gave her a hug when she came to work on Monday. Grandma said later that she was sure the police never really tried to find out who had been trying to shoot John or why. What she heard was that it was only because he had been on the "white" side of Forest Avenue talking to the son of a family whose grass he cut.

That's how John earned a little money in the summer months. It left him far from rich, but he reappeared at the Shapiros' house a couple of days later with a great heart-shaped box of chocolates. "Answer the door," Grandma told Pearl when she heard someone knock.

"Miss Pearl," said John, "these are for your mother. Will you write a card for me?"

After her embarrassment at the dinner table, Pearl was happy to play an adult role in the drama. "I certainly will, Mr. Davidson," she said. "What do you want me to write?"

John thought about it. "Well," he said, finally, handing her a small white card, "just write, 'To my friend, with thanks.'"

8

Marriage to a Jewish Football Player

Since the Shapiros' generation of Russian immigrants arrived without birth certificates, they often didn't know just how old they were. My mother, for one, chopped a couple of years off her age, even when she approached ninety, as if by then anyone cared. Her gravestone gives a birth date that shortens the truth by a year or two.

Aunt Fannie says Grandma Lena placed her birth at two days before Passover. "So," said my aunt, "I just decided my birthday must have been April 8th. That's what I thought until I wrote to Washington, D.C. and found out that Pesach that year was earlier. So April eighth isn't really my birthday, it's March eighteenth. But who cares? I go on celebrating it on April eighth!"

My aunt fudged on another thing, her name. "It's not really Fannie," she confessed, "it's Sorafegal. But when I was eight or nine, I read a book about a Sara who was a bad woman. I thought, who wants to go around with that? So when we moved to Dallas, I told the school my name was Fannie. Pearl was the only one in the family who would call me Sara. She knew it was prettier than Fannie, and it is. But it's too late to change everyone else."

Those constitute perhaps the sum of the lies that Aunt Fannie told in all her ninety-six or ninety-seven years. Her congeniality outdistanced even her honesty. "I went to the bank today," she'd report, "and the prettiest young woman was working behind the counter. 'Ooo, you are so pretty,' I told her.

"'Why, thank you, ma'am,' I heard back."

This dialogue got repeated in groceries and dry cleaners, beauty parlors and drug stores, wherever she went.

All the Shapiro sisters were pretty or at least "cute," as my mother complained about being typed. Fannie added to that a dimension of vulnerable southern charm, which men besides her father found irresistible. "The house on Forest Avenue was bursting with fellows who came to see her," Mother said.

One of them came over one night, sat on the porch and asked to take her to a movie. "I can't go with you," replied my aunt. "You're not *Jewish*."

"Well," he said, "I *can* be."

Fannie could have married any Jewish boy in Dallas, according to my mother. I have an old photo that testifies to Mother's assessment. It has Aunt Fannie and me standing in the back yard on Forest Avenue by the ungainly fig tree. With her auburn hair and oval-shaped face, she wraps her arms around my narrow shoulders. I was no more than four, sporting the cherished white boots that were Grandpa's gift. Aunt Fannie was about thirty-five, garbed in a brown woolen dress with a large velvet bow across the front. In that dress, or for that matter, in whatever she wore, she looked richer than she was—a phenomenon, she said, that could be attributed to genes inherited from great aunts who had been dressmakers to the Russian czars.

Those were the days of her tenure at Bagby and Long. Despite her improvement in typing, she sensed that Mr. Bagby might take her up on her suggestion to resign or initiate it himself. So she left Bagby and went to work in the credit department of Neiman-Marcus. "But any excuse to go traveling, I'd quit my job and do it," says my aunt. "The best trip was the one to Chicago. Becky and Henry, who by then were married, were going there to a convention, so I tagged along."

When Fannie got to Chicago, she thought it was "simply heaven"—so new and exciting compared to Dallas. She lodged with my dad's sister Sadie, and when Mother and he were ready to go home, Sadie said, "Fannie, don't go. What do you have in Dallas? Stay here. We'll go out on double dates."

"But I've got to make some money," Fannie told her. "There's a house we're paying for in Dallas." Sadie thought that Fannie wouldn't find it hard to get a job in Chicago and sent her to an employment agency. My aunt told them she had worked with attorneys and in a department store, and that same night the lady called to say she could start work the next day.

"So I went to Pines & Morse, a fine law firm on Michigan Avenue," says my aunt. "Mr. Glick was my boss, and he said he'd like to invite me for dinner. 'Sure,' I said. We went to the stock market, to every place. But I was finally ashamed to go out, the way I was dressed.

"'Oh, don't worry,' said Mr. Glick. 'I have accounts all over Sheridan Road. Just go and buy what you need.' Mr. Glick was a wealthy man, but about twenty years older than me. I never took advantage of his offer. Wasn't I a fool!"

The Chicago stay lasted about a year, and the only reason it ended was that Aunt Pearl, who had not yet moved away from Dallas, drove all the way to Chicago with a friend and said, "You're coming home with us!" "That was probably Mama's idea," Fannie says. So she went back to Dallas with Pearl and got a job at a small real estate office where they didn't recognize typing errors.

Rose and Morris, the only ones of their family who were able to finish high school, were about to get their diplomas and go to work. Together with Fannie and Pearl, they had enough so that Grandma could stop taking in sewing at last. Between them, they bought her a silk, flowered dress for the High Holy Days. "Lovely," she exclaimed when she opened the big box. "I'll wear it to Mrs. Rabinowitz's." Helen was standing by, looking on.

"But, Mama, it's for Rosh Hashanah," Fannie said. "We bought it for you for the synagogue."

"Going to Rosh Hashanah services is not fun," Grandma replied. "I'll wear it to Mrs. Rabinowitz's." She looked to see what Helen thought. Helen smiled.

Soon after that, in 1932, Grandma took sick. They stayed with her constantly, but the doctor said she was worn out, and she died early the next year. With my mother married, Fannie was the eldest one left on Forest Avenue and figured she ought to stay at home and be sure that Grandpa Max was taken care of, even if she didn't like him. "Helen put up with him better than the rest of us," Fannie says, "so we let her do most of the caring of him."

"Around that time I got engaged—twice, in fact," Fannie says. "First it was to Jack Rosen, then to Max Gordon. Max kept calling, he wanted so much to go out with me. I felt sorry for him, so I got unengaged to Jack and engaged to him. I don't like to hurt people's feelings. Getting engaged didn't seem to mean much then, anyway."

"Papa died in 1938, and it was a relief," Fannie adds. "His synagogue friends came to the funeral, then we all met to say Kaddish at Becky and Henry's house on Grand Avenue. Within a year, we lost Helen, too. We all walked with her family to her grave in the Negro cemetery. I cried more that day than when we buried Papa."

▶▶▶

By the time Grandpa Max died, Aunt Fannie was thirty-seven. Though my mother was only three years older, she had three growing children: my sister Florence, who was sixteen, my brother Jerome, fourteen, and me, six. Fannie decided it was time to look seriously at the idea of marriage.

The engagements to Jack, followed by Max, did not lead to marriage. "I loved going dancing with those boys," she says, "but Arthur Feldman was different from the others."

Feldman was settled in a jewelry store that he owned with his twin brother Harry. It was on Deep Elm Street, the part of Elm away from the department stores, where inexpensive jewelry and clothing and pawn shops were assembled.

"We had known his family for years," says Fannie. "One day when my sister Rose walked in his store, Arthur said, 'Are you Fannie Shapiro's sister?'

"'Yes,' Rose said.

"'Well, tell her I said hello.'

"'Listen,' Rose said, 'if you want to say hello, say it yourself.'"

He did. That same night he called Fannie and invited her to go out for a drive in his car. Three days later he proposed.

Fannie asked my mother what she thought. Though he offered security, Mother was surprised at the man Fannie chose. Still, she thought it would be okay. So Arthur and Fannie decided to get married.

I was only seven, but I had my own reaction to her engagement, and it wasn't good. Arthur Feldman had been a football player in school, and I didn't know any football players. I wasn't sure Jewish people ever *were* football players. It didn't seem right that my beautiful aunt was about to go live with a burly man who smoked cigars and owned a store where he sold cheap jewelry. Especially since Mother kept insisting that she could have married *anyone*.

Fannie and Arthur were about the same age, but he had that bloated look of a man whose large muscles of youth had grown soft. He looked older than she, and people sometimes mistook her for his daughter. "Sometimes I felt like a child by comparison," she says.

I remember their wedding. It was in the Rabbi's study on a drizzling September afternoon. Fannie was dressed in a cream-colored suit and she wore the heavy, sparkling ring that Arthur had given her. I was crouched in a corner, in awe of that woman, miserable to think our days together might have ended.

Decades after that day and even after Arthur's death and her divorce from Dave, her second husband, Aunt Fannie expresses wonder about her past. "Stanley," she tells me, "you know my friend Rosalie. When her husband Sam died, Rosalie recovered so fast. She was out in the world again so soon. I couldn't understand it. One day we had lunch together, and I asked her.

"'Rosalie,' I said, 'tell me, confidentially, how did you get over Sam's death so quickly?'"

"Rosalie leaned over close to me. 'Fannie,' she said, 'it's because I had such wonderful memories of the years he and I spent together, all the good times we had.'"

"I was amazed," says Aunt Fannie. "And Sam didn't leave her rich!"

My aunt turns away sadly. "I don't have those kind of memories, Stanley," she tells me. "Looking back on the past gives me no consolation."

No consolation? After being engaged to Jack Rosen and Max Gordon, then married to Arthur Feldman and Dave Bern, there followed a score of others—an unbroken queue of suitors until my aunt needed a cane, turned ninety and showed the effects of aging that nature hurls at most people at sixty. Even past ninety, she retained that southern laugh that drew men to her all her adult life.

She shakes her head, though, and says to me with eyes no longer dancing, "No, Stanley. My memories give me no consolation."

9

No Consolation

"All those boyfriends didn't give you consolation?" I ask. "I wish I had had half as many!"

There was a reason, of course, for my aunt's feelings. By the mid-to-late 1930s, Jewish families were no longer new immigrants in Dallas, but they still huddled together within a dozen blocks in old South Dallas. My parents, together with Dad's brother Sam, had bought a one-story duplex house on Grand Avenue, a misnamed street not far from the Shapiros on Forest Avenue. It's where we lived until July 1940 when I was nearly eight years old.

Fannie and Arthur went for their honeymoon to the shore in Galveston, the same place where my aunt first set foot in America. When they returned, they moved to a two-story, four-unit apartment building on a corner of Park Row, only a few blocks from Grand Avenue.

With the suitcases barely stored away, Uncle Arthur lit a cigar and said, "We've got to go see Mother. She'll never forgive me if I don't go to see her first thing." Fannie put on a solid navy blue suit and little makeup, and they went to Mama Feldman's house on South Boulevard. They arrived just as she and a couple of the other Feldman sons were intent on a game of poker. "Not a one of them stood up," my aunt remembered. "Not a one said hello. They couldn't have cared less that we were there! I was tempted to point that out to Arthur, but decided I better not. What a family, I thought!"

That was not the end of her surprises from the Feldmans. In the apartment upstairs from Fannie and Arthur lived Arthur's twin brother, Harry, his wife Minnie, and their two sons. Harry and Minnie had already been married for half a dozen years, and it had become her custom to feed and do laundry for her husband's bachelor brother as well as for her husband. She didn't see why Arthur needed a wife.

"Even after we were married," Fannie said, "Arthur would come home from the store tired and hungry, and after he ate he'd often go upstairs to play cards with Harry. Once, when I was ready to serve dinner, he came in and said, 'Oh, I already ate upstairs.'

"That was one of the few times I let him know what I thought. 'If you ever do that again,' I yelled, 'I'll go up and break every one of their tchotchkes (knickknacks).' After that, he ate at home."

"Even after our son Wade was born," Fannie recalled, "I realized that in a way Arthur would never be as devoted to us as he was to his brother. I told him once that the person he really should have married was Harry."

Aunt Fannie was thirty-eight when she gave birth to my cousin Wade. She was in labor for hours, and in our house my mother paced nervously for news from Baylor Hospital. "I was barely conscious when the doctor came into the hospital room," Fannie said. "I heard him tell the nurses to fill me quickly with penicillin. The drug had just been discovered, and I think I would have died without it."

Wade was a healthy child, with thick locks and a bouncy manner. Past the age when most women of that era were having children, my aunt walked her baby in an elegant carriage down Park Row for the neighbors to see. "A beautiful boy, Fegal! Such blond curls! You sure he's Jewish?"

As the eldest of her family, my mother assumed that it was fitting that she render advice to her siblings, an activity she willingly undertook. After Wade was born, she lost no time in sharing counsel on child-raising. "You're going to spoil that baby by coddling him so much," she told her sister.

"Maybe so," said my aunt, "but I didn't care. I knew I'd never have another child."

His parents furnished a nursery for Wade in a room that faced the side street, and one night just before his second birthday, they heard a noise from his room and rushed in just in time to see a man hurrying out through the window. "He had grabbed a scale and a few other things," Fannie recalls. "We called for the police and they came, but as long as Wade was all right in his bed, I didn't care about anything else. After that, Becky said that I sheltered him even more. Well, who wouldn't?"

Her husband, for example. "When Wade was a little baby," says Fannie, "Arthur used to play with him, because he was so cute. After that, Arthur got too busy and absorbed with his brother and the store."

Aunt Fannie's remark that Arthur should have married his brother was not totally a joke. Arthur Feldman was one of a family of eight or nine children, but it was Harry with whom he had the closeness. When their days of playing football had ended, he and his twin went on to smoke cigars together and, after opening the jewelry store on Deep Elm, to spend most of every day together. Arthur told Fannie that, without knowing what the other was wearing, he and Harry would often put on the nearly identical suit and tie.

When my mother sought an inexpensive gift, she would drive to Deep Elm to shop at the Feldman Brothers store. Occasionally I went along for the adventure into what seemed like an alien world. Harry would always look at us in silence, but, cigar temporarily taken out of his mouth, Uncle Arthur would greet us in a loud voice, and usher us in.

At home he was less talkative. "Sometimes Arthur would bring in a pistol that someone had pawned, and he'd hide it in the house," Fannie says. "'Honey, why did you bring that here?' I'd ask. 'Suppose Wade finds it while he's playing.'

"'Don't worry,' was all Arthur would say. 'Nothing will happen.'

"He refused to talk more about it. Arthur may have been chatty at the store, but at home he was as quiet as his brother."

▶▶▶

By early in the decade of the 1940s, Dallas was changing in ways that would leave it a different city, life in it different from what we'd known. As the city grew, many Dallas Jews expanded their businesses and secured government contracts for manufacturing uniforms or shoes or linens for the war. "The rabbi lectured us against reaping wealth from battles that were taking place on the same lands many of us had come from," Mother said, shaking her head. "Of course, that didn't stop people from doing it."

That, according to Mother, was a time of deeply mixed feelings. Anxiety over loved ones far from home was a daily companion, but the gnawing struggle of the early years as transplanted Jews was over for many people. They were making money and were ready to show it, to put their beginnings and first languages away as history. The first streets they knew, Park Row and Forest Avenue, were left to other Jews who couldn't afford to move and to black families who wouldn't have been welcomed elsewhere even if they could afford to move. A migration began north, to large, open lots of land that allowed the building of comfortable houses. The migration turned into a feverish caravan that went on for most of that decade. In 1940 my family left Grand Avenue and moved to Stanhope Avenue, into a semi-paved neighborhood called University Park.

When Fannie and Arthur talked of leaving Park Row, she suggested that it might be the time to have a place away from Harry and Minnie. But her idea got rejected. Arthur and his brother consulted agents, and on Normandy, a street a couple of blocks from Stanhope, they bought a two-story duplex. It was to house Arthur and his family upstairs, Harry and his downstairs. "I looked so disappointed about that whole idea," Fannie says, "that Arthur loaded me up with a new diamond ring."

Our two new homes had the virtue of being near to one another, and there was hardly a day when Aunt Fannie didn't drop in to our house and no day when she and my mother didn't talk. Mother volunteered warnings about overly spoiling Wade. "You're always on top of him," she said to her sister, "with his clothes and his food and his homework!" If Fannie heard the counsel, she practiced ignoring it.

▶▶▶

After we moved to University Park, Aunt Fannie got in the habit of joining my parents and me for Rosh Hashanah and Yom Kippur services at Shearith Israel. (Uncle Arthur went in for football but not much for religion, and Wade followed in his footsteps.) My parents and I would drive in the

Dodge back to the old building in South Dallas, and Aunt Fannie would go alone in her Chevrolet, should she opt to depart early.

Yom Kippur services, of course, last from morning until sundown, which it seemed to me got pushed later every single year. If you lasted from the previous sundown through that long day without food or drink, the wise ones must have decided, any notion of re-engaging in last year's sins would be abandoned.

At age ten, I approached Yom Kippur without argument, since my future was still to include confirmation and bar mitzvah, reserved for those who had demonstrated seriousness in prayer. But after an hour or two of standing and sitting and standing and reciting Hebrew words I didn't understand (Hebrew school notwithstanding), my strength would ebb. Mother began to look pale herself, but if I glanced her way, she would straighten up to her full five feet and adopt a stoic expression.

That's when Aunt Fannie might give me the nod. "Back in a couple of minutes," I'd whisper to Mother and tiptoe out after my aunt. Casually, we'd amble toward her car, parked at a safe distance from the schul, from where she and I would make quick escape to the old South Dallas Pig Stand, around the corner from Forest Avenue. There, barbecue sandwiches with tangy sauce and cold Dr. Peppers awaited.

"What if we run into someone we know?" I asked my aunt, tearing open the wrapping.

"Then," she said, "they'll be as guilty as we are."

Even if we shared a second sandwich, we never tarried over lunch, afraid to be absent a suspicious length of time. I'd carefully wipe away the sauce before re-entering the synagogue, since often it was my father who was stationed at the door.

"Where were you?" Mother asked, once we were back in our seats.

"Just outside, getting some air."

"Umm," she muttered with a quizzical look, going back to the prayer book.

Aunt Fannie usually called it a day before the day was wrung out. Not my mother. No matter how tired it left her, she never failed to complete the Yom

Kippur fast until sundown when we would return home for dinner, a light one with soup, as dictated. She didn't ask Aunt Fannie or me whether we had fasted. I thought maybe I fooled her into believing that I had, but it's doubtful.

Aunt Fannie says that those were some of the few times she ever defied her older sister. "I miss her now," said my aunt, much later. "Sometimes I still go to the phone to call her, and then I have to remember, oh, Becky isn't here any more."

▶▶▶

In 1945 the war ended, and the next decade was spent becoming happily re-accustomed to gasoline, meat, and nylon stockings.

The Feldman store prospered, but Fannie confided in Mother that Arthur's distant moods at home grew longer and more troubling. "One day he called me from Dr. Wolfe's office—he went there once in a while for treatments of some kind," Fannie recalls. "He never bothered to tell me what they were. But that day he was practically crying on the phone. "'What ever is wrong, dear?'" I asked.

" 'Please, come get me,' he said. 'I don't know what the doctor did to me, but I'm awfully sick.'

"Wade was home from high school, and he drove to pick Arthur up. When he came up the stairs, I asked, 'Honey, what's the matter?'

"'I don't know,' Arthur said. 'I feel terrible. I hurt all over.'"

Fannie called Dr. Wolfe. "I didn't do anything new," he said. "There's nothing wrong with Arthur. But he ran out of here like a crazy man!"

"It was never the same after that," says my aunt. "Arthur kept claiming that Dr. Wolfe had done something to him that day, and he kept hurting."

They started going to other doctors; they went to half a dozen. Fannie always went with him. Finally, doctors diagnosed what Arthur had as depression. It was in the late 1950s, and for the next two years he was in and out of hospitals, including for shock therapy. Nothing made much difference. The last doctor Arthur saw, someone who was very kind to him, said to my aunt, "Fannie, you're wasting your time. There's nothing you can do for what Arthur has."

"By then he had stopped driving," Fannie says. "If Harry had already left for work, I'd drive Arthur downtown to the store. In a few hours he'd call and say, 'I'm sick. I've got to come home.' And I would go and pick him up. Eventually there were days when he didn't want to go to work at all; he'd tell Harry to open the store without him. Sometimes he spent the day in pajamas.

"I'd call Becky and Henry or some other friends and ask them to come over to play cards at night. But he'd just sit the whole evening and hardly say anything. It seemed as if I was living with a different person. Or with no one."

One day Arthur said to her, "Honey, if I continue going to doctors and hospitals like this, there won't be a thing left for you and Wade."

"Don't worry about the money," she replied. "You're going to get well."

"Well," he said, "I don't know how I can live through this."

"There came a time when even Harry stopped coming upstairs," says Fannie. "He didn't understand. He was angry for being deserted by the brother he'd always leaned on."

Why wouldn't he be? For decades he and Arthur had played sports and cards together, owned a business together, ridden to work together, ridden home together. The only thing they didn't do together was to commit suicide. Arthur did that alone.

It was in 1960, about six years after Arthur first got sick. "We were in the bedroom, the two of us," Fannie says. "A quiet afternoon after a couple of days when Arthur had hardly spoken. He was getting dressed. Suddenly, he opened a drawer where he kept his underwear, and without saying anything, he took out a gun he had hidden in there. Before I could stop him, he shot himself . . . and he fell right at my feet."

My mother remembers Fannie calling her and blurting into the phone a frantic plea to come over. Mother rushed the couple of blocks to their house and found Fannie and, lying on the floor, her husband. "I'd never seen Arthur look so peaceful," my mother said later, sounding incredulous. "It was the last cruel thing he could do to her."

It's hard to condense the effect of an event like that. "Harry, the inseparable twin brother, was nonchalant," says my aunt, angrily. "All he did was come upstairs and take Arthur's clothes, as soon as he was buried.

"But for me . . . it was a long while before I could see anything but Arthur lying there on the floor.

"If I didn't believe in God, I wouldn't be here today. I thought, I don't know what it's all about, but surely the Lord knows. I'll do the best I can."

After a few months, Harry found that he couldn't continue to manage the store on Elm Street alone. He decided to close it and take home the remaining inventory. Joseph Gold, Fannie's old friend and attorney, told her not to let Arthur's brother put anything over on her, that she was entitled to half of everything that remained in the store. "So I asked Harry about it," Fannie says, "and he claimed that nothing remained of any value, and that's why he was closing the place. But later, I happened to be in their brother Joe's store—he had a jewelry store, too—when a woman came in asking for a particular cut of diamond. Joe called Harry at home to see if he had one. He did."

"So Harry and Minnie cheated me," says my aunt, "but I don't care. Those things never meant that much to me. And I didn't have the strength to fight them."

Harry died five years after his twin brother, and they're side by side, even now, in adjoining graves in the Shearith Israel Cemetery. Soon after Arthur died, Fannie sold her share of the duplex and moved to an apartment. "I should have furnished the new place first," she says, "then disposed of the rest, but I couldn't wait to get rid of it all and get away."

"And Wade?" she says to me. "Your mother was probably right. I spoiled him. But you know, he never had a father. So I had to be mother and father. I tried, though I don't think I did a very good job of it."

10

Heavy on the Gravy,
but Hide the Pots and Pans

"If you have money, you are wise and good-looking
and can sing well too."
Yiddish proverb

If my father's parents hadn't also bypassed Ellis Island, I wouldn't have become a first generation Jewish Texan. But they did. Like the Shapiros, and at around the same time, they debarked in Galveston. Unlike the Shapiros with their Russian heritage, the Elys set out from Romania. But they weren't Elys then—rather, something like Elyavitchs. Jewish immigrant women jettisoned their heavy shoes and wigs when they touched America; men shed their hard-to-spell names. Both left their memories behind. Of Romania my father remembered what my mother remembered about Russia: nothing.

Recently I learned of a Federation of Jewish Communities in Bucharest, Romania, and I wrote to see if they might be able to furnish any information about my father's family. Unfortunately I had little to help them go on.

However, the director of the federation answered my letter and included the following facts, which were quoted from Dr. Carol Iancu's book, *The Jews in Romania (1866-1919)*, published in Romania. They help to explain the Ely's migration.

There was an 1866 constitution which provided that Romanian citizenship be recognized only for Christians. Then, according to Dr. Iancu:

▶▶▶
The unique quality of exclusion lies in the country's legislation that debarred Jews not only from politics but also from various facets of social

life. Many trades and functions were expressly forbidden them: law, teaching, administration, the army. By the famous 'numerus clauses' they were progressively excluded from schools and universities.

This legal status, together with the activities of nationalist organizations and sometimes violent popular movements, led to 'en masse' emigration to the United States, western Europe and Palestine.

It is only at this later date (1919) that the Jews were accepted as full Romanian citizens, with all the rights attached to this designation.

▶▶▶

What the Elys and the Shapiros did share in common was their departure from the old country with empty pockets and the talent for keeping them empty. Grandpa Max Shapiro seems to have arranged failure in his grocery store, and Grandpa Solomon Ely, for whom I was named, masterminded a missed real estate windfall. Early in his days in Texas, he put together enough cash to buy several plots of inexpensive, unpromising land. That parcel, near South Dallas, later turned out to be in the core of downtown and worth more than enough to enrich several families. It did so, but they weren't ours. Calculating incorrectly that the land would remain undeveloped, Grandpa sold it years earlier, for a few dollars profit. If I ever feel the need to justify my lack of business acumen, I attribute it to loyalty to both grandfathers.

Grandpa Solomon Ely, a short, round-faced man always pictured wearing horn-rimmed glasses and a hat, was more successful in his association with the synagogue. Unlike Max Shapiro, whose pretense at religion got him out of work, Solomon served in 1906 as founding vice-president of The First Romanian and Austrian Benevolent Association in Dallas, later reorganized as a religious congregation. A small group of Orthodox Jews gathered for services in a tiny wooden building in South Dallas, just as they had in the old country, men and boys together embracing the Torah downstairs, women and girls dispatched upstairs. Though my Uncle Morris is a Shapiro and not an Ely, he and my brother Jerome both had their bar mitzvahs in the "Romanische" schul. However, the Orthodox side of Judaism was not as widespread in America as in Europe, and for it to survive, the little congregation had to merge with a larger one. That was Shearith Israel, the Conservative synagogue that my family attended.

Burial grounds assume high importance to Jews, who often take care to lay their dead to rest in the best possible places, not infrequently an improvement over what they enjoyed in life. So, in 1881, fifteen years even before the benevolent association was formed, the Romanian and Austrian group dedicated a cemetery that they called Anshe Sphard in old South Dallas. It today is the Shearith Israel Cemetery, that lonely but finely maintained remnant of Judaism in the south part of town that, like Jewish families, might have been moved north were that possible.

▶▶▶

In many traditions, Jews name a child only after someone deceased, so I of course never knew Grandpa Solomon. I did know Bubbe Esther, who lived until 1942, when I was ten. A small, sharp featured lady who spoke only Yiddish, but a lot of that, she gave birth to four sons and two daughters, half of them before the family had left Romania. With all those children around— and no Helen to help out—Bubbe could mostly be found in the kitchen of the Elys' wooden house on South Boulevard, a couple of blocks from Forest Avenue, one street over from Park Row.

Mama Ely, as she was called, baked eggplants stovetop, chopped in handfuls of bitter spices, added vinegar, sloshed it together and served it in large portions from glass jars, cold. After my parents were married, my mother reproduced that Romanian recipe for the benefit of my father, turning out a dish that he liked and the single version of eggplant that I've ever eaten and not liked.

Bubbe also fried chickens by the group, encased them in thick crusts, sheltered them in heavy gravy and offered them up alongside platters of buttered biscuits. Sam, Henry, Izzie, Rose, Sadie and Ben got the idea that in calories there was nothing villainous, a philosophy they adhered to the rest of their lives. It was from those early years that my father got the notion of skimping on other things, but not on food.

On the road to a freer life in America, most immigrant families stuck together, with particular obedience to the commandment of honoring father and mother. There was not one Ely or Shapiro son or daughter who didn't offer support to his or her parents, although sometimes begrudgingly.

My father, for instance. "Come live with us in University Park," he suggested to Bubbe as he planned our family's move away from Grand Avenue. "We'll make a room for you in the new house." But Mama Ely didn't picture herself as part of any change. She informed my dad and her other children, should they have a similar idea, that she intended to live out the rest of her life just where she was on South Boulevard, with the schul a short walk away and near friends of her age who also refused to leave the neighborhood they knew. And that's what she did. Once we had moved, my dad, like his brothers and sisters, had to go well out of his way to pay his respects after work. But his daily visits continued as long as Bubbe lived. Our dinners simply got delayed.

Settled on Stanhope Avenue, I started in the third grade in Bradfield School. Florence began college at Southern Methodist (referred to as SMU, its initials making it easy to ignore the religious affiliation). Jerome lacked one year to complete Forest High, so he stayed in South Dallas and lived with Bubbe Ely for a year so that he could finish in his old school. He would come across town to visit us on weekends.

I was then going on eight, short and thin, and Jerome was going on sixteen, tall and thin. Mama Ely took it as her mission to change her grandson's profile during his residency. "She sure loaded me up with eggplant and chicken soup," he'd report to us on Saturdays. By the end of that year, when Jerome moved back with the rest of us, he was a little heavier and Bubbe was sadder. Yaakov had become her little prince as I, Shlomo, had once been Grandpa Max Shapiro's.

▶▶▶

One time my sister was asked who was the stronger of her two parents. "Mother," she responded without hesitation. Maybe that explains in part why, for Florence and Jerome and me, it was the Shapiros who from the very start we thought of as family. Even though Uncle Sam and Aunt ("Big") Becky Ely lived for a while on the other side of our Grand Avenue duplex, they and all the other Elys got categorized in our minds as the more distant relations, viewed with a certain skepticism. That perception was given birth if for no other reason than that the Shapiros always were closer at hand, maybe a reflection of my mother's dominant role in our family.

There was also the issue of money. Though not scorned by the Shapiros, in the lives of my father's brothers it assumed a more central, at least a more apparent, role. Even as young men downing Mama Ely's fried chicken around the table on South Boulevard, talk among them centered around how they would avoid the kind of struggle they had seen their parents and their parents' friends endure. They set out for a future built around work and family security.

And not through the corporate life. That was hardly known in those days and wouldn't have had much appeal if it were. Among my father's generation of Jews, it became a goal, if possible, to avoid working for someone else. And since in Dallas many Jewish families knew or were related to one another, they consciously or not started to divide up the pot. The Lewises seemed interested in the retail liquor business, so that would go to them, and it was somehow understood that no one else would compete. To the Siegels went dairy products, and the Markowitzes could corner the bread products franchises. So it went in that mannerly way. For those families whose vision was more modest, there was always room for one more small dress manufacturer or wholesaler or another retail jewelry or apparel shop. As their first customers, those families could count on the Lewises, Siegels and Markowitzes.

Such early dreams emerged as realities on the Dallas landscape and brought wealth to those families and generations of their heirs.

The Ely brothers set out to find an open niche. Market researchers didn't exist then, but common sense and footwork served as well. The winning idea came one night from Sam, the eldest brother.

"What do you think of a wholesale house that sells men's leather goods and accessories?" he asked Henry, Izzie and Ben. (Rose and Sadie, the sisters, weren't polled since it was assumed that they would marry and be the responsibilities of their husbands.) "I've looked around—no one else is doing it. I'm talkin' about a business where we travel out of Dallas, to other cities, even the little towns that everybody else ignores. We divide up the territory."

"I like that!" yelled Izzie, the thin brother with eyeglasses. "Provided we connect with good lines to sell. No junk. Quality belts and wallets."

"And maybe small clocks and tie racks," added Ben, the youngest. "The bigger we get, the better discounts we can demand."

After the shake of hands, which sealed the deal, funds got pooled so that Sam could take the long train trip to New York City to persuade manufacturers to lend the young brothers credit lines far off in Texas. Sam was a handsome, well-built man in his mid-twenties—a persuasive salesman—and he succeeded. Soon he was back home with the news that three well-known New York companies had agreed to work with them on a trial basis. He and his brothers quickly rented warehouse space and a small office and hired one or two Jewish young men to run the office, promising them a share of the profits. The brothers expected to be on the road most of the time, agreeing on how they would divide the territories of Texas (itself no small plot), Louisiana, Arkansas and Tennessee, all to be reached by car. With that, the Ely Company was formed.

But there was a holdout: my father, the second oldest son. While his brothers were unpacking the boxes of new merchandise and setting up travel schedules, Dad said no thanks for the invitation to join them and went to work instead as advertising manager of a small retail clothing store. His refusal to join the partnership had nothing to do with laziness. "He just had to work by himself," my mother always explained.

One morning when Florence and Jerome were still young kids and with a depression hovering nearby, Dad arrived early at the store and found a sign posted in front saying that it had closed and was out of business. After that, like his contemporaries, he swore never to work for anyone else.

From his own market research, my father had heard about what for his part of the country was a fledgling business, that of life insurance. He met the manager of a major New York company about to enter the South and in the late 1920s was taken on as an independent insurance agent, the very first to represent that organization in Texas. He remained with them for the next fifty years, his own boss.

"Your dad probably would have gotten richer in the wholesale business with Sam and I.G. and Ben," Mother said to me, "but it would never have worked. He had to do things his way."

Mother was right. There were times when the only similarity between my father and his brothers seemed to be their family name. While Sam and Izzie and Ben succeeded in patronizing Cadillac dealerships, my father was satisfied to drive to work in our old gray Dodge for as long as it agreed to make the trip. All my Ely aunts and uncles eventually joined lavish Jewish country clubs, sometimes more than one, but my father's club was the Masonic Lodge. The split carried over to religious affiliations: while my parents remained in the Conservative synagogue, the other Elys joined Reform temples, newly fashionable and the antithesis of the old "Romanische" Orthodox schul that Grandpa Solomon had founded. "So conservative!" Uncle Ben, a dozen years my father's junior, said, derisively, of my dad and his approach to life.

▶▶▶

Uncle Sam married tall, stately "Big" Becky. She was a beautifully groomed lady whose bearing and speech belied an upbringing as humble as my mother's. For years Aunt Becky and Uncle Sam lived well, traveled and saved little, and when Sam contracted leukemia and died in his fifties, he left Big Becky poor. "Even when Sam was near the end, you never saw Becky not looking her best," my mother declared, somewhere between admiring and contemptuous. Even when Aunt Becky lost her husband and her wealth, she retained her elegance.

Izzie apparently didn't like his name and opted for what seemed to me the even less appealing nickname, "I.G." He married Bessie, a goodhearted woman who later volunteered to raise a young orphan girl along with her own two children. Aunt Bessie was a champion and generous producer of kosher-style dill pickles that she let age in a dark cellar and that I loved. Far less stylish than Aunt Becky, she'd periodically deliver a jar or two of her pickles to our house with instructions to my mother that they be given to me.

Many years later, Aunt Bessie became widowed, forgot she had ever been poor, and turned into a demanding, daffy old lady. She'd insist on being an unwelcome part of a group of younger folks who were on their way out for an evening's dancing or partying.

Beyond being the youngest of the sons, Uncle Ben was the most brash— "the big shot," as my father characterized him in a tone a little short of admiration. Cousin Ann remembers Ben as a popular, freewheeling young fellow, six feet and fair, with large handsome features and a deep voice. I suspected that our cousin might not have minded becoming Mrs. Ben, but he didn't ask her. The right wife for him would be someone regal and strong, like Sara, who became his wife for more than a half century. She bore him a good-looking son, Jerry, and a pretty daughter, Marilyn. She shared his ambition for success and helped him finally to become the wealthiest of all four brothers.

Aunt Sara was a slender, tailored woman of fine, straight features who appreciated and sought fine things, an arranger of houses and lives. She had been part of a cultured German Jewish family. As long as I knew her, her health seemed tentative and her appearance perfect. "Sara might be laid up with one of her kidney attacks," said my mother, "but let an emergency arise and she's out of bed, dressed in a smart outfit, her hair done, and ready to take charge."

As I was growing up, my aunt urged me join their Jewish country club in Dallas as a junior member. Though I was certainly snobbish enough to like being invited there, it was a place where I never felt I belonged. Aunt Sara seemed hurt when I declined. Had I agreed, she might also have appointed herself to track me down a wife. She would have located a good one.

But all that was later. My first recollections of her and Uncle Ben were terror. "I'm afraid that . . . uhh . . ." I would say in front of my towering uncle, the words fading off into silence. "Afraid?" he'd bark back. "Don't be afraid of anything!" He certainly never seemed to be.

Sooner or later I dropped the "uncle" or "aunt" that preceded those relatives on my mother's side, but I would never have entertained doing that with Ben and Sara. As long as they lived, they remained "uncle" and "aunt" and I find myself addressing them so even now when I go to visit their graves.

While their husbands were out selling on the road, Big Becky, Bessie and

Sara, the wives of the three partners, banded together for lunches and furnishing of houses. But there was a competitive edge to that fellowship, and if one of the three emerged with a new mink coat, the others usually followed. They lived like that for years, changing on a moment's notice and with no apparent explanation from best friends to silent adversaries.

My mother was of course another Ely wife but never a member of that triumvirate. If during the shifting alliances of her sisters-in-law she participated mostly as a distant player, it was, I thought, with some enthusiasm. My mother and father, though less affluent than the others, had avoided the rivalries their partnership produced by never being part of it.

It happened that Aunt Becky and Aunt Sara were in a period of not speaking when Uncle Sam died. Uncle Ben had no use for grudges, and knowing that Big Becky had been left poor, he offered to help her, seeking reconciliation with his sister-in-law for himself and Sara. Aunt Becky wouldn't have it. She elected instead, at a not young age, to start work as saleswoman in an exclusive dress shop in Dallas. My mother often invited her for dinner at our house, and I looked forward to those visits with my stylishly dressed aunt. Big Becky spoke and looked as if she had come from buying costly outfits rather than selling them.

Uncle Sam's death was not the only event that altered the Ely Company's makeup. It was followed a couple of decades later by I.G.'s decision to strike out on his own. He withdrew from the partnership and, not to compete with it, he and his family moved to Atlanta where he started the I.G. Ely Company, a similar business, with his son Bernard. Ben and I.G. parted in the most brotherly way, once more making certain not to overlap territories. They coordinated buying trips to markets in New York to make joint purchases and benefit from greater discounts. For years afterwards, Ben counseled his older brother and nephew on the running of their Atlanta business and seemed genuinely sorry that it never prospered as much as his own had.

▶▶▶

Every Sunday between mid-1939 and 1940, my parents and I drove in the Dodge the six or seven miles to watch our new home being built on

Stanhope. I could hardly wait until we finally moved on the first day of July 1940. The house was airy and pretty with two bathrooms , enough that I could finally linger awhile. Until I went to visit the Ben Elys, it seemed to me as nice a house as I had seen.

They, of course, had also moved, to a new home a mile or so away from us, on an elegant, tree-lined street in Highland Park (a step up from University Park). On a block zoned for two-story dwellings with considerable footage between them, their house looked forbidding, painted outside in grays and cool, dark greens. If it evolved that most visitors came in to see us through the back or side entrance, the front door was the port of entry at Uncle Ben's. You rang the doorbell, which was answered by Bernice, their maid, whether anyone else was home, or busy, or not. My aunt's collection of Lalique crystal and Baker furniture got installed behind heavy folds of living room drapes, richly patterned and pleated, that tumbled from high ceiling to floor and forbade the entrance of any interrupting light.

Occasionally I would ride my bicycle—the one I nagged my parents to buy and then rarely used—over to visit Marilyn, who, a couple of years younger than me, is the only Ely cousin approximately my age. In her bedroom on the second floor, her parents had built shelves to house her collection of hand-made dolls. "Marilyn," I said on a visit one hot summer's day, "I'm thirsty. I'm goin' in the kitchen to get some water."

"No, you don't need to do that!" she replied, urgently. "Bernice will get it for you." Bernice, who I figured must have had better things to do, was summoned to the job.

The truth is, I wasn't so thirsty. I wanted to peek into Aunt Sara's kitchen, an adventure I relished because I had never seen one that, though used, seemed so unused. Neither she nor Bernice (by her instructions, I supposed) left out a thing, anything, on any counter or appliance or table top. A thorough inspection wouldn't reveal one clue to hint at the room's being used to prepare the fried chicken and gravy that Uncle Ben loved.

The move to North Dallas prompted annual invitations for Thanksgiving dinner at Uncle Ben's, occasions when it would have been a toss-up as to whether my father or I was the less comfortable. Had the gathering been anywhere else, I'm sure Dad would have found an excuse to bow out. Though agreeing to go, he found no reason to get dressed up just for dinner at his younger brother's. It was my mother who found some rationale in it. I sported a new shirt and ironed pants.

"Dear Stanley," Aunt Sara would smile, as she greeted me in a long, elegant dress, her hair done, as always, in a complex coiffure. After nervously shaking hands with Uncle Ben and saying hello to Jerry, their son, five years older than me, I'd go upstairs to see Marilyn and await what I figured would be a wonderful dinner.

Which it always was. Silver dishes heaped with turkey and dressings and vegetables and condiments were offered in Uncle Ben's elegant dining room under a sparkling crystal chandelier. The presenters were Bernice in starched uniform, aided by one or two others arrived for the occasion. A few smaller tables had been set up to the side of the dining room, for "the kids," and I liked being assigned there since it gave me the distance to watch a pageant unfold. I wondered how Bubbe Ely, tough and simple worker in her modest household, who by then had passed on, would have viewed her youngest son's banquet.

But, having gorged on the evening's bird, what really intrigued me was how so much food had come out of that immaculate kitchen. If I summoned enough nerve, sometime before leaving I'd sneak back there just to see if late at night, when the lights were out, anything from all those dishes and bowls and cups and saucers and, presumably, an army of pots and pans, may have accidentally been left out. Nothing, of course, was.

Finally, I'd shake hands with Uncle Ben and thank him sincerely. Ready to depart, my father looked happier than when we had arrived. "Good night, brother," Uncle Ben would say to his elder sibling, grasping him affectionately by the arm and smiling at the event he had sponsored.

"Goodnight, brother," responded my father tentatively.

Decades later, I visited Marilyn when she was married and herself the mother of three. We passed through her kitchen as she escorted me from the front of her house to the family room. "Oh, Stanley," she pleaded, "please excuse this messy kitchen!"

The least observant visitor couldn't have helped wondering when a meal had last been prepared in that room. It was as ominously clean, as vacant of all sign of use as what I remembered seeing in her mother's house years before.

There was no way I could suppress a grin and a feeling of affection. "It's okay, cuz," I said.

Mother's grandparents in Russia, c. 1890

The candlesticks from Russia

My parents' engagement, 1919

Mother's wedding photo, 1920

Aunt Pearl, c. 1920

Mother playing in Galveston, c. 1921

Grandpa Max Shapiro in his Dallas grocery store, c. 1915

Stanley and Grandpa Max, c. 1936

Mother and Stanley, c. 1936

Aunt Rose, c. 1930

Aunt Fannie, c. 1918

Aunt Pearl, c. 1918

Stanley and Aunt Fannie, c. 1941

Uncle Herbert, c. 1935

69

Aunt Fannie and Stanley, c. 1936

Aunt Rose and Aunt Fannie, c. 1955

Part Two

Closer to Home

11

Henry—As Much Salt As You Want, but No Pepper

If Jews from "up north" are merely taken aback when they get the bad news that they don't have a monopoly on American Judaism, they're astonished to find out that off in the provinces, their cousins manifest no yearning whatever for their big-city lifestyle. This always seemed to me especially true of Texans.

None of the Ely brothers harbored affection for New York, my father least of all. Now and then he traveled east to visit the head office of his insurance company—sometimes, in the old days, even setting out in the wrong direction, from Dallas south to Galveston. There he would board the boat that descended through the Gulf of Mexico, sailed around Florida and up the Atlantic along the East Coast. That trip, now thought frivolous and stored away as history, sounded like a magnificent adventure to me, one on which I would gladly have taken his place. But Dad stayed away no more than ten days, the minimum needed to travel, check into headquarters and charge the trip to business.

"You can have that place!" was the verdict he pronounced after every visit to New York. Or, as Mother wrote to her friend in Houston, "Henry gives New York to the New Yorkers."

Little Becky and Henry moved to Grand Avenue and in a couple of years became parents to Florence (1922) and Jerome (1924). "I am only good for raising babies," Mother wrote to Rose during that decade. She might more accurately have said "having babies," since she shared a good part of their raising with one or another black ladies who became poorly paid but loyal household helpers. Laying plans to support those babies became my father's task, one that he shared with no one.

Without any education except that which he pursued on his own and without the partnership that his brothers enjoyed, my father aspired to become an honor roll businessman: energetic, informed and dependable. At times generous and discreet, as well. To avoid having his clients lose their insurance coverage, he would quietly advance their premiums when they couldn't afford to cover them. Cousin Ann says he loaned money to her and others in the family when they wanted to take night-school classes.

Dad also grasped the notion of how a businessman presents himself. Building on a good start from nature, he retained a slender six-foot figure, a healthy complexion and a strict adherence to whatever diet got prescribed by his trusted physician, Dr. Joe. Even into his early eighties and feeble, and though the process may then have stretched out for an hour, he continued as he had for decades to dress for work. After buttoning a clean white shirt, he would tie his own paisley or polka dot bow tie, meticulously slip a fresh handkerchief into the coat pocket of his suit and top the outfit with a proper hat, cloth in winter, straw in summer. He placed a small black pad with reminders of things to do in his inside coat pocket. Unlike Fannie's husband Arthur, who finally refused to go to work, Dad refused to stay home. He continued to make the trek downtown until a couple of months before he died, long past the time when one could be sure he still knew the way.

▶▶▶
The walls in my father's office grew ever more crowded with certificates for contests he'd won in the insurance business: "Henry Ely, Million Dollar Club, 1945." "Henry Ely, Leaders Club, 1950." He and Mother often went away for conventions, entrance to which had been garnered by winning those awards.

Someone seeing that collection of framed certificates might have assumed that in Henry Ely's office sat a man needing only to open the door to clients who had been jostling one another impatiently in line. That would have been a mistake. Those honors didn't disclose the struggle it took to get the world on his side.

Many evenings my father spent phoning potential clients, his voice taking on a particular warmth that seemed to start and end with the call. At Shearith Israel, he volunteered to take charge of seating reservations for the High Holy Days (on Rosh Hashanah, you didn't think you could simply walk in and expect to find a seat!). That job entitled him to stand at the door and shake hands with the congregants as they entered the sanctuary. "Gut Yontif, Sol," he would greet, "L'Shana Tovah," his presence serving as visible reminder that he would be around past Yom Kippur to attend to their insurance needs.

Away from business but never away from it, my dad's walk through life was rarely a peaceful stroll.

He even half, or less than half, jokingly asked my friends whether they wouldn't like some life insurance. Years later, he visited the office where I was working in New York and did the same among my colleagues, a moment for me of terrible embarrassment. Though I was unmarried and childless, he loaded me up with insurance policies enough for the head of a large family (policies I canceled after he died).

The compensation for his hard work, if there was one, was at home, with children whom he loved without understanding them and a wife whom he called from his office at noon every day for fifty years. "Hello, anything new there? Just wanted to check in." If he became irritated by the shady action of some competitor, however—and it happened regularly—he would place Mother at the receiving end. "You never help me in business, like Sara does with my brother Ben," he'd complain loudly.

"Henry," she would reply, looking him directly in the eye, "when I have tried to help, you said that I did everything wrong. So I'm not offering any more!"

I heard these stances voiced and revoiced at home, and I used to puzzle over which of my parents was right. Finally I saw they were both right, and both had gotten the arrangement they sought. The dialogue merely served to verify their positions and allow them to continue.

Dad never understood why neither Jerome nor I, and Florence least of all, felt any urge to take over his insurance business, an idea he tried to promote with the promise of a good start from his list of clients and commissions from renewals of policies he had sold. He saw no connection between his children's antipathy and his unending portrayal of the insurance business as a profession burdened with slimy salesmen. The effect was so obvious to me, I couldn't imagine how it wouldn't be to him. But I never bothered to explain it. I just liked saying, "No thanks."

Eventually Henry Ely managed to do what every Jewish husband was expected to do: provide shelter and food and a certain status and respectability for his spouse and children. Affectionate understanding, if it came along, was a bonus, not required of male heads of families. Above all my father set out to leave his wife financially independent, if he died before she. And he did.

▶▶▶

If by dint of labor Dad prospered in business, many of the rest of life's satisfactions eluded him.

The independent streak that made him reject a partnership with his brothers plus his success as insurance agent were only a corner of the picture. They were not enough to counteract the insecurity in which he seemed so trapped that dogmatism presented itself as the constant escape. His grand-daughters Elissa and Marcia remember him as a stern old man who preached "good behavior" and would give them a nickel or a dime as a reward if they toed the line.

My father's opinions stepped forward without need of examination through any weighing process, and once reached, never had to stand up to review. As a room immediately brightens when the light switch is turned on, his convictions got born in an instant.

"Russians, they're all crooks!" he stated during the years of communism, forgetting, I figured, that without them, he would have been without his wife. "Those other insurance agents—and most lawyers? Shysters!"

"All?" I'd ask.

"All!"

Long hair was dirty hair, and he even held to the belief, gotten who knows where, that though salt is healthy and should be used unsparingly, pepper is unhealthy and ought not to be used at all. There was no point trying to persuade him that he had gotten it turned around. Pepper was banished from our dining table, and if I had a sudden craving to ruin my health, I sneaked into the kitchen and sprinkled a dash of the stuff directly on my plate.

The untrustworthiness of other insurance agents was a frequent topic but not as frequent as the subject of marriage, on which my father's opinion was unequivocal: marriage is right, bachelorhood, like pepper, ought not to be on the table. Florence and Jerome did their duties in that regard, and when Dad and I had nothing else to converse about, which wasn't infrequent, he would renew the subject. "Your brother and sister are married now, you know." ("Yes, I do.") "Are you dating anyone, a nice Jewish girl?" ("Umm.") "You're past twenty-five, it's time to settle down." ("I thought I was!")

I searched for limp excuses until the game became infuriating. "If I ever do get married," I yelled at him once, "it'll be to please me, not you!" It was a moment of dishonest rage, since I knew I was not going to marry for his sake or mine. I withheld the real reason, telling myself that he wouldn't have understood. In truth, I enjoyed the withholding.

When everyone else had long since understood that I was not a candidate for marriage, when my father was so old that he couldn't name the day of the week, he managed to remember that I wasn't wed and would unearth the topic yet again. In his need to see me married to confirm his success as a father (and, I assume, to see me happy), I confess that I found something horrible and poignant.

▸▸▸

People who are bound by routines may be unexciting, but they offer the advantage of rarely surprising anyone. Once all his children were away, my father wrote letters, with carbon copies, to all of us, two or three times per week. He used his office typewriter. "Dear kids," they started. "Nothing much new today. Maybe it'll rain. Called home awhile ago, but nobody there. Mom must have gone to the beauty parlor again. What a waste of money, eh?" The letters would end, "We're proud of all of you. Love, Dad." I figured that any day, on the copy he sent me, he might add a P.S., "but we'd be prouder if you got married."

Dad's preoccupations were as dependable as his routines, and they usually centered around small matters: closing the faucet not to waste water (which in Texas, one pays for). Those sermons could be expected. But even for we who are predictable (and I'm one, too), there are occasional lapses. With him, it happened when I took up smoking, around the end of my high school days.

For two or three years I had fallen into obsession about Larry, a handsome friend a year or so older than me. Since he started to smoke, it was inevitable that I would follow. Furtive revolt was my way, so when I joined my pal for cigarettes—non-filtered killers—it was at his house or behind my garage.

But soon after high school, I went north to college, by then no longer dizzy from inhaling and without the need to retreat to the alley for a smoke. There were no parents to hide from, only new friends to offer companionship in the habit, and purchases of cigarettes started to be made by the carton. But as the Christmas holidays approached—my first trip home from school—I got nervous. After discussing the matter with my co-smokers, I decided it was time to come clean about the habit. I wrote to my parents to give them the news.

Dad picked me up at the railroad station in Fort Worth. The train arrived there, rather than Dallas, rendering the trip to our house longer. He looked pale and bleary, plainly upset. "We got your letter yesterday," said my father, "and I hardly slept last night."

Hardly slept? "Oh?"

"You know," he continued, "you're the only one—the only one—in our family to smoke. Who ever smoked!"

Of course I knew. That added to the appeal.

"Yes," I murmured, "but everyone at school does it. Just everyone. Girls and boys! It's not a sin."

We rode the rest of the way in silence, with me resolved that if I was going to smoke, I'd do it in front of family as well as Larry. For the ten days of that vacation, while Mother characteristically avoided engaging in the affair, the number of distressful looks from my father kept pace with the number of cigarettes I lit at home, and vice-versa. Neither of us compromised.

Finally, the holiday ended and the day came to go back to Fort Worth for the return trip to school. At the railroad station, Dad and I embraced awkwardly. "Well," he said, "take care of yourself up there," and reaching into his pocket, he added, "here's a little gift."

A gift? A little gift? "But . . . thank you!" I stammered. When had I ever gotten a gift from him?

I boarded the train, settled into my seat and waved tentatively through the window. As soon as the train pulled away, I tore open the wrapping. Inside the package was a silver cigarette lighter.

▶▶▶

My brother often characterized our dad as "a good man," and Dad was that even if he sometimes simply was wrong. Jerome accepted that paradox better than me. In later years I wondered why my mother, the smarter of our parents, didn't offer occasional corrections. But she didn't.

Certainly my mother had her faults, but faults were easier to find in my father. Many nights he coached young applicants in Masonic Lodge work, though he showed no interest in my schoolwork. He didn't take me to baseball games (which I wasn't so eager to go to, anyway). My mother's sisters, with whom he never felt comfortable, he called by demeaning nicknames like "Emmy Schmaltz." While overlooking my election as editor of the school newspaper, he dwelled on minor infractions like my leaving on the lights in rooms where they weren't used or forgetting to lock the back door. He often reminded me that, to save the four-cent carfare years before, he had walked to work downtown—unlike me, who wasted gasoline today. The faults that he spotlighted I always found unremarkable.

And when he continued to obsess on my unmarried status, it seemed that he finally could focus only on what I wasn't, blind to all that I was.

My mother would comment on what a fine teacher a neighbor of ours was to his son, a close friend of mine. "Mr. __ was such a good teacher!" Mother remarked, with a curious kind of frequency. Was she pointing out the opposite about my own father? I'm not sure.

As a child, I remember Dad, as the Sabbath ended at sundown on Saturday, offering his family the traditional wish: "A Gutte Voch." ("Have a good week.") Thinking back on it, I wonder that not once did I ask what the phrase meant. And never did he explain it.

The result of this disharmony was that for most of my adult life, he and I engaged in a battle in which only one side kept at the fight. Mine. As most boys need to love their fathers, I needed, sorry to say, to reject mine. In case he didn't appreciate that a war was still on, I found ways to send reminders: persisting in smoking (which he hated notwithstanding the lighter) and especially as we exited the synagogue; growing a beard (which even I wasn't sure I cared for and which he found dirty); and not getting married (though leaving the reason unexplained).

The final clincher came when he was very old and I would return to Dallas for a visit, chat like a parrot with my mother, then grow nearly silent when he entered the room. By that time all the vitality of youth had left him. "Is there anything you'd like to discuss with me?" he would ask, almost plaintively.

I'd pause as if to ponder the question. "Noo," I'd reply, slowly, "no, I don't think so." I would see him retreat, a lonely loser.

▶▶▶

My wall of near silence continued until Dad's final illness, a few days in a Connecticut hospital following a series of strokes. (The hospital requested an autopsy, to which we agreed. The doctors reported amazement that the man had been able to walk, so blocked were his arteries.)

I resisted going into his hospital room during those final hours, and did so finally only because a valued friend insisted that I must, that I would regret it later if I didn't. In the room I saw Dad lay struggling, in a coma, and I approached his bed reluctantly, not at all sure what to do. Whether or not he heard my words, I have no way to know, but if he did they must have amazed him as much as they did me. Through my tears they blurted out, unplanned. "I'm sorry, I'm so sorry!"

"So sorry?" For what? Being a poor son? His being a poor father? Both things? I never knew!

He died the next day, and his body had to be returned to Texas. That occurred during a period when I had a phobia of flying so deep that I had stopped doing it. Stubbornly, I took the train to Dallas—a day and a half's trip—and missed his funeral. My sister gave me a furious look. My mother said I would have been proud to see the number of persons who came to the funeral home and then to their apartment to say Kaddish that evening. The rabbi said he was sorry I didn't like flying.

▶▶▶

More than two decades since his death in 1975, I light a candle on the day of my father's Yahrzeit (the anniversary of his death).

I realize by now that when he was wrong, it was without malice, and that what he denied me were gifts like sensitivity and companionship that he didn't know how to give. On issues of importance to me, such as my choice to go to a university up north (that region for which he had no use), he offered willing support.

These are facts I've seen only lately. Admitting to my father's good side, the side that I don't think Florence ever saw but that Jerome understood all along, has come haltingly to me. It wasn't until three or four years after Dad was gone that I could agree with his contempt for smoking, and with his belief that the beard was unappealing. That's when I stopped smoking and shaved the beard. Today I'm even more rabid against smokers than he was, and without the emphysema that made smoke painful for him.

One of his most engaging moments took place when I wasn't around. A college friend visiting in Dallas long after college paid a courtesy call on my parents, and my father, trying to be the hospitable Texas host, offered a drink. Inexperienced in the art of bartending, he poured what my friend described as the strongest Scotch ever made. "He must have emptied the bottle in it," my friend advised me.

▶▶▶

Recently I've had to face a new discovery. Since he was forty when I was born, Dad always seemed old to me. "Old" meant "Dad," and vice-versa. Now, I was getting older—nearly old—and to me that meant . . . him, the person I had tried hardest not to resemble.

Ironically, he is the person whom I resemble the most. Physically, first of all, even to the reluctant smile that often slips into disdain. And our similarities grow stronger as I grow older. On trips back to Dallas, persons he knew never fail to notice: "Yes, indeed, you sure are Henry's son!" In the mirror I see reflected other qualities of his: overreactions to small upsets, anger at minor injustices, fury at petty misdemeanors. They are mine as they were his.

The ultimate copying of an attitude concerns one I despised, the exclusive sanctity of a heterosexual union. Though it seemed to me impoverished nonsense, I've struggled for years to extricate the notion from my own head. The success has been mixed. As Jews sometimes make good anti-Semites, gays are often fine homophobes. In this, my father inked the pad well, then put his stamp on me. It's an imprint that I'm still trying to erase, to persuade myself that bachelor—along with pepper—equals okay.

12

Little Becky and Us

My father never interfered with Mother's passion for daytime card playing, nor even for her occasional exodus from Dallas to visit Florence and her
children in Denver or Jerome and his children in Stamford, and me later in
nearby New York. The trip that challenged Mother's strength and forever put
an end to her image as merely cute was the one she took to Stamford when
Jerome had been diagnosed with cancer. That was the fall and winter of
1962-1963.

Jerome's illness was discovered on a routine chest x-ray taken in May
1962, and by early November he was unable to work. In October my mother
came east and stayed throughout the remaining four months until my brother's death the following February.

Shortly before Christmas, Jerome's doctors referred him to the care of
cancer specialists at Memorial Sloan-Kettering Hospital. When he moved into
Manhattan, Mother and Paula, Jerome's wife, decided that they would share a
room in a residential hotel in midtown, from which they could walk to the hospital. Paula's mother left her home on Long Island and moved to Stamford to
take charge of her granddaughters Elissa and Marcia; I often joined them on
weekends. Paula returned to Connecticut regularly to see her children, but she
remained mostly in Manhattan. Mother was a long way from her home in
Texas. For a couple of long months, it seemed as if no one was where they
belonged, everyone was in a strange place.

When my mother arrived in Stamford, she brought a knee length white
wool coat with a leopard skin collar, the sort of cover that can get you through

most days of a Texas winter. As New York weather got colder, she wore it every day until it seemed too light in weight and the white of the wool darkened into gray. Mother was unconcerned with how it felt or looked—she may not have even noticed. She didn't take care, either, to eat the proper breakfast that she had prepared for us as youngsters, endorsing it as a fundamental opener to good health. Her day focused around the hours spent at Jerome's side, long ones that started early every morning.

I was working in a marketing job in an office nearby and often would go to the hospital after work. I'd visit with my brother and wait until Mother and Paula were ready to end their day, not before eight or nine o'clock. Then I'd accompany them for a supper nearby.

The hospital hours passed with awful slowness, and my mother drew close to some others who were keeping vigils at the bedsides of loved ones. She particularly befriended an elegant young woman who had come from Colombia with her husband, who was suffering from leukemia. Our mother easily fell into the role of her mother, now and then accompanying her to the cafeteria and even the nondenominational chapel downstairs in the hospital. "You want to go to the chapel for a little while?" Mother asked her. "Come on, I'll go with you." The young woman's knowledge of English was slight, but she understood.

One night I saw her walking slowly down the hall corridor with her husband leaning on her arm, both of them looking spirited by the fact that he was at least momentarily able to be out of his room. Only a night later, the woman was absent. "What happened to—?" I asked. I knew the answer when I saw Mother's eyes fill with tears.

"She left," I heard.

My father came to New York for a couple of brief visits during those weeks, but he was without words in the hospital. He remained mostly in Dallas. Mother made sure that friends invited him to dinner, but otherwise she did not seem to notice her separation from him.

Life ebbed ineluctably from Jerome, and as he grew weaker, Mother's supervision grew even more constant. On the morning of the last day of my brother's life, a bitter late February day heading into a snowstorm, Paula went home on the train to Stamford with sudden fever and flu. "Go home and take care of yourself," Mother told her. "I'll stay."

By six or seven that night, it became clear that the end may have been near, and we called Paula to come back. There was also the question of Dad. In unemotional terms, my mother approached the doctor in charge. "My son's father lives in Texas," she said. "Do you think . . . I should call him to come?"

"I believe so," replied the doctor, quietly. So she did.

A sign was posted on the door to Jerome's room, indicating that oxygen was in use, forbidding visitors. Conversations among Mother and Paula and Paula's sister and me finally ended. Time seemed to stop. I paced the hallway and barely cracked open the door to Jerome's room. I could hear the very dimmest of breath. Finally, toward eleven o'clock, the doctor, a tall handsome woman, asked me to step away, and she went into the room alone. After a long while she came out and softly told me, standing in the hall, that my brother was gone.

I went back to the waiting room where the others sat, silent and exhausted. I didn't think about what to say. "It's all over," I said. "Oh God!" I heard cried aloud. We all collapsed, but Mother for only a moment. The doctor asked us to allow an autopsy. Mother looked at Paula with a silent "yes."

There was a last look before we left. On the side table beside his bed were Jerome's eyeglasses. Without thinking, I picked them up. I started to hand them to Mother but stupidly, practically, dropped them in the wastebasket as we left his room.

People marvel when I tell them that the next morning, before returning with Paula to Stamford, my mother went down to the beauty shop in their hotel to have her hair done. I was taken aback when I found her there. Only later did I come to believe that her action had nothing to do with vanity. She said to Paula that there wasn't anything else she could do. To me it seemed that at a most hideous moment she was grasping for a hold on life.

I left Mother and Paula and reluctantly boarded a bus to the airport to meet my father when he arrived from Dallas. He walked off the plane stiffly, and I guided him to a small private room that I had requested, to tell him that Jerome had died late the night before. We went outside into the cold to wait for cousins of Paula who came to pick up him and me and drive us, silently, to Stamford. When Dad entered Jerome and Paula's house and saw my mother, he broke into sobs. Mother looked at him coldly, with a glance that seemed to say, "Get hold of yourself."

That day, my young nieces Elissa and Marcia went to play at a friend's house. The snow arrived, and I was glad when it began to stick in the driveway and I could go outside to shovel. Later, we realized that the more proper place for Jerome's burial might have been in Dallas, but he was laid to rest the following day in Paula's family's plot on Long Island. Though my father was seated just on the other side of her, my mother leaned her head on my shoulder as we drove to and from the cemetery in the limousine.

After a week of sitting Shivah in Connecticut, my parents undertook their trip back to Texas, my mother's first return home since the previous October. I accompanied them to the airport, and as Mother started to board the plane, I noticed that she was still wrapped in the white coat, the coat that remained gray.

One day, a month after Jerome's death, my father was driving to a town near Dallas to call on a client. Around noon and in bright sunshine, he fell into a deep sleep at the wheel of his car. The car rolled off the highway and turned over into a ditch. Perhaps Dad was saved by the fact that he was asleep and relaxed, because he incurred deep bruises and contusions but was otherwise uninjured. The car was junked.

That was 1963, by which time my brother and sister and I had all been away from Dallas for years. My parents decided to put the house on Stanhope on the market. Mother took charge of the search for a new home. She quickly found a spacious ground floor apartment for her and my father with a second bedroom for TV watching and guests. The house that I especially loved, that all of us had lived in, that my parents continued in for a total of twenty-three years, got sold and the move made within a few weeks.

Once in their new apartment on Edgemere Street, Mother characteristically never looked back to Stanhope. Though it hadn't been Jerome's home for well more than a decade, my parents' leaving that house stamped a final seal though hardly the final memory of the life of a beloved son.

▶ ▶ ▶

Mother found the height that nature didn't give her in her straight posture and determined walk and even her dark, deep eyes that somehow met whoever she was talking to on their level. If you were to ask me whether she was a spiritual person, I would quickly say yes. At the end of the day I often saw her walk out on the deck behind the Stanhope house, look to the sky, fold her hands together and pray. Paula remarked that even as Jerome was sick, Mother lit the Sabbath candles with quiet and serenity.

Her visits with the young Colombian woman to the nondenominational chapel in Memorial Hospital marked perhaps the only times in her life that she went beyond the bounds of Judaism for religious support.

Even so, I doubt that what she discovered in Judaism was joy (though she would probably disagree). Obligatory holidays got observed in our house, to be sure. Mother bought a new dress and hat for Rosh Hashanah, made gefilte fish from scratch for Passover, and those silver candlesticks from Russia got used every Sabbath. But as I was growing up, I remember no talk of exchanging gifts on Chanukah, and Passover Seders were spent without song. Perhaps her generation found no need for those things. It seemed to me, though, that while we followed the rules inside, the delight of Judaism remained outdoors. Even so, when as an adult I attended fewer and fewer religious services, my mother said to me, with what I recognized as sincere conviction, "You should go! You'd get a lot out of them."

Involving herself little in religious organizations, Mother had immense admiration for women like her friend Jenny who gave of herself to the Jewish community. And fixing the person's religion was a mental exercise that Mother engaged in automatically when she met someone new, a leftover habit and discomfort among strangers from early immigrant days, I figured. The fact that I didn't go through the same process confounded her. After I departed that Jewish landscape in Dallas and stepped out into the wider world. I would mention a new friend and she would ask, "Is he (or she) Jewish?"

I'd stop and think for a minute. "I don't know," I'd answer. She would shake her head, trying to imagine how that was possible, wondering if I was trying to be funny.

During one of the brief intervals after college when I was living again at home, the mother of a college friend was visiting in Dallas and I invited her to our house. She was a theater director, in town on theater business. My mother didn't seem excited by the prospect of having the lady to dinner, but she agreed to it. Our guest arrived, a buxom, talkative, ebullient lady with pronounced Jewish features, and it wasn't long before I could see my mother relaxing. After Mrs. T. left, Mother said to me, in a tone of some annoyance, "A theater director—and Jewish? Why didn't you tell me before she came?"

If I wanted to evoke a rise out of my mother, I had only to observe that in my opinion the best marriages in our family were the mixed ones, Jewish and gentile: Uncle Morris', Aunt Rose's, cousin Wade's. "What are you talking about?" my mother would uncharacteristically holler back.

▶▶▶

Those last four months of Jerome's illness when my mother and Paula lived together, the last two in the same hotel room, cemented a bond that lasted the rest of Mother's life.

But they had already formed the rare friendship between wife and mother-in-law. "Your mother used to bake cookies and mail them to us," Paula says. "And she'd send gifts when there was no special occasion. I saw such spirituality in her, and a different lifestyle from what I had grown up with. If she bought a piece of jewelry, it was because she really loved it—and could foresee leaving it later to one of us. She never did it to impress people."

Elissa and Marcia are themselves now grown and married, both to men who are not Jewish. (Two more good mixed marriages, I'm thinking.) Before marrying, both agreed with their future husbands that any children they might have would be raised Jewish. "That was your mother's influence on them," Paula tells me. "Not mine."

Paula says she isn't sure how much my mother loved her, but I am. At some point Mother stopped referring to her as "daughter-in-law" and simply called her "daughter."

▶▶▶

Uncle Morris claims that my mother was the smartest one in the Shapiro family. "She would have been a good business person," he often stated in the years when, as a widow, she would consult with him about investments. She kept intact most of the capital that my father left to her.

Had society not damned the notion, I think Mother might even have made a good professional gambler. She coined an understatement when, as a young mother, she wrote to her friend Rose in Houston: "I do like to play cards, for I don't often lose."

But she didn't need to pursue either of those full-time, since the business side got taken care of by her husband and the gambling by her brother Morris. Expressing irritation or anger at my father was one more thing she didn't have to do, since I served up enough of that for both of us.

Born in 1932, eight years after Jerome (and ten after Florence), and at the height of the Depression, I assume that my birth was a surprise. Since I was growing up with something like two sets of parents, the actual ones plus a much older sister and brother that at times seemed like parents, Mother said that they intended to have a fourth child to give me company. That kid never got born, and considering what I might have passed on at home to one smaller than me, I figure he or she was better off unrealized.

My tardy arrival as a third child provided no novelty, and Mother would often take off for the afternoon and leave me in the care of Marietha. (It was she who walked me to school on my first day.) Aunts Pearl and Fannie and Rose, all then unmarried, also were around to help out. "Becky never minded leaving you with one of us so she could play cards," Aunt Rose recalls.

Around age two, I developed an ear infection so serious that a doctor detected the scars only recently, sixty years later. With antibiotics not yet discovered, I had to stay in bed for a number of weeks, after which, I'm told, I needed to re-learn to walk. "You were always hanging on my skirts after that," Mother said, and therefore concluded that I needed emancipation from her.

She embarked on a conscious effort to leave me more.

A few years later, as an extension of the same idea, she and my father started to let me stay home alone when they went out at night—"earlier than we did with either Florence or Jerome," she explained. That later idea was fine with me, but at the first stage, when I was three or four, I'm not sure I didn't find desertion in her idea. The photo of Aunt Fannie and me in the back yard of the house on Forest Avenue shows a blond boy with a pair of tall white boots but a sad face.

▶▶▶

Decades passed. Mother's letters to her friend Rose in Houston told of Fannie's marriage in 1938, Florence's in 1944, Jerome's in 1954. My going away to college, then into the army. Trips with Dad to insurance conventions, with and without him to Denver, New York, and occasionally to Houston. The births of grandchildren. The deaths of friends. Bits of gossip.

From her mother and Bubbe Ely, her mother-in-law, my mother early on learned about and practiced good cooking. She continued to do so when there was a gathering of our family for Passover or some anniversary, but the novelty of preparing pot roasts and Romanian style eggplant had worn off by the time my parents' marriage turned into its third or fourth decade and children's departures had shrunk the number at the table. Then, my father would come home from his office and seeing my mother's disaffection for the kitchen, would say, "Honey, you want to go to Wyatt's for dinner tonight?"

"Yes, Henry," Mother would respond and quickly change clothes and drive with him to the cafeteria a couple of miles away. They'd arrive early in the evening, before the line grew long with other older couples who had lost the fondness for home cooking, especially on summer nights when even an air-conditioned kitchen might not manage to shake away the remains of a 95- or 100-degree Texas afternoon.

My father was not the most popular customer at Wyatt's because when he ordered the $3.95 prime rib, he invariably added, "Now be sure that's on a *hot* plate." He repeated that every time he went there, frequently to the same woman standing patiently behind the counter. If I was present, I'd turn away with embarrassment. Mother may have been uncomfortable, too, but she didn't wish to spoil her chances for future evenings at Wyatt's by pointing out to my father that they were not dining at the Adolphus Hotel or that in fact the plates *were* hot without the need to request it. Uncle Morris had less at stake, and one time when he went with my parents, he said to his brother-in-law, "Henry, one of these days that girl is gonna put the hot plate on your head!"

By 1983, when Rose sent back the package of letters she had saved, my father was gone. With his death in 1975, Mother's task ended as caretaker of a man whom she would never publicly criticize but whom, in a moment of rare candor, she later admitted to me that she had outgrown years before. While his passing marked the end of a fifty-five-year marriage, it also released Mother from what had turned for her into the role of forbearing nursemaid.

Even after his death, Mother loved the cafeteria experience and never understood why I did less so. When in Dallas, I would chaperone her to the Shearith Israel Cemetery for a visit to Dad's grave, and on the way home she would say, "Stanley, what about a cup of coffee at the Highland Park Cafeteria? We'll pass right by it."

I never cherished the idea because I knew how slowly she moved and that the cup of coffee would expand to cottage cheese, sliced carrots, a muffin, and at least an hour's time. But for someone whose childhood had been spent having to help feed four younger siblings, those ladylike moments of enjoying food that she didn't need to prepare were satisfying to her. So we went. "Too bad you don't have a nice cafeteria near where you live in New York," she'd say, following up with a question to which I never had an answer: "Why don't they have cafeterias in New York?"

Earlier, when she had traveled east, I had put her on to Schrafft's, which I figured was as good an alternative to Wyatt's as Manhattan could offer. She loved going to Schrafft's and once even admitted that it might have surpassed her hometown cafeterias. There she would linger for two hours over muffin and coffee and almost always exit with a new lady friend whom she met—and learned the life story of—at the next table.

▶▶▶

With no responsibilities at home, Mother continued to take an occasional trip to visit Florence in Denver where she played bridge with her daughter and her friends. If there was a bat mitzvah or a graduation of one of Paula and Jerome's daughters, she'd make her way back to Stamford. For fun, she would give a reprise to Elissa and Marcia of "I Love You a Bushel and a Peck," the song she tickled them with when they were tiny. She seemed genuinely happy when Paula remarried in 1970.

For another few years she continued driving, and when the doctors, at our request, told her to stop, she did so with an angry protest. She wasn't fooled by the source of the command. "You're making me do this!" she protested to Florence and me.

In the late 1970s, Mother and I made two summer trips together, one to San Francisco, the other a year later for a couple of weeks to a rented house in Cape Cod. I was sure those would be near the end of her traveling days, and they were. She reveled in both journeys.

For years Mother spawned her particular notion as concerned travel in the direction of Texas. "We only want you kids to come here (to Dallas) if you really want to," she'd repeat. Every time she said it, it struck me as an odd remark, and I finally realized why. Turning the statement around, it became, "If you kids don't come to visit, it's because you don't really want to." (And then, what kind of kids are you?)

But I did go, three times every year. If it was during the summer, I'd take part of the afternoons and escape to the swimming pool that had been built for the residents of her apartment complex. It was a quiet spot, a pool surrounded by nicely clipped grass, lush Texas ferns in baskets hanging from oak trees, and tall, red-tipped shrubs. Since the residents on Edgemere were principally of my mother's generation, others would appear at the pool mostly when grandchildren had come to swim. For July after July I would seek that quiet, float back and forth on my private warm water and wonder how many more Julys Mother would be able to continue living in her apartment—whether that might be the last one before she was deprived of her independence and I of my personal tarn.

But those visits weren't just fun. I worked to make them the time to smooth out wrinkles between me and her, between me and Dallas. Mother and I would take early evening walks around her neighborhood and play the card games that I inevitably lost, and I'm sure she realized that I was trying not to let my relationship with her end in as ruptured a way it had ended with my father.

There were times as we would drive away from the cemetery that I would find myself saying, "I think I came to see the good side of Dad too late."

"Yes," Mother would reply, but dwelling on the past didn't suit her. "My friends come here to the cemetery, but as soon as they leave, they ask, 'Well, where's the next bridge game?'" As soon as she finished the coffee at Wyatt's Cafeteria, so did she.

During those later visits I discovered that Mother had accepted my homosexuality with seemingly less conflict than me. Sometimes I would go out alone in the evening and finally got to the point where I didn't offer a destination. She never asked. Only once did she say, quite suddenly, "You know, Stanley, you haven't always been honest with me."

I was startled by the unexpectedness of her comment, the context of which didn't need explaining. It left me silent. "You're right," I answered, finally. There seemed to be no need for more discussion, and there never was.

After AIDS struck, Mother kept up with news about the epidemic, and when I told her that I had started to do volunteer work with an AIDS service organization, she wrote a check in my name and asked me to donate it to that group. I smiled at the gesture of approval, but with the check went a forthright warning. "I don't know what I'd do if anything happened to you," she said with a stern look.

▶▶▶

My mother gathered in her spirituality and understanding to finish the final years of her life. She would continue to do her correspondence at the quiet end of the day, eleven or twelve at night, her letters often carrying the calmness of that hour. The ones to Rose were filled with particular affection. "I can never tell you how I enjoy your letters," she stated in one of the later ones. "They always remind me that I have my friend. I am rich when I think of what a dear sister you have been."

She urged me to take the gold-rimmed dessert plates that I had loved since childhood; to Florence and Paula and her three granddaughters she gradually gave all her jewelry (and not to exlude me, since I had no wife, she gave a jeweled pin); she labeled items of furniture for the person she wanted them to go to (instructions we didn't quite follow); she guided me through the contents of her safety deposit box. "You'll find everything in here," she said, making sure that the lady in the bank knew who I was. She still occasionally mailed her cookies and froze her home-made blintzes for the arrival of an out-of-town relative, but gradually her life slowed into one that was more narrow and more lonely.

When Mother no longer drove, I saw that her card playing friends, the ones she had hosted many dozens of times, began to desert her. "What happened to Mrs. Goodstein?" I'd ask. "Or Mrs. Frank?"

"Oh," she said, "I don't hear from them much."

Ironically, it was then—with my father gone—that who she did hear from were Uncle Ben and Aunt Sara. With their apartment only minutes from hers, they assumed the role of guardians, keeping track of her and inviting her to dinner at the country club my family never joined.

Finally, Mother suffered from a crippling arthritis and had to choose between having an aide come to live with her or moving to Golden Acres, the Jewish senior home in Dallas where she said she hoped never to be. Not wanting a stranger living in her apartment, she moved in 1985 with some of her own furniture to a sunny suite in Golden Acres, where she remained for her final two years. Aunt Rose and Uncle Herbert sold their house and moved into my parents' apartment on Edgemere. Mother never returned there, and I never went back to swim in the pool.

At Golden Acres she was courteous to the nurses and custodians and they made sure she was up for breakfast every day and that she got plenty of physical therapy. Before long, she was slowly walking again. Her skin retained a shine, even as she grew more bent. The other Becky Ely, "Big Becky," had also spent her final days there, and Mother often remarked about the coincidence. "Isn't it odd," she said, "two Becky Elys have been at Golden Acres, and no one here ever comments on it!"

Only occasionally did Mother complain about having given up her apartment. "I don't know where any of those dishes and glasses went!" she'd moan. But in fact those things held less and less importance to her. She beamed like the young girl in the family photos when a visitor came to break the confining routine of the retirement home. The only coldness I saw in her was, of all things, when her sisters Rose or Fannie arrived. That, I figured, came from her no longer being able to benefit from her eldest sister status and dictate the location of the next family dinner.

▶▶▶

No matter Mother's smile, visits to Golden Acres took on a special urgency. It's the final address. She and I would sit in the shade of the patio and talk, or I would escort her out to the car for a drive or a meal away from the dining room. She attempted some effort at independence by pushing the wheelchair rather than riding in it.

It was clear that Mother was using the time to reflect back to early days. "I made so many mistakes back then," she said, looking at me earnestly.

Which mistakes, I wondered? Her campaign to emancipate me? Her lack of effort to help my father and me connect? I could offer a few mistakes for consideration—leaving me in their bedroom for the first years could surely qualify—but it seemed pointless by then. "They weren't important," I replied. I suspected, though, since we weren't very good at fooling each other, that neither she nor I wholly believed that.

In June of 1987, my mother broke her arm and died a couple of days later of heart failure during surgery. She was ninety. A son-in-law, a daughter-in-law and three of her grandchildren along with her two surviving children came from far away to see her buried next to my father and not far from Pearl and their parents and a host of friends in the Shearith Israel Cemetery. It was a sunny Sunday. The next day we took a drive to Golden Acres to pack up her things and say goodbye to the nurses. I told them I thought Mother had been ready to leave. They agreed.

We went out for dinner at a seafood restaurant the last time I saw her, in March, a few months before she died. It was for the kind of food she liked and never got at Golden Acres. Perhaps I sensed that time was almost up. "Do you ever regret that you never went back to Russia?" it suddenly occurred to me to ask.

"Oh, no!" Mother said. "Israel, yes, that's where I've wanted to go. That's the place I regret never seeing. I wonder whether I still could get there?"

"Perhaps," I said, in a gentle lie.

Memories of my own came rushing by: licking the bowl as she made chocolate cake; getting dressed to go with her to town to see her long-time saleslady where I'd get fitted for a pair of woolen slacks; her coming (without my father) to my college graduation, standing tall for a photo next to me in cap and gown.

Finally, her repeated statements of love and support when I visited Golden Acres. "I'm proud of you and what you've done," she said, insistently, as if to offer a final piece of reconciliation and sustenance to hold on to in years to come. I have held on to it, though, along with much of her own Russian melancholy that, without wishing to, she also left implanted in me.

I had no way to know as we separated that night that it would be the final time. Kidding about the fact that she seemed to be getting shorter, I bent over to give her a kiss and felt the same knot in my throat that I had experienced at every hug goodbye, starting when, nearly trembling with anticipation, I set out from Texas for college in faraway Illinois at seventeen.

There was only one thing I didn't understand: once in Golden Acres, Mother attended their Friday night Sabbath services and I even accompanied her to a couple of their Passover Seders, but she gave up a lifetime habit of playing cards. When I asked why she didn't join in the bridge games that I saw other women playing there, she sat up straight and said, "Well, I don't know them! What if they're bad players? If I get started in those games, I won't be able to get away."

Of course.

13

Uncle Morris,
a Gambler in the Bedroom

"Why ever did your uncle move in with you all—*and* into your bedroom?" asked Tommy, my almost only non-Jewish friend for the first seventeen years of my life. "Why doesn't he have his own place?"

"I don't know," I confessed. "I know my mother likes it this way. Maybe, with her younger brother to look out after, it's like having another son around."

"That seems mighty strange to me," Tommy said, in his slow way of speech. "My daddy wouldn't put up with it." Tommy abided by the venerable southern custom, regardless the age of the parties, of referring to his father as "daddy." It was similar to my hanging on to "Tommy" instead of "Tom."

"I don't know that my dad likes it," I said in my own slow, southern way, "but he doesn't usually argue with what my mother wants." I thought about Tommy's question another minute, and added a different idea. "I guess my dad likes the additional rent."

My friend and I were stretched out on chairs on the screened porch, the only place in our house on Stanhope that stood a chance of catching a breeze. It was July of 1947, the usual hot middle of a long Texas summer. Still a couple of years before Tommy and I would finish Highland Park High, the small voice that told me, "You've got to go away" had already whispered in my ear. It was not too early to relish the expectation of enrolling in a college up north, a plan I had confided to Tommy.

"Well, you're lucky," he drawled. "When we graduate, you'll be getting away from this hot box."

"You could, too, if you wanted to," I insisted. "Anyway, where I am lucky is that I'll be getting away from Uncle Morris. You don't know what it's like, us living in the same room this past year."

"What is it like?"

I looked away. "When I'm getting up to go to school, he's just coming home—or maybe he hasn't come home yet. If he is home, he's asleep, so I have to be real quiet. Then, everything is so secretive. You don't ask him any questions, but he asks you plenty. 'You're going to a play again, Stanley? Not going to the football game? Where did you go last night?' And so on."

"You don't have to apologize for wanting to see a play," Tommy insisted. "But where does your uncle stay out to so late? Someone told me he goes out to gamble. Does he?"

I stood up and walked over to the edge of the porch, my back to my friend. "Let's change the subject," I said. "Let's eat. Mother left us lunch in the kitchen."

Tommy and I had been friends since our paths crossed in the third grade, the year my family moved to University Park from South Dallas and his moved to Dallas from Mt. Vernon, a small town in East Texas. Their move enabled his father, an attorney, to work for a large oil company. I had been promoted and had skipped a grade, so the Jewish kids of my age whom I knew were a year behind me in school. Installed in Bradfield School and knowing no one, I took to Tommy, who I quickly discovered shared my liking for talk and disliking for sports.

Sometimes, at one or another of our homes, we would close ourselves off in a bedroom to play "school," wherein we'd alternate roles of teacher and student. I naturally thought I should be the teacher and relinquished the part to him only when he finally insisted.

Later, around seventh or eighth grade, our friendship spilled over to visits for talk and lunch that I never told any other friends about. We would analyze school and the kids whose popularity and apparent comfort level we envied. Those meetings were a sabbatical, for him from his church group, for me from my synagogue crowd.

When lunch was scheduled at Tommy's, his mother, an impeccable woman, laid out artistic sandwiches with accompaniments of delicate, fresh potato chips, iced tea and cloth napkins. At my house, my mother left us whatever happened to be around, though at times I suspected that she arranged for it to be something like chopped liver or corned beef, in case Tommy forgot that he had crossed over into Israel.

At four o'clock on that July day, I walked Tommy to the corner a couple of blocks away, where he would catch a bus for home. Going back, I thought again of our conversation about Uncle Morris, Mother's brother who had moved in with us in 1946, the year before, when he came home from service. Tommy asked a good question, I thought. Why did Uncle Morris have to live with us? That night, he had said he wouldn't be home, which caused no objection from me.

Before the war, my uncle had a bookkeeper's job at A. Harris', the same department store where Aunt Fannie and Aunt Pearl had worked. Short, slight, balding, and distant, a younger looking Grandpa Max: that was how I remembered him from those days. "Morris is furious at being the only male in a tightly-knit family of females," Cousin Ann once explained to me. "He came to West Texas to visit my family one summer and didn't say anything for a week."

The army was unconcerned about his conversational skills and drafted him in 1941 at age thirty-two. Instead of being sent to one of the war zones in Europe or the Pacific, he drew the card that said "Alaska," and that's where he was stationed for three years. Not yet a state, Alaska was cold and deserted, and Morris had not much to do, except to gamble. The Shapiro aptitude for cards got awakened at that point, and when he came home he bought a shiny car and new clothes and never went back to his job at A. Harris'.

Neither did he seek his own place to live. Instead, he moved in with us, specifically with me, since Jerome had exercised seniority and taken occupancy of bedroom number two.

What I told Tommy, that Uncle Morris gave my mother someone else to look out after, wasn't altogether accurate, since he embarked on an independent routine: sleeping until afternoon, going out late, coming back very late. His phone calls were private and hushed. He certainly didn't announce that he was playing cards; when he went out, the destination was left unlisted. We just pieced the story together, a story that was embarrassing to me at fifteen, though less so to my mother.

In fact, Mother benefited from an expert bridge consultant when Morris moved in. "You didn't play that hand right, Becky," he'd whisper to her, peering over the afternoon game that she shared with her friends.

"Tell me later," she'd mouth back silently.

I would hear her and Uncle Morris spend long times reconstituting who had bid what and who had played what, from a game that had finished hours earlier. To me, the memory of this information ranked as remarkable and uninteresting on the highest level. But I figured maybe that advice was part of his rent.

"Do I really have to share a bedroom with Uncle Morris?" I moaned, as I started clearing part of the closet.

"Yes!" Mother stated. "And why not? Your uncle has been off in the war, defending us. Anyway, he won't be here forever."

"Defending us in Alaska?" I asked. "I'm not going to be here forever, either!"

Whether or not I concurred didn't matter. Uncle Morris arrived, becoming a roommate of marginal compatibility. Aside from our opposite schedules, he didn't take to my language. If I let out with something like, "I really love that song," or "that house," he would bark back, "Men don't love things."

I harkened back to Tommy's question. Why did my dad put up with this arrangement? (If I ever had called my father "Daddy," which was doubtful, I had reclassified him to "Dad" in training for leaving the South.) Dad's perspective on Uncle Morris was different from mine. Given Morris' routine, the two of them rarely even met. My father was usually coming home from the office around the time my uncle was getting ready to go out.

Mother had reasons others than advice at bridge for wanting her brother at home. Morris would help her around the house when he got up at two or three in the afternoon, vacuuming the rug or cleaning up dirty dishes. What was an assist to Mother was an embarrassment to me. Damn, I thought, if I came home from school with a friend, there was Uncle Morris in his green G.I. undershorts again, gathering up the laundry.

Conversation with him rarely ventured past his questioning my dad or me as he dressed for an evening out. "Henry," he'd ask, "does this tie go with this suit?" Before long we understood that Uncle Morris was color blind, so my dad or I would replace his green tie with a blue one. (This discovery simultaneously explained why I would find a freshly-washed white sock of mine paired up with a gray one of his.)

In all, I did not like the new sleeping arrangement. It was a big enough bedroom, maybe fifteen feet square, but not big enough for the belongings and different schedules and moods of a nervous teen-ager and a cranky thirty-eight-year-old uncle. If the tension soared and I complained, my dad deferred to my mother, who reminded me of Uncle Morris' contribution to our national defense.

▶▶▶

In spite of our contrary natures, there seemed to be a kind of underground mentality that bound Uncle Morris and me. "Here, Stanley," he would say at unexpected moments and in the middle of nothing related, "stick this in your pocket. Use it when you go out on a date."

I'd look down at a $10 or even a $20 bill, currency with which I had had barely any experience. "Oh, I can't take that," I'd mumble. "I really don't need it."

"Take it!" he'd snap. "Put it in your pocket!" So of course I did.

With a couple of tries, we got the routine down pat.

It also was good to have someone like Morris around if I got in trouble, which didn't happen often but threw me into chaos when it did. As with the Fort Worth speeding ticket.

Every Texas kid (Jewish and otherwise) waits for the sixteenth birthday to be legally set loose behind the wheel of a car. Jerome had been teaching me to drive our old stick-shift Dodge, to go slow when I saw children playing near the street. By the time I turned sixteen, I was ready. And a day or two later, I was licensed to drive.

"Can I use the car tonight?" I asked one Sunday afternoon shortly after that, when I saw that my father was relaxed and not in an insurance selling mood.

"Where are you going?" he wanted to know.

"I'm gonna pick up a couple of kids. We'll just go over to the Jewish Community Center."

"Okay," he said, proffering the keys, "but be careful. And . . . don't waste gas driving around!"

"You know I won't."

You know I will show off in front of those other kids, some of whom were also learning to drive, but in their parents' Cadillacs and Lincolns. I don't remember whose idea it was, mine maybe, but we drove all the way for dinner to Fort Worth, traditional rival town thirty miles west of Dallas. To enhance the experience, I snapped on the radio and accelerated the Dodge up to fifty or fifty-five miles an hour.

My timing was bad. Just inside Fort Worth, we came zooming under the nose of a policeman, pleased to stop a bunch of teen-agers with a license plate from a hostile neighboring city. He sirened me over to the side of the road and sauntered up to the car with half a smile. "You in a hurry, son?" he asked.

"I, umm, have to get back for my dad's birthday party."

"I'll help you," he said with a grin. "Here's a gift you can hand him."

I returned with a $12 speeding ticket, bad enough, but with "Fort Worth" printed on it I feared that my driving days, which had hardly begun, may have already ended. The rare time I dared to disobey!

For a day or two I sat on the ticket, scared to tell my parents. Suddenly, it occurred to me to try my roommate. "Uncle Morris," I said politely, before he went out that evening, "I've got a problem."

He looked at me quizzically, since sharing problems had not been our habit. Maybe he thought I had gotten a girl pregnant. Maybe he hoped.

"You see, I got this speeding ticket."

"Oh?"

"Yeah, but it was in Fort Worth. I drove over there with a couple of kids.

Dad didn't know I was going there. It's $12!"

He smiled in a fatherly way and patted me on the back. "Just give me the ticket, Stanley," he said, offering bail. "I'll take care of it. No one else will have to find out."

I got the ticket out of my desk drawer and handed it to him. I never asked what happened to it, but the case seemed to end there, and true to his word, no one else did find out.

Uncle Morris' own transportation was a new maroon Oldsmobile that provided a shiny contrast to our homely car when they were together in the garage. I coveted that vehicle of his. On Saturday afternoons I'd even douse it with a nice soapy shower and warm water rinse.

Perhaps my misguided venture to Fort Worth had heightened me in his eyes, because on the occasional Friday or Saturday night that he stayed home, he would ask, "You going out tonight, Stanley? You want to use the Olds?"

I'd restrain myself from sounding overly excited. "Well, sure," I would answer, casually. "Thanks." If I didn't have a date, I quickly arranged one. Being at the wheel of that Olds vastly improved my status among my friends.

▶▶▶

The fact is that my trip to Fort Worth *was* relatively daring, as the late 1940s, a period when having a rum and Coca-Cola on New Year's Eve was venturing into the risqué.

Particularly in our Jewish milieu, Uncle Morris stood out. Besides his unconventional lifestyle, he spawned unconventional theories such as the one about lying down. "There's very little use for chairs," he'd say. "A fellow either should be standing up and walking, or lying down." He practiced it, too; when not vacuuming the carpet, he could usually be found in bed.

He became a favorite topic among my pals. "Morris," my friend Mark got up the nerve to ask on one of the days when we were all together and awake at the same time, "where is it that you go at night?"

Larry and Stanley, the other members of the pack, were gathered around in my bedroom, too. "Come on, tell us, Uncle Morris," Larry said with neck strained. "We won't tell anyone."

Uncle Morris gave them a look. "Where do I go?" he repeated. "First I drive downtown. Where it's dark. I park the car in a garage underground. Then, when I make sure no one sees me, I go around the corner to a private club, and meet up with three or four gangsters. We smoke hashish. And we screw some cheap women."

"You dooo?" Stanley asked.

By that evening, a score of Jewish mothers in University Park had heard the tale and were passing it on to their husbands. My dad heard it, too. "Becky," he said, with unaccustomed authority, "your brother's filling those kids' heads. And everyone around is hearing about it."

"Oh, well," Mother replied with a nervous grin, "they're just kids."

At moments like that, when he sensed he had gone too far, Uncle Morris would go out and shepherd home some new luxury gadget, the kind that my parents traditionally eschewed.

"Henry," he announced a couple of days later, "I'm going to get one of those new window air conditioners for the house. I've been hearing about them. Stanley and I'll try it out in our room."

"That's very nice of you, Morris," my father said, "but I don't know if we need an air conditioner."

"Sure we do," I yelled.

Uncle Morris ignored my father and brought home a chunky thing that he had installed in a side window in our bedroom. I waited expectantly for its debut, since until then refrigerated air was what you knew only from Saturday afternoon movies or trips to a department store downtown. Finally the machine got turned on. It whirred loudly and blew fiercely. But it cooled, and offered a major move forward into luxury.

Somehow, the roommate picture seemed to be improving. As Uncle Morris and I emerged refreshed from the air-conditioned bedroom, my low opinion of card playing was passing through a surprising transformation. Hearing me brag about the cool air, my mother hesitantly approached the room in the afternoon heat. The contrast to the rest of the house became hard to resist.

"Henry, I think we ought to have dinner tonight in the boys' bedroom," she surprised my father one day. "You'd be amazed how much more comfortable it is in there."

"In the bedroom?" asked my dad, a man of tradition, which included not to eat dinner in a bedroom.

"It'll be easy. We can set up some card tables. Stanley will help."

I agreed and as usual, my dad gave in. Dinners got relocated out of the breakfast room. The two twin beds, the dressers, the bookshelves, the desk, the closets, and the uncle half the time in bed were augmented by a couple of card tables and even less privacy than before. But dinners were cooler. And before long, Uncle Morris had financed air conditioners that were buzzing everywhere in the house. Surprising themselves, Mother and Dad became converts. Outside doors got closed and that screened porch, the scene of many tranquil summer gatherings, was relegated to a dusty souvenir.

▶▶▶

My cohabitation with Uncle Morris came to an end when I got my wish to go away to school. But a month before high school graduation, I came home one afternoon to find a large rock lying on the floor in the breakfast room, which faced the street in the front of the house. A shattered window was the clear marker of the rock's path of entry.

This happened at a time when my parents were out of town at an insurance convention, and not knowing what to do, I left the room the way it was until Uncle Morris could look at it the next day. He turned sullen when he saw the damage—then the rock—and he quickly arranged to have the window repaired. "I'll clean up the mess," he stated.

"I guess we have to tell the folks, eh?" I asked.

"Yes, sure," he said, hesitantly.

My father's customary passiveness vanished when he heard the tale. "Don't worry, Henry," my mother insisted. "It was probably an accident."

"It was no accident. Not even a robbery. Nothing was missing. It was a warning. You know who to!"

I told the story to Tommy, and confessed to how frightening it had been within our small, protected world. "Maybe he does hang out with gangsters," Tommy said. "Maybe they were threatening him."

There was no way for me to dispute that. But my uncle seemed sure that it wouldn't happen again, and it didn't.

Perhaps Uncle Morris agreed with my father that the rock affair be taken as a warning, since after I went off to college my mother wrote to me that Morris was staying in more at night, entertained by yet another new invention, television, which he had bought and watched, of course, from bed.

A few years later, after I had moved to New York, Mother wrote something more startling: that my uncle was dropping hints around the house about a new lady friend named Dorothy.

14

. . . and Dorothy,
the Best Draw of All

It wasn't as if women had not been part of Uncle Morris' life, but he kept them as unexplained and separated from us as his card playing. Even while I was still living at home, there were occasional calls from a female voice saying, shyly, "Hello," and asking, "Is Morris there?" If he was, the phone got carried on its long cord from the kitchen to the bedroom for talk behind closed doors. There being no point in asking who the lady was, no one did.

It seemed to me that Uncle Morris suffered from a case of overactive secrecy. Occasionally I spotted a female in the front seat of his Oldsmobile, parked in the driveway while he rushed in to pick something up. But none gained entrance into our house, and I felt sorry for those hidden ladies.

That changed with Dorothy.

"Last night we met Morris' new friend," Mother wrote to me in New York in 1960. "He brought her home—I mean, inside. It was nice to meet her. Her name is Dorothy, she's blond and pretty, younger than he is. I don't think she's Jewish . . . ."

With that exit line, Mother started folding in a dash of blemish along with praise. Her keen eyes told her that if, after living on Stanhope for eight or nine years, Morris for the first time brought someone inside, it must be taken seriously.

Florence by then was long gone to live in Denver, a mother of three; Jerome was in Stamford, father of two; I was a bachelor in Manhattan. Was Mother going to applaud seeing the only remaining younger one become involved with some dame, particularly one whom she correctly guessed wasn't Jewish? Not likely.

When I returned to Dallas for a break from the eastern winter, I got awarded Jerome's old room, and Uncle Morris invited his new interest for a brief visit home. "Dorothy," he said, smiling, "this is my nephew Stanley. We used to be roommates. Stanley, this is Dorothy. Isn't she beautiful?"

While Dorothy grinned, I assented. She was. Beautiful, round-cheeked, buxom, smiling and open, with a healthy glow and a head of thick blond hair. Uncle Morris, I thought, had managed to find his opposite.

The next day I risked inquiring. "Who is Dorothy, Uncle Morris?"

"Who is she?" he answered, in his Biblical habit of repeating the question. "She's an executive secretary for an oil company, and very smart." It turned out that the oil company was the very one where my friend Tommy's father worked as an attorney.

It fell to my mother, who by then had met Dorothy several times, to explain that she had been married before, a miserable episode, not to be discussed. She and Uncle Morris had met through a mutual friend who was a card-playing associate of his. She was some thirteen years his junior.

Subsequent letters from Mother expanded the tale. "Morris has been in a very good mood," she wrote. "He bought a new television set for the den so big that it has to sit on the floor. Last night, for the first time, he brought Dorothy over for dinner. I made gefilte fish, a big pot roast and kugel."

I grinned when I read Mother's decidedly-Jewish menu for her first time as hostess to Dorothy. It was no accident, of course. If Dorothy were as smart as Uncle Morris says, I figured, she'd get the message.

But if my mother was trying to sow doubts, Uncle Morris ignored them. Dorothy became his steady companion, and the next time I visited Dallas, my parents invited them for dinner again. I saw that Dorothy had found a couple of topics—business and stocks—to talk to my father about, something no one else ever bothered to do. And she laughed when I told her that my friend Tommy's father worked as an attorney at her company. "Of course I know Mr. Wilkinson," she said. "A fine, old fashioned gentleman. He's told me that his daddy was an attorney, too." (Welcome back to the South, I thought. His "daddy" must then have been about ninety-five.)

"Come on, Dorothy, let's do the dishes," said Uncle Morris, as the meal was ending.

"You do them yourself this time, Morris. I want to talk to Stanley." Guiding me into the den, Dorothy said, "Now sit down here and tell me all about you and what you're doing up there in the big city."

My uncle flashed me a stare, but he proceeded into the kitchen alone. When I had finished my story, Dorothy smiled and said it sounded wonderful to her, and that she was proud of me. By then, of course, I was her fan.

Before I left to go back to New York, Uncle Morris invited me to join him and Dorothy at one of the new, expensive Italian restaurants that were turning Dallas into a big-time town. I helped him select a tie of the desired color, put one on myself, and slid into the back of the Olds. We picked up Dorothy at her apartment, and at the restaurant they walked in hand-in-hand.

Morris suggested ordering shrimp cocktails (missing from the standard home fare) and asked, "So how's your job in that advertising agency going?"

I was taking in the fancy decor, so new in Dallas, and not listening. His interest in my career was so unexpected that I didn't realize he was talking to me. After a long moment in which no one else answered and I saw two people sitting forward, staring at me, I got the point. "Oh, me?" I said. "Well, fine, thanks. Yeah, it's going fine." (Only someone as naive as I was then would say that a New York ad agency job was going fine and believe it. Going fine can immediately precede getting fired, which is what happened.)

Uncle Morris sat back in his chair, and Dorothy smiled. She seemed to get prettier by the day.

Before I returned to New York, Uncle Morris extended a hand of equality. "Stanley," he said, "you're old enough to drop the 'Uncle.' Just call me Morris from now on."

"Well, okay," I said, uncertainly.

A year later, my uncle presented Dorothy with a sparkling diamond. With qualified glee, my mother wrote me the news: "It looks as if Morris and

Dorothy are going to get married and he'll be moving away. I'll miss him, but he hasn't been here much lately, anyway."

▶▶▶

Uncle Morris—okay, just Morris—was a couple of years past fifty when he embarked on this latter-day engagement. It was one that introduced changes for persons beyond himself. My father seemed relieved to terminate the long epoch of his brother-in-law as boarder, rent and household appliances notwithstanding. Aunts Fannie and Pearl and Rose were delighted at the prospect of a new, pretty, younger sister. Only my mother, the eldest Shapiro, held out reservation. "He's been so comfortable here," she commented to my dad.

"He'll be comfortable somewhere else now," he advised.

Then there was the reaction of his former roommate. Realizing that marriage was not in my future, I had created an imaginary bond with this unattached uncle, the sole other male family member who was single. There we stood together, two unlikely candidates for wedded life, at least in my mind. The tableau had taken on a quality of permanence. With the announcement of his engagement, I suddenly had the feeling of having been betrayed.

Jerome picked up on it. "It sounds to me as if everyone is happy about that marriage except one person," he remarked.

"No, no," I claimed, loudly. "I'm happy."

In a small, private ceremony in 1962, Dorothy and Morris got married. There was no talk about anyone converting to a new religion. With their assets pooled, they furnished a new apartment, sunny and far enough from my parents that a visit required effort. From too few rooms in our house on Stanhope, there arose a surplus. Like the screened porch, Morris' old bedroom fell into disuse.

"Morris and Dorothy had us over for dinner last night," Mother wrote. "Then this morning he hurried by with a bunch of oranges that he'd gotten at the farmer's market. I asked him to sit down for a while, but he said that Dorothy was at home, waiting to make their fresh orange juice. They had already gone out and played golf. All this by ten in the morning!"

Morris continued occasional trips to Las Vegas but fewer than before.

Aunt Rose learned that Dorothy would accompany him and patiently wait in the hotel room the hours that he played in the casino. Before long, there were enough winnings that neither cards nor Dorothy's job, which she left, were necessary. In their places came early morning walks, occasional car trips, housekeeping and investing, in the latter of which Dorothy was probably the smartest in the family.

She also was cleverly trying to win over a reluctant sister-in-law. "Dorothy offered to come over and give me a permanent this morning," Mother wrote. "She said that Morris grumbled, but she came anyway, and now my hair looks very nice. She's invited us all for dinner when you get here for the holidays."

I got there, looking forward to dinner at their place. With all of us seated around a beautifully laid table, Dorothy turned to my dad and played the expert on Jewish cuisine. "Come on, Henry," she sang, "have some more matzo-ball soup. It's good for you."

My father smiled broadly as he passed his plate. "Dorothy," he said, "you'll make a good little Jewish cook."

"Oh, shoooot," she responded, grinning.

It was a delicious dinner.

"Well, it seems to me that Morris has landed himself a fine wife," my father announced as we were driving home, sounding happier by far than he was following Thanksgiving dinners at his brother Ben's.

After that, I tried to grab a conversation with my new aunt whenever I returned to Texas, but to avoid incurring Morris's jealousy, it had to be on the run. If we were having dinner at my parents' home, Dorothy and I would exit into the kitchen to start doing dishes, and privately she would state: "You know, Stanley, you make your folks so happy when you come home for the holidays." Or, she might offer some advice. "You should start saving a little money, putting it into some kind of fund. You'd be surprised how fast it'll grow." That same counsel had often been issued by my father, but it somehow sounded better from her.

Though he would have preferred a dog, Morris agreed to Dorothy's wish for a cat, Sam, followed by another, Sol. When at home, they all four watched television from bed. And visits with the rest of the family became curtailed to special occasions. Morris granted his wife leave to be with others sparingly.

Content to be mostly by themselves, with their cats, they let the years unfurl.

▶▶▶

By the time my father died and Mother moved into Golden Acres, Morris had ceased to be the little brother who helped vacuum the rug. He had become her principal caretaker. Before she left her apartment on Edgemere, he and Dorothy checked out the facility and made sure she got the best suite. "Jews know how to run a home for old folks," he assured me. "It's a classy place."

Mother griped that her living at Golden Acres was costing too much money, but Morris persuaded her otherwise. "You don't have to worry, Becky," he said, "you've got enough." He and Dorothy took care of paying Mother's bills and taxes.

It seemed as if, though at least twelve years his senior, my mother had become Morris' little sister.

Between Dorothy and Morris, however, the marriage was never anything but a partnership of equals. Aunt Rose says that no one was changed by marriage as much as her brother Morris. Even my mother began to see her sister-in-law differently. When I pointed out to Mother how much more relaxed Morris was since his time with Dorothy, she assented, at last, with only slight equivocation. "Yes," she said, slowly, "you're right."

I have said, only partly in jest, that in all their married years, Dorothy and Morris weren't physically apart more than the total of the hours in a week. The uncle who seemed to me least likely candidate for "best married" finished twenty-five years in as ideal a relationship—Jewish, mixed, or any other—as I had seen. If Dorothy had not contracted cancer, it surely would have continued decades more.

▶▶▶

Dorothy's illness came as a double blow to someone who had been so strong and had maintained a lifestyle of healthy food and exercise. Already sick (though we didn't know it), she made an elegant Passover Seder for our family when I visited there in the spring of 1985, just before Mother went to Golden Acres. "Dorothy never should have done it," Aunt Rose told me much later. "She was in terrible pain that night."

While the cancer hit, retreated, and returned, Morris monitored all of Dorothy's activities. On my next visit, I launched into the talk with her that I always looked forward to, reporting that I finally was putting away a few dollars into savings. She nodded in approval. Morris kept watch nearby and interrupted. "Now, Dorothy," he said, "you've used your voice enough for today. Go upstairs and lie down awhile."

"Yes, honey," she answered, and proceeded up to their bedroom.

Only when Morris had a spare minute would he go into another room to watch a sports program. "I have to keep up with football," he told me. "It's the only distraction I've got."

Before long my visits ended with Dorothy's smile diminished slightly. "Pray good thoughts for me, Stanley," she said, anxiously.

"Yes," I said, "I will."

The cancer finally dug in and stayed. Long-distance phone calls revealed that it was difficult for Dorothy to speak clearly. Ruefully, she said to me, "Well, now it's taken the things I was most proud of—my hair and my speech—even my handwriting!" Soon the morning walks stopped, and she took to bed.

The last time I saw Dorothy, on another spring visit in 1988, she was nearly a skeleton. She lay in bed at home in the apartment that they had bought and loved. No more medical treatments, only husband's care. Morris walked into her room, filled with sun and the African violets she grew, and cheerfully announced that I had come from New York to see her.

Dorothy nodded slightly as I talked. Through the entire visit, I held her still-manicured hand. Finally, she seemed exhausted and hardly able to stay awake, and I knew it was time to leave. Though I was certain that I would never see her again, I followed her lead and said, "Dorothy, I know that the next time we meet, you'll be all well."

She strained a hint of a smile and a barely whispered reply: "And I know you wouldn't lie to me, Stanley."

Everyone misses Dorothy. I remember her cheerfulness and optimism even as she grew sicker. Aunt Rose says that she was the best friend she ever had, the most compassionate person she ever knew. "She never let on in those early days when she thought that Morris liked Becky better than her," Rose says. "Or how she hated sitting in that Las Vegas hotel room while he played cards downstairs."

▶▶▶

Morris has disproved everyone's expectation that he would fall apart, with Dorothy gone. But we forgot that he's never been conventional. Now that he's past eighty-five, his hands tremble, but that doesn't prevent his continuing their early morning walks or the fresh orange juice that he and Dorothy made every day together. Friends have given him a list of interesting women to call, but he prefers to spend his days mostly alone, finding new recipes to cook for himself, caring for a small garden, and doing his own housekeeping, without the company of Sol or Sam, who have died as well. Brown and blue socks still get mixed up, but that's no longer important.

On the Jewish High Holy Days he goes to Shearith Israel and sits in the row that he shared for years with my mother and father. "I don't recognize many people there any more," he says, sadly. Nieces and nephews of his and Dorothy's are welcomed into his apartment. In the living room he leaves an old marble lamp lit all the time, though he hasn't explained why.

Morris and I seem to have come full circle. With my parents gone, he and I share the same house when I'm back in Dallas. This time, however, it's his home, and I'm the one who comes in late. Before going out, I go upstairs to his room to talk a minute, and he asks whether I wouldn't just as soon stay home and try some of his mashed potatoes. He never fails to lay in a big jar of the herring that I like.

Aunt Rose is now ninety, and Aunt Fannie, the unexpected survivor of two heart attacks, died in 1996 only a few years short of 100. When the two of them became widows, Morris assumed the role of responsible big brother as he had earlier with Pearl and with my mother. But he doesn't overdo the attention. When he feels it's safe to leave town, he takes advantage of an invitation to escape to Las Vegas for a poker tournament. Going now for companionship rather than card playing, he's treated like one of the elders whom old pals present with a flashy nylon Las Vegas poker jacket. "No one else understands why I like that trip," he says. That may be true, but everyone still encourages him to do it.

On a visit of my own to Dallas, I suggested taking everyone out to dinner.

"What?" he asked. "Go to a restaurant on the second night of Passover? Suppose someone sees us! You take the others."

I expressed surprise to Aunt Rose about the depth of Morris' religious feeling. "What are you talking about?" she asked. "He wants to stay home to watch a baseball game!" Nothing puts him, as he describes it, "in heaven," quite like football and basketball on the same night. One he may follow by radio, the other on television.

I don't share his interest in those sports and haven't attempted to go back to playing bridge, but now when there are silences between us, they lack the tension of old. Occasionally he snaps at me, and if it's unreasonable, I bark back. But I try to keep a respectful quiet. I remind myself of great burdens he's shouldered for me in my absence from Dallas.

We discuss investments, and he surprised me by asking if I would be the executor of his will. He's concerned that things of value not get lost, such as the set of sterling silver flatware that Dorothy brought into their marriage. "I never asked her where she got it," he says.

Even inviting my friend Tom to his apartment feels comfortable now. "Why don't you ask Tom to come and use the pool?" Morris suggests. When Tom does come, somehow the questions about Uncle Morris moving in with my family that he and I pondered so long ago on the screened porch seem not to need an answer.

▶▶▶

Dorothy rests in the handsome plot that Morris and she bought years earlier. It's in North Dallas, part of a manicured, multidenominational cemetery, more accessible than that of Shearith Israel. Uncle Ben and Aunt Sara are buried there, too, in the Jewish section. Dorothy rests in the "mixed" area. Morris pays a visit every few days. When I'm in town, I go, too.

"Honey, here's Stanley," he said, when we went together recently. "Stanley's come to see you." He chats with Dorothy as he did in life, keeping her abreast of the news. "Well, the market's down a little today." Then, on a more serious note, "We've got a nice place here. See, that little tree is growing. It'll give us shade before long. I'll be with you soon . . . but not just yet."

On the dark marble double stone that lies flat into the ground, he has had his name and date of birth engraved to the side of hers. Between the names is chiseled, "Together forever."

Morris never leaves his wife's grave without fresh flowers. He brings them, arranges them in a small urn, adds clean water and changes them when they've faded. Often they're products of what he and she planted in their own small garden. "What do you think about these roses, hey?" he asked me when I was there in the fall. "From our patio. Bet you don't have roses growing outside in New York in October!"

He remarks that he seems to be the only one in the cemetery. "Don't those other people go to see their family?" he wonders aloud.

Overhearing a conversation between me and Aunt Rose, he realized when I was there on that October visit that it was soon going to be my birthday. "Here, Stanley, for your birthday," he said tersely. "Stick this in your pocket!"

I looked down with amazement at a $100 bill, one more denomination with which I have scant experience. Suddenly, memories of long-gone years, air conditioners, traffic tickets, a snazzy maroon Oldsmobile, stories about cheap women, $10 and $20 bills, flooded through my head. This time, though, I didn't feign a protest. I just smiled and put the bill away.

"Thanks, Morris," I said.

15

Tom—You're from Texas and You're Not Jewish?

When we were nearly nine and met in Bradfield School, Tommy and I both hoped not to be noticed and stood back from other boys who crowded on to the softball field. Our bodies were too skinny for heights they suddenly needed to support, and we were called unwillingly into the fraternity of those saddled for a lifetime with eyeglasses. Taller, finally to six feet, we remained thin and unathletic.

Of certain facts I have a less perfect memory than Tommy does. I had forgotten that he made his sole trek to South Dallas in 1945 to attend my bar mitzvah in the old Shearith Israel building. "I was astounded," he says, "to see the congregation divided by sex and afraid that I wouldn't be allowed to sit with my mother, but we did." That first time in a Jewish house of worship he calls the moment when he realized how different we were in some fundamental ways.

In 1953, right after finishing college, we were called at the same time for the obligatory pre-induction physical exam for the army. Though it's another event I've pushed out of my mind, it stayed in his. "I have a vivid picture of our whole group of guys," he says, "in a huge circle, all of us naked, while the doctors proceeded around, poking us for hernias and I guess VD. You were across the circle from me, and it was the first time I ever saw you naked." Because of some unfatal flaw, Tommy got excused from the military service that I was drafted into the next year. It was a moment that made me feel manly and envious.

As time passed and we sought to subtract rather than add years, he complained that he looked older than I by more than the six months that separated us. He was annoyed with his early loss of hair. Today we look about the same age, a point of satisfaction for him.

Tom went through college in Dallas and even stayed on for work and a few changes of apartments. But during all those thirty years, he remained at heart an East Texas small-town guy. Like his parents ("Mom" and "Daddy"), he finally chose to escape Dallas' crowds and rush hour traffic that begins at six-thirty in the morning and doesn't let up until past dark again. "You know," he pointed out, as he planned to return to Mt. Vernon, "Dallas is no longer the city we grew up in."

Mt. Vernon is still the place where Tommy started. With a couple of thousand citizens, an array of churches and a new retirement home, Mt. Vernon retains a mentality that says that's enough. It's located 100 miles east of Dallas, going toward Arkansas, on rolling land that interrupts the flat Texas landscape, a place where you don't have to hold office to be addressed as "Sir" or "Ma'am."

"They can't all live much longer," Tommy said of the older generation of his family as he decided to move back to East Texas. So sure was he of their limited endurance and a corresponding inheritance that he took early retirement from a job teaching English in a Dallas college.

He underestimated them. Tom's grandfather, a judge, defied a couple of near fatal heart attacks and hung around to age 101. His father endured a long illness and lived nearly that long, and his Aunt Agnes was still teaching piano until she died at ninety-five. Aunt Gladys also lived until past ninety.

Dismayed by the longevity of his predecessors—all except the one he was closest to, his mother, who died instantly of a heart attack at seventy-four— Tom had no choice but to go back to work. He joined the faculty of a community college that was about to open in the middle of pasture land with an enrollment of 2,000 students. There, with his long limbs and cap, tie and corduroy jacket, he goes to instruct East Texas folks in art history and humanities. Some of his students are women returning to school as adults, others are rural boys and girls from families where college is considered a luxury. He is found an interesting oddity by all of them.

▶▶▶

But this is today. Like my mother trying to recall her first letters to her friend Rose, it's hard for me to reconstitute my early contacts with Tom. "Did your parents ever hint at anti-Semitism, when you started coming over to my house for lunch?" I asked him recently.

"Not a bit," he said. "Did yours try to prejudice you against gentiles?"

"No," I replied, not quite lying but relieved that he seemed to have taken no note of, or maybe been polite enough not to mention my mother's luncheon menus.

Other kids at school started to group Tommy and me together, and there may have been an occasional whispered "sissies." I didn't mind the pairing, but I early on got in the habit of sectioning my friends, Tom on one side, on the other all my Jewish friends, whom he knew only casually from school.

As we neared high school, I would tell him about parties I had gone to, making them sound more drunken and wilder than they were. He was impressed by my story of the Fort Worth traffic ticket, in which I enlarged on the velocity at which I had driven. Tom was the only one with whom I could play the role of a daring one, and I didn't miss the chance.

Eventually, long after school days and into adulthood—and in the unlikely case that he hadn't long since figured it out—I realized that it was past time to tell my old friend that I was gay. I did it the least courageous way—by letter—in 1959, when I was living in New York. Our next meeting occurred in September 1960, when Tommy was on his way to a short-lived stay at Yale. We talked long into the night in the bar of the Roosevelt Hotel, near Grand Central, where he was staying.

"Okay, Tommy," I said, "the cards are on the table."

He looked eager, then timid. Slowly, he twirled a plastic stick around and around his drink. "Yep, they are."

"So . . ." I asked, "what do you want to know?"

"Well . . . what do you do?"

I sat up straight. "Well, you know, I have these three roommates on West 12th Street, and they're very straight. They think I am too, I think. So I can't bring anyone home."

Tom looked at me with a we've-known-each-other-a-long-time look. "Then," he asked, with a sharp point in his voice, "why do you live with them?"

"I *like* them. They give me some security."

He looked unsatisfied, but let it pass. "Okay, so you can't bring anyone home."

"That's right. Not that I much want to, anyway. I haven't been with anybody more than once or twice. I go a lot to the baths."

"The what?"

We did a duet of twirling plastic sticks around our glasses. "The baths," I repeated, in a near whisper. "Guys go to have sex." Before he had a chance to explore that topic, I went on. "Did I tell you about the guy I met in Washington Square?"

"You haven't told me *anything* yet!"

"Well, it's a couple of blocks from the apartment, and I went down there early one evening this July. I found a bench and started to read. A tall young black fellow came up and began to talk. *He* started to talk. He seemed nice, very sweet—an artist. Nice looking guy. So we talked some . . . about art."

Tommy put down his plastic stirrer. "But that wasn't what he really wanted to talk about."

"That's right. He invited me to his place a couple of blocks away, in the Village."

"Did you go?"

"Yeah."

"So, what happened? Were you nervous?"

"Yes, I was nervous. And . . . umm, he wanted to . . . enter me through the rear."

"He *did*?"

"Yes, and I'd never done that."

Tommy's eyes grew wider. "Did you let him?"

"Yeah. Well, it was his place."

"Ohh!" he said, almost spitting out his drink. "That's not enough reason!

Did you like it?"

"I didn't like it. It hurt. As soon as we finished, I left."

"Is that it?"

"A day or two later, I started to itch."

"Itch?? Oh, my God!"

I turned somber. "All around my crotch. And I didn't know what it was. I didn't figure it was something to discuss with my roommates. Finally, I got the name of a dermatologist and went to see him."

"What'd he say?"

"He said it was crabs. Gave me a prescription."

"The crabs! Umph! Did that work?"

"Sure. Later I felt stupid because I found out that a lot of guys get crabs . . . from other guys. Nearly everyone!"

Tommy looked doubtful again. "Everyone?"

"Well . . . They're easy to pass. And you don't need to go to a doctor. There's a bottle of oily stuff you can buy over the counter. You rub it in good once or twice, and pretty soon the crabs are gone."

It was one o'clock in the morning, and the hotel bar was about to close. As the waiter started dimming the lights, the two of us grew silent. "Of course," I added softly, "I had to keep the bottle hidden."

Tommy finished his drink. "So, you saw that guy again?"

"Absolutely not! Crabs, they're not a big deal. But they're not nothing. They're . . . embarrassing! And uncomfortable. I don't need to go looking for them."

My friend from grade school looked at me with a little smile of amazement, as we called to the waiter and paid the check.

▶▶▶

Nowadays Tom lives in a new two-bedroom house on a quiet cul-de-sac in Mount Vernon.

His three cocker spaniels yelp, and Tom throws on his cap and lopes out the front door as I pull up into his driveway. For me, it's an overnight East Texas getaway during a trip to Dallas. It's my first visit to his new home, acquired when he sold his grandparents' fine old Victorian house on Main Street a few blocks away.

"You're one of the few friends who still comes down here," he says, giving me a warm Texas hug.

"But I enjoy coming here," I state. "I also like to get away from Dallas traffic."

"This'll be your room," he says, ushering me into the front bedroom, "your" lying down and stretching into four or five syllables. "That's the canopy bed I used to sleep in as a kid, when I stayed over at my grandparents' house." (A canopy bed, I thought? Would my grandparents even have known what one was?)

At night, we two bachelors go out for a Mexican dinner in nearby Mt. Pleasant, and Tom pays the fee to join a "private club." That enables us to order margaritas, going counter to the East Texas staple of beer I see being consumed by the young cowboy-hatted crowd.

After dinner, Tom stokes up a fire in his new fireplace and turns down the overhead light. With shoes off and feet propped up on a couple of fine footstools, we settle in for the kind of unhurried talk we've had on scores of evenings since Highland Park days. Eventually the subject turns into joys and burdens of travel.

"It'd be easy to just stay home," I say. "Sometimes I have to force myself not to. Once I'm gone somewhere, of course, I'm glad. My mother used to say that the only trip she regretted was the one she didn't take."

"She was right," says Tom. "But, oh, the getting there!"

"Neither of us likes flying, but I can't go back to not doing it," I announce. "I've decided I don't have to like it, I just have to do it."

"It's hard getting away, with the dogs, and the yard."

"We find reasons. I have a cat. It's hard for me to get away, too."

That seems the moment for Tom to stretch and for the spaniels to yelp a demand for a nighttime snack. Tom goes to the kitchen to oblige them, and returns with hot tea.

"You don't mind my saying so," I suggest before the night runs out, "you're getting more and more like your father. I remember, when Mr. Wilkinson retired and didn't have to fly any more, he said he never would again. He didn't want to leave Mt. Vernon once he came back here."

"He didn't want to leave his room!"

"We have to try not to mimic the worst of our fathers."

"That's true," Tom agrees, hesitantly. "Yeah, that's true."

"I always think how much nicer you were to your parents than I was to mine. Living in New York, I didn't have the day-to-day care for them as they got older."

"Yes," he says, ironically. "You've really missed out!"

Tom looks wistful. "I wish," he adds," that my daddy . . . my father had taken a more assertive role, like yours."

"You've got that wrong. My mother was the one in charge. Jewish fathers weren't even supposed to help raise kids. But that cost my father something; he didn't get back much love from his three children—only from Jerome. I'm not even convinced how sincere that was."

Tom smiles a faint smile. "It was so easy for you and me to feel close to our mothers, wasn't it? Such unequal affection for parents."

"Yep," I sigh.

"How many nights we've spent thrashing out our problems with parents! Dozens! Have you ever done that with anyone else?"

"Not as often. Or continually."

"Do you think there's enough left for a few more years of heart-to-hearts?" asks Tom, stretching once more.

"Wouldn't be surprised," I say. "I'm not finished with my father. Maybe even my mother!"

▶▶▶

Perhaps to guarantee that there *is* material left for more heart-to-hearts, I find a one-night stop in Mt. Vernon sufficient. And I keep thinking that Tom is a misfit staying on in that static little burg. But I seem to be wrong. He has spoiled the three dogs, which I see you can do as well in a very small town as anywhere else. Against obvious hurdles, he's also found a circle of interesting friends, many of them other teachers.

Tom said "no" when I asked whether he missed the grand former Wilkinson home on Main St. With no plumbing problems or weak foundation, his new place features lots of windows and skylights. Perhaps most appealing of all is the view from Tom's bedroom. "Look here," he says, guiding me to the back of the house and throwing open the drapes in his room. Beyond the window, behind the house, lies a huge grassy field populated with horses and cattle, an undisturbed picture of serenity that stretches wide under the blue Texas sky. It's far from the crowds in Dallas, universes from New York.

▶▶▶

I am grateful for my good luck in meeting Tom so early. Aside from friendship, I acquired through him one acquaintance who lived in a world of which I was ignorant.

Family life, for instance. If big-city Jews think that they have no relatives in an outpost like Texas, Jews everywhere seem to feel they have a monopoly on close-knit families, often under the jurisdiction of a commanding matriarch. With Tommy, I learned that that was not true. His relationship, especially with his mother but also his father, aunts, uncles and cousins was closer than mine was to the same people in my family. When I told Tom that I had finally gotten to the point of going out without listing a destination for my mother's benefit, he said, "That would have been impossible for me."

Beyond a look at gentile family relationships, Tom gave me my first view as to how Christmas gets celebrated by well-off folks. In elementary school, I would come back after the December holidays, and when Tommy and other kids were talking about their parties and comparing gifts, someone would ask me, "What did you get, Stanley?" I never had the courage to explain that we were Jewish and didn't celebrate Christmas, so I'd invent a received present or two, items sufficiently modest that they wouldn't outrage my parents should they happen to find out.

I still felt the sting of Christmas when we lived in South Dallas and at age five or six, I insisted on climbing on the lap of a department store Santa Claus. Uncensored by my mother, he told me that he would come to see me at my house on a certain evening. I waited eagerly for that night, and when it came around, I watched anxiously—finally, despondently—for his arrival. No one at home warned me that that it was a hoax.

I'm not sure I fooled Tommy any more than myself with my made-up Christmas presents. He had certainly heard about Chanukah, and probably wondered why I didn't talk about those gifts. He didn't know that I would have, if (and here I trust my imperfect memory) there had been any.

▶▶▶

Others I knew in Texas, of whose society I was much more a part, live for me now mostly on pages in a scrapbook. But that first meeting between Tommy and me in 1940 set in motion a friendship that, without any obvious reason to last and with our adult years living far apart, turns out to have endured past a half century. We never exchanged vows, of course, but I laugh to think that if we had, it would have produced another example of lasting interfaith marriages.

There were many times when we were young that I envied the attention that Tom benefited from by being an only child. But I see now, as we both face a future without parents or siblings or partners, that I have something he lacks, the closeness of nieces and nephews. Tom's road and mine are solitary ones today, but having lacked sisters or brothers, his turns out to be even more unaccompanied than mine. That seems more important for me to remember than some of those past events I've forgotten.

I don't fill all the gaps for him, nor does he for me. But we do what friends should do. We try.

16

Florence—A Near and Distant Loss

In my family's album, just a page or two past the snapshot of Aunt Fannie and myself behind the house on Forest Avenue, there is one more fading portrait of me that was taken around 1937, when I was five. Standing in front of a swing in the back yard of our house on Grand Avenue, I am naked but for a lady's pocketbook hiding my genitals. The photo was set up by Florence and Jerome.

"Well, isn't that cute!" Aunt Fannie said once when we leafed through the album and came upon that picture. *Cute*, I thought? *No*. A little boy covered only with a woman's pocketbook, and then immortalized in a photograph? Not cute. All these years I've felt degraded when I ran across that image. I may have been manipulated by people older than me into its being taken, but there have been decades since when I had the chance to tear the picture up. Why I haven't done so, I'm never sure.

The picture jumped back into my mind after Florence died in 1992. I had an oddly bland reaction to her passing. Could it be rooted in that photo shot half a century ago? Maybe.

What I know is that after her death, I felt neither as blurry nor teary-eyed as I did each time another of my family passed away. I ordered a basket of nice food to be sent to John, her husband, and I wrote him a letter. Those, with a donation to my preferred charity, were the total of my acknowledgment that I had become like Tom an only child with no parents, that the last of our immediate family had gone.

My sister was buried in Denver, the city where she moved when she was married, where she then lived for the next nearly half century. Thousands of miles away, her funeral took place without me. But it was more than the miles from New York that kept me away. The opposite ends of the country in which we had been living mirrored the distance between us. If I were to chart our relationship over the last several decades, the line would simply hang its head and go downward.

▶▶▶

Since Jerome and Florence were eight and ten years older than me, they seemed like a cross between siblings and parents to me, in any case a lot bigger than I was. But being only two years apart from each other, they were buddies. The Forest Avenue High paper photographed them smiling together as brother-and-sister members of the school's debating team. Before Forest High, they had attended the same South Dallas elementary school; after high school, Southern Methodist in Dallas. The Jims and Daves and Bettys that used to come to our house were friends of one as much as the other. Years later, during Jerome's illness, Florence came to visit him from Denver. I could see the affection that they shared, a partnership in which I never participated. To my brother and sister, I must have seemed a cross between spoiled little brother and, when young, a child to be played with. At their choice. Family stories tell that Florence had set her heart on a little sister, if there had to be another sibling at all. I turned out to be the disappointing gender. Perhaps the photo in the back yard was a sort of revenge.

Never mind that I was frightened on the occasions when, very young, I was left in the custody of those two. Forget that I hid birthday gifts in fear of their being pirated (even if in reality they never would have been).

Ignore her part in the following dialogue:

Florence: "No one's going to be home today, you won't be able to get in."

Aunt Fannie: "Stanley'll be there."

Florence: "That's like I said."

Notwithstanding all of that, my sister and brother were handsome, for me heroes more than villains, opening the door into their worlds at unpredictable moments, such as when, at twenty, Florence persuaded her boyfriend to take me along on their date. That happened a few times. At age ten I loved that kind of treat, going to the outdoor summer musicals with two grown-ups. Only later did I come to think that it was a severe test of a boyfriend plus a misleading message to an impressionable younger brother.

Like the Shapiro sisters, Florence was not tall but a slender, pretty blond with a sexy figure. To that she added a sensual walk and slow southern speech that she retained long after leaving the South. She was cool and unrevealing like the good card player that she turned out to be. Following Aunt Fannie's lead of the generation before, she attracted swarms of boys. "She's so scatterbrained," they'd say, adding, "but she always gets the best grades in the class!"

On December 7, 1941, Bobby, a beau of hers, was at our house when the news came on the radio of the bombing of Pearl Harbor. I was nine, and I remember his look of distress, a look shared by everyone in the house: my parents and brother and his friends. Bobby was a carefree fellow who quickly enlisted in the air force, became a pilot and before the war ended was killed in action in the Pacific.

In 1941, Florence was studying science and in a training job as a laboratory technician at a local hospital. She worked there for two or three years, living at home, driving off before sunrise every morning. One day she spilled acid on the back of her hand in the laboratory, and it caused a burn so severe that she was laid up in bed for days thereafter, instructed not to move. Going into her darkened room was strange and disturbing, made all the more so by the foil that had to be put on the burn and whose stench filled the house. That burn turned into a scar that never went away.

In those years Ely cousins of Florence's age, Bernard and Freda and Morris and Louis and Evelyn, all started to become engaged. There are photos in the album of the girls attending engagement luncheons, Florence on a break from the hospital, wearing her lab technician's uniform.

She took her turn in 1944. It came following a blind date, then a few more, with the cousin of a friend of hers who was visiting from Denver. John, the Coloradoan, was a young Jewish man, tall with strong features, full lips, thinning dark hair and a deep announcer's voice. He had studied architecture, then gone into building apartment houses with his father. Soon he was pursuing Florence with flowers and telegrams. Though she debated about moving so far from Dallas, she finally accepted his proposal for marriage. In doing so, she passed up some local fellows who temporarily were away in military service but whom she knew much better.

My sister was nearly twenty-two, almost as sheltered as I, when she got married in November 1944. At her wedding in a small ballroom of a residential hotel, a friend of hers sang, "Always." Before getting dressed for the ceremony in a smart woolen suit, Florence paced nervously around the house on Stanhope in her bra. She looked seductive.

While everyone else beamed that day—what *was* known of John was that his family was well-off—I staggered from what I at age twelve saw as a great impending loss. And I was right.

In a couple of years she would become a mother, then twice more. With manifold adjustments to make—a new city where she went knowing no one except her husband, and him not well; a powerful mother-in-law who kept her son locked in permanent dependence; three children to raise later on, my sister surely would—did—forget the times she took me along on dates and the Sunday morning ritual in which she and I often climbed in bed to read the comics together.

Her marriage wasn't betrayal, of course. But, like Uncle Morris', it felt so to me.

▶▶▶

Perhaps there was something else that also made her forget our erstwhile closeness. Her husband. John later became something of a local personality by appearing on television at wrestling matches that he promoted. That sideline seemed to me appropriate, since I found him nearly as coarse as the wrestlers. His was the sort of joke that went: "You know the definition of a poor Jew? He's the one who washes his own Cadillac."

From the earliest days, he joked about the fact that I spoke with a Texas twang (actually, not a heavy one), couldn't whistle and didn't play baseball. He simply tolerated me as Florence's dates had earlier—maybe somewhat less. He certainly didn't like me, a fact that he spit at me in a moment of anger years later. "How much do you make in that teaching job?" he embarrassed me, by asking when we were at a party among strangers. If over the years I tried to placate him, it was bribery, from fear more than affection.

Since his in-laws lived so far away, John must have reconciled himself to our stay-over visits, and since Colorado is paradise compared to Texas in the summer, I exploited the chance to go to Denver during school vacations. Overnight by train, those were my first and much anticipated ventures outside Texas. John's parents had built a large, comfortable house (there they called it a cabin) in the mountains, and we'd escape for the weekend into those hills. It was a wonderful treat for a young Texas kid: to stop along the road and buy fresh cream from a farm, pick mushrooms out of the ground and cook them over a fire at night. They were the best of the moments with John and his parents, immigrants like mine but with heavier accents, more serious religious commitment and much more money.

I wanted the Colorado trips for more than the climate or the food or the brother-in-law, principally to see my sister, to have her notice that I was growing up. But that's not altogether true, since part of me—in fact, a big part—sought the opposite: to put a brake on growing and recapture the relationship we had before she left Dallas. Whatever my motives, she seemed disinterested in what I said about school or friends. Perhaps it was his influence? I didn't know. In any case, there started a pattern in which I continued to seek a closeness that she continued to withhold.

Those summer visits, which I anticipated with hope and then discomfort, diminished as the years passed. Longer stretches went by without my seeing my sister and brother-in-law. If I wrote or sent a gift, it did not get acknowledged. Faithfully, though, she would send me a check for my birthday, even if months had passed without our being in touch. "Have a good time," the card would usually say, with nothing more.

First imprints do not give way to easy erasure. That early relationship with my sister, and its veiled sexual component, remained difficult for me to let go of. All that changed was that later on anger got stirred in with my other feelings, since with me she manifested ever more detachment, sometimes needing to turn her head away when I spoke.

On dozens of occasions I went to tear that awful early photo from the picture album. I never did.

▶▶▶

In time Susie, my niece, and Arden and Ed, my two nephews, finished school, went off to college, and moved away from Denver. With less responsibilities at home, Florence stepped up the hours that she spent playing bridge or golf. ("You know, I never worked again after I got married," she commented once in a manner that to me seemed strangely proud.) John started to suffer from intermittent, at times serious depression, nearly an echo a couple of decades later of what Uncle Arthur had suffered in the late 1950s. The man who had never enjoyed socializing wanted more and more simply to change into pajamas and spend evenings watching television, from bed. Perhaps in compensation, he regaled his wife with an expensive car and beautiful clothes, and the freedom to build a life outside their house, which she did not only at luncheons but on trips with women friends to health spas. I wondered whether, maybe unconsciously, Florence wasn't staging an updated, more affluent version of our parents' marriage.

What was sure was that her daytime companions became her intimates. Mother remarked, "If you want to know what your sister is thinking, talk to one of her girlfriends—or maybe Martha, their housekeeper." Ironically, I thought, the freedom that John gave her to be with those women friends could have been what kept her married to him.

▶▶▶

No bulletin ever got sent to tell Florence that her brother Stanley had turned out to be gay.

As with my parents, I never confronted her or her husband with the blunt fact. I was having too much trouble confronting it myself. Anyway, I didn't need to. When we were together, he or Florence would loudly comment on some piece of my behavior such as, "Only sissies do that!" I suspected that he had primed her for an ambivalence about homosexuality, and I thought that coming from him, well, those remarks were what you'd expect. But why the slurs from her? Were they really hers, or had she found that being his good pupil just made her life easier?

Only one of their children, Arden, the older son, married, and a few years later he revealed that he and his wife were separating. At first, Florence held to the idea that it was Arden's wife who wanted the separation, rejecting the reason that Arden gave her: that he was gay. "I don't know that I can approve of that," she told him angrily. Though she had witnessed our mother accepting my sexual leaning, she seemed unable to profit from Mother's example for herself. Later, she became more reconciled with Arden's ex-wife than with him. If he called long distance and spoke of his new male lover, she asked, "Who?"

I've naturally wondered how much my sister blamed me in this scenario—uncle and nephew plotting against the established order. If so, she'd have been wrong, since my nephew's change of lifestyle took place long before I knew about it. But finding me an accomplice must have been irresistible if it helped displace any doubt she harbored about her responsibility for his being gay. Anyway, I had no idea what she was thinking—and I didn't consult her girlfriends.

My sister and I didn't discuss things like that. I might have wanted to, but she didn't. In fact, she and I talked mostly within the safe zone: recipes or family gossip. Today, I would push for more—then, I didn't have the courage.

Some of our best communication came, oddly enough, when we had to deal with issues concerning our mother, after she was widowed. With Jerome long since passed away, Florence and I remained the surviving children. Suddenly, when Mother's name came up, it would seem as if Florence inhaled a rush of warmth and allowed the barriers between us to topple. Our ideas concerning Mother's future were usually in sync, and I enjoyed that infrequent closeness. But it didn't last. When we had finished discussing business, we'd conclude as if a meeting were adjourned and part hastily, with a polite goodbye or an uncomfortable hug.

The same happened when I'd leave Denver after what had evolved into infrequent visits. "Well, this was a really good time," I'd say, bending over to kiss a hesitantly turned cheek.

"Yes, it was," she'd reply with a warm smile, only then to seem to retreat before it went on too long.

I was sure that sooner or later Florence would offer to make me one of the handsome sweaters that she hand-knitted for everyone else in the family. But I was wrong.

▶▶▶

From 1987 on, I was with my sister just twice, one of those times at Mother's funeral in Dallas, in that same year. It had been a while since Florence and I were together, and I was surprised to see that she had let go the svelte figure she retained for so long. "Taking care of John has been a full time job lately," she said, without being asked. "I couldn't do that and watch my weight."

Florence's relationship with our father had been, if anything, worse than mine. It seemed to me that she held a thinly veiled antipathy toward our dad because he was not as strong a figure as she would have liked.

So, while she may not have missed Dad, she would miss Mother. Mother's trips to Denver had been so frequent that she became a bridge player and friend to Florence's friends. If Mother spoke of my sister and caught a cold reaction from me, she'd remind me that Florence had endured a difficult marriage, including the time that John was discovered to be having an affair with another woman, the time that a near-divorce took place. With Jerome gone, Mother especially would have wished for my sister and me to be friends.

Over several days during that funeral trip, Florence and I were alone only half an hour. I seized the time to air a matter that was much on my mind: the fact that I was to receive a larger share of Mother's estate than her.

"I hope you're not angry about that," I said.

"But that was *my* suggestion," Florence stated.

Her suggestion? Was that possible? Long before, my mother had explained to me how she had written her will, and why, based on need. She never suggested that it was anyone's idea other than hers. Whose was it, really? I've never known.

I was concerned, too, about what lay ahead. "If we don't make a real effort to stay in touch," I added, "we'll drift apart. We have to *make* it happen."

Florence responded with an uncomfortable giggle.

After I received my share of Mother's estate, the birthday checks with the brief messages from my sister stopped. Most phone calls, too, in both directions. I came to realize that with me Florence had managed the exact relationship she wanted: not openly hostile, since that might have provoked response. But not loving. A non-existent relationship. None at all.

In the fall of 1988, I got a call saying that she was coming to New York with friends from Denver (though not her husband, who preferred to stay at home). She asked me to arrange a dinner with Paula, Jerome's former wife, and Marcia, their younger daughter, who by then was also working and living in New York. I was delighted at the prospect of a visit with my sister and I requested some private time—a brunch, maybe a chance to show her my apartment.

It turned out, though, that she was on a tour with a full agenda. We met just once, at that dinner with Paula, Marcia and Andy, Marcia's future husband. I picked Florence up at her hotel, and she remarked to me a couple of times, in a tone that sounded more surprised than pleased, "Well, you look really well!" At dinner, she cooed over the others but again looked the other way when I spoke. She was unable to make the brunch date, and the apartment remained unseen.

That was the last time we were together.

▶▶

Breast cancer struck Florence when she was fifty. She underwent a radical mastectomy and a long recovery, and for years after that, she often kept her arm wrapped tightly to lessen the pain. I cringed when I saw her force a laugh at John's joke about a "woman with big boobs!"

Dormant for a decade and a half, the cancer reappeared in other parts of her body in 1989. Then a stroke in 1991 left her partly paralyzed and in need of help to walk or dress. By that time, she and I had become politely, permanently distant. But suddenly her life had changed: she was seriously ill. I thought of my mother, who had read my feelings about Florence so well, whom I could hear from her grave exhorting me to rebuild a closeness.

But I didn't. If I no longer felt envy of my sister's wealth, there remained a leaden residue of disappointment and sadness. And an unwillingness to fulfill the wishes of my mother, who used to point out that Florence lacked good relationships with men. Well, I thought angrily, she had a second brother who was still alive, not just a man but also a good candidate for a friend.

She missed the chance.

I made a few phone calls to Denver—not many—and since for me writing was easier, I sent occasional photos of family or trips and brief cards of good wishes. If I thought of visiting, I could only foresee discomfort. It seemed too late to feign an attachment, or to apply bandages to so deep an emotional wound. I had waited too long, I thought. In truth, I just didn't want to go.

As Florence had been devoted to John when he was ill, he provided full-time nursing care at home after her stroke. In his protectiveness of her, he hurled anger at me. "Only a card from her brother!" he yelled once on the phone. "So distant!"

His remark left me off guard, as his remarks had on many occasions. I didn't know what to say. "I've never been encouraged to be anything else," I blurted back, finally.

At the end of August 1992, with help from a couple of aides, Florence managed to fly to a bridge tournament in Las Vegas and play a few hands. Back in Denver, she collapsed in her driveway with a heart attack and died a few hours later. "Perhaps she just couldn't stand to spend another night in that house," said her son Ed.

And so my sister's life ended, cared for by her husband of almost fifty years but apparently unreconciled to the fact that her elder son was gay, and lacking any goodbye from her brother, the only other survivor of her immediate family.

Do I have regrets? Sure, though I've claimed that they are not of my doing. Ask me, and I'll tell you that, for me, Florence kept the door half closed, not half open.

"I understand why you didn't come to Mother's funeral," my nephew Arden said to me. "Even so, I missed you."

I appreciated his thought, and I could imagine my mother shaking her finger my way.

A part of me missed being there, too, so maybe I shouldn't have been so proud. Who knows if an effort that loomed pointless might have been less so, had I tried. If my sister didn't work to bring us closer together, she didn't wish me harm. Perhaps, for her, there would have been danger to do anything more than that.

Or maybe, alas, our relationship simply was not as important to her as it was to me.

▶▶▶

The last time I was in Denver was in 1982. I wanted to buy Florence something special for her sixtieth birthday, so we drove across town to the studio of a glassblower whose work I had seen. She selected a lovely perfume bottle.

Despite the distance that had grown between us, I asked John after she died if he would save some personal item of hers for me. I couldn't think of anything I could use, but I did remember the perfume bottle and the fact that she chose it. That was what I asked for. A while later, I received a package that contained a perfume bottle though, one less fine than the one I had given her. John's note said, "There were several of these on her dresser and I don't want to give away any of the others."

John also died, in 1997, at around age eighty. I had made no effort to keep in contact with him, though I heard roundabout of his pursuit of women, mostly younger than the youngest of his offspring. One romance with a young lady ended with her death from a mysterious, perhaps drug-related accident. It was a sensational story that a local Denver paper reported at length. I was grateful that my mother wasn't alive to read it.

Florence's daughter was angry that some of her mother's fine jewelry intended for her ended up with a girlfriend of her father's. "I realize now how much Mother must have intervened for us," she told me.

▶▶▶

I started here by writing that I had scant reaction when Florence died. In rushing around, I didn't think about it more than to focus on being left the only survivor in our family. Was my scurrying about a way to say that my sister wasn't worth mourning? Or that I'd been a bum?

I'd like to push that door open, late as it is, to allow back in even the imperfect love of sister and brother and the acknowledgment that I had a right to my disappointment. I'd also like to consider that Florence probably long ago forgave me for—or hardly noticed—what I didn't do.

Pretty soon I may go and tear up that old photo. Or not need to.

17

Jerome—One of Two Quiet Adventurers

Before Shearith Israel caught up with the migration of its congregants north, more than a decade had passed. By the late 1950s, the synagogue collected enough cash and pledges to begin erecting a sprawling new home over several acres of valuable, tree-filled North Dallas land. The new building would be modern and low slung. If anyone thought it lacked the warm character of the old South Dallas structure with its tall stairways and balconies and arches and stained glass windows, they found it better not to say so.

Until the new home was completed, young folks from North Dallas who were enrolled in Sunday school had to travel. That included me. Early every Sunday morning, in a fresh shirt and slacks, I would meet friends at the Highland Park Shopping Village, where we'd catch a chartered bus for a ride of several miles to the old synagogue. Those Sunday classes were more obligatory than engaging, but we had the weekly bus rides where we could cut up and make jokes about school. The driver was a burly South Dallas type who clearly wouldn't have minded a different Sunday-morning assignment. North Dallas Jewish kids, he informed us correctly, were a spoiled bunch.

So by bus we got to Sunday school. But the Shearith Israel elders must have realized that for Hebrew lessons, it was a different matter. They'd be pushing their luck to ask boys to undertake a trip across town every Monday through Thursday afternoon, after public school was over. (In those days, females were excused from Hebrew, something like jury duty.)

As an interim measure, the synagogue rented a small three-room structure on Preston Road, a couple of blocks from our house on Stanhope. That's where North Dallas Hebrew got taught to pre-bar mitzvah boys and the persevering few who continued after bar mitzvah. With a fragile wooden frame, peeling green shutters and a weed-filled garden, the building seemed hardly a school or a house, a glaring anomaly among the spacious, well tended dwellings of University Park. Its oddity appealed to us boys, but the house provoked plenty of talk among homeowners who would have voted to see it vanish. (And those feelings weren't altogether anti-Semitic, since they emanated as much from Jews as non-Jews.)

I didn't much take to Hebrew School. The school administrators seemed to have agreed to keep the classes as uninteresting and impractical as possible. You could forebear with Hebrew for six years—as I did—and, though expert in prayers, not have learned enough to locate food or a bathroom in Tel Aviv.

There were periods during those years, however, when my brother Jerome served as our teacher, and then the picture changed. Jerome and his friend David Zesmer, his fellow teacher, were half as old as the other instructors, closer in age to us than to them. Every day they would come after classes at SMU. Jerome shared with his students his interpretation of a tree swaying back and forth in the wind, even the variation between its dance in a gentle breeze and a lusty gale. I can't recall that any of that had much to do with Hebrew, but it was a ploy that made us eleven- and twelve-year-olds smile and stay awake. "Give us the tree again!" we'd yell at the start of class.

"After the lesson, chaverim (friends)," he'd respond, with a knowing bribe. "You want soft breeze or hurricane today?"

"Hurricane!"

"Okay, chaverim, hurricane. After the lesson. Now let's go to page thirty-nine."

And, willingly, we'd open our books from the right, to page thirty-nine.

Once Jerome left Dallas for the air force and then graduate school in Indiana, his career as Hebrew teacher was over. We missed him, and if the prospect of a bar mitzvah hadn't lain ahead, I would have found scant wish to continue with the lessons in the house on Preston Road. Actually, the question never came to a vote. Hebrew school wasn't looked on as an elective; like preparing in Sunday school for confirmation, it was just what good Jewish boys (anyway, boys of good Jewish parents) did. I was no protester in those days, anyway.

For Jerome, Hebrew was a different thing. He, rather than I, should have written about Jewish life in Texas since of the two of us, he was by far the more committed Jew.

And his interest in Hebrew wasn't born at home. Despite so many years of attendance at Shearith Israel, my parents' acquaintance with the language extended no further than the half dozen most frequently recited prayers, and those transliterated into English. (And they made no effort to teach us Yiddish.)

Jerome and his friend David had a passion for Hebrew and Jewish culture that was nurtured by Jacob Levin, head of the Shearith Israel Hebrew program. Levin, then around forty, was a passionate supporter of Zionism, a tanned, slightly balding, muscular man with a commanding voice. Florence seemed to have no interest in Mr. Levin, and the eight years difference between me and Jerome left me too young for the circle of Levin's admirers. But he was dynamic enough to draw Jerome and David enthusiastically into his classes and politics.

Levin ran a summer camp, Camp Bonim, on lakeside property outside of Dallas, and for years Jerome and a group of his pals went there as campers and later as counselors. (For camping, girls were allowed to come along.) I don't think even Levin's magnetism could have involved me in a quest for Hebrew study. Beyond that, his authoritarianism frightened me. Still, at the insistence of my parents and brother, who probably figured that some weeks at camp would toughen and/or draw me into Judaism, I went to Camp Bonim the summer when I was ten.

Jerome was then eighteen, already an inch or two past six feet, filled out a bit from Bubbe Ely's fried chicken, but still slender with an oval face, dark eyes and a long, intense glance, more a countenance of the Shapiros than the Elys. At Camp Bonim, he was not only counselor and swimming instructor but, his most renowned status, camp bugler. It was Jerome's duty to blow reveille every morning at six and he had mastered doing it from a horizontal position in bed, eyes closed. He'd lay down his bugle, turn over and go back to sleep as soon as the last note was out.

My family's hope that camp life would convert me didn't work out. One night per week, initiation rites for a secret society took place in a darkened corner of the camp ground; of those I attempted to remain ignorant. Though I attended obligatory lectures, I brought along as little interest to them as to the sports program. If people treated me kindly, it wasn't because of me or my participation in camping; it was because I was Jerome Ely's little brother.

My clearest recollection of Camp Bonim was one afternoon when I was swimming in the lake. I somehow floated under a large wooden platform and was unable to find the way out for air. There were a couple of horrible minutes when I thought I was dying. That day completed my half-hearted attempt at camping; that summer ended my brief trial as a young Zionist.

▶▶▶

While he was interpreting the swaying tree for us at Hebrew school, Jerome was an undergraduate psychology student at SMU. Part of that curriculum involved learning to administer intelligence tests. He would take out his test materials and round up neighborhood folks to whom he could administer the Stanford-Binet test. He was sure my mother would have done well, and he was no doubt correct, but, "Oh, no, not me!" she replied, when he asked whether she would be a candidate.

For me and some neighborhood kids, the test provided a diversion from the hot days of July, and we were impressed that someone we knew was doing grown-up work like that. So, seated on the screened porch on Stanhope, I agreed to have my I.Q. checked out. "That was really good!" Jerome announced at the end of the test. "'Very smart fellow!" My grades in school already were giving testimony to that fact, but validation from an older brother carried more gold, especially as my parents seemed to take my academic record for granted.

Once, I remember Jerome chastised me for behaving badly when Mother was sick and he had cautioned me not to upset her. Other than that single incident, what my brother gave me was the kind of praise that accompanied the I.Q. test. No matter how I didn't fit in or even attempt to fit in that summer at Camp Bonim, he went on introducing me as if I were the camper of the year. It surprised me many times over the years to meet his friends and discover that they already knew about me, introduced by him with a resumé skewed on the good side.

When I was young, it was he who would occasionally invite me for special moments: dinner (without parents) at Sammy's, a nice restaurant in Highland Park Village. It was he who took me to the school playground to play tennis. He was the one who taught me to drive our old Dodge, to be on guard when children were playing near the street. One night, just as I was ready to get my license, our family was going for dinner at some friends' home, and Mother suggested that Jerome drive. "Oh, let Stanley do it," he countered. "We're not in that much of a hurry." My mother, of course, acquiesced, though with some reluctance, it seemed to me. I proudly slid into the front seat behind the wheel.

Jerome, then, became the one who knew I could learn some Hebrew . . . produce a respectable I.Q. . . . and be trusted to drive the car. He was the single relative, in my mind at least, and probably in truth as well, who saw me as an individual, more than another kid stamped from a mold.

▶▶▶

If the summer at Camp Bonim foreshadowed our future relationship, it also told a lot about my brother. A popular teen-ager saddled with a misfit younger brother nearby would have mortified most eighteen-year-old boys. But it was my brother's nature not to let something like that bother him, and apparently it didn't.

Life usually seemed to be at his command.

While he kept pulling down "As," I never remember seeing him sweat over or hardly even study for a test in school. My mother told the story of overhearing Jerome when he was in the third grade. "Well," he said to himself, "Miss X said we should spend half an hour on this assignment. If I hurry, I'll get it done in ten minutes. Then I'll have more time to play." Mother wasted no time in going to Miss X to tell her that her son Jerome Ely needed to be given more challenging work in school.

Mother also recalled the time, years later, when Jerome brought home a friend from SMU and found her in an old dress, on her knees scrubbing the kitchen floor. She relished the fact that he introduced her as proudly as if she were turned out in her finest outfit.

Jerome and Aunt Fannie were the ones who never burdened anyone with their concerns but who could be counted on to listen to yours. He possessed a gift for painting rosy pictures like the swaying of the tree. He contracted hepatitis while he was stationed in Germany, but he wrote funny letters from the hospital designed to cheer up the family at home.

If I look back today, I see twin exaggerated pictures, the one he painted to his friends of me, the one I painted to myself of him. But as I was growing up and Jerome was away at school, I eagerly awaited his visits home, since he was the only one in the family who was available to discuss "the real me," whom I could bring up to date on my unhappiness with Uncle Morris or my parents or whoever. To keep our conversations private, we occasionally tried communicating in Spanish.

The most recurring theme of our conversations was the future. They'd take place in pajamas, late into the night. "What are you thinking about studying?" he asked.

"Journalism."

"At SMU?"

Jerome didn't have to wait for my answer. "Not if I can help it. I want to go away."

"Yes," he said quietly. "I understand."

Soon, it became clear that what really bound my brother and me was the need to find our futures somewhere away from where we had grown up. By going to Indiana for graduate school, he set the process in motion. He made it look more natural and inevitable than I was able to do, but distancing himself from home seemed to be as necessary for him as it was becoming for me.

There was something else that put us on common ground: we both approached the journey with determination more than fanfare. He recognized that long before I did. "You and I," he would say to me at the conclusion of one of those long talks, "we don't jump up and down and shout about what we do—but we do it. We're adventurous in a quiet kind of way."

Later, it occurred to me that, in a sense, that also gave us a connection to our father, since he had chosen to pass up that lucrative partnership with his brothers and quietly forge his own way. In any case, Jerome's assessment of the bond between himself and me sounded fine when I was fourteen or fifteen. It was something I liked then and, fifty years later, still do.

▶▶▶

My first trip east was in mid-March 1953 when my brother invited me to visit him in Connecticut. By then, he had completed a Ph.D. in industrial psychology at Purdue University and moved to Stamford to join a firm that specialized in human engineering. With a friend, he shared a rambling old two-story house set back among trees and hidden from a main road.

It was the spring vacation of my senior year in college in Illinois, and I could hardly wait for a look at New York. As we drove from the airport up the Merritt Parkway, I thought that I had never even imagined such a burst of green, so many hundreds of trees ready to open into early spring bloom. The trees I knew from Texas had mostly been planted by landscapers, not nature.

Jerome's housemate was a colleague, a handsome blond southerner on whom I quickly developed a crush. They were both around twenty-eight, and their bachelor lives seemed perfect to me. "You want to go into New York Friday night, after I finish work?" my brother asked me, after I looked around his house.

"Of course!" was my instant reply.

Friday evening, we drove into the city in his little Chevrolet, the thousands of lights seeming to shine me a welcome to Manhattan. "Shall we try Italian food?" Jerome asked as we headed down the West Side Highway, alongside the Hudson River, and parked near 14th Street.

"Oh, yes!" I was ecstatic with the idea of what sounded like a glamorous New York evening.

We parked near 14th Street and walked down Greenwich Avenue. I got my first look, albeit a furtive one, at a gay neighborhood. Young men strolled by, tidy young men with careful haircuts and well tailored herringbone sport jackets, white shirts and flannel trousers. Handsome young men, some of whom looked our way. Later, I wondered whether it was for my sake that my brother had chosen that route.

Near Bleecker Street, we stepped down into a café filled with the aroma of garlic, the sound of a nickelodeon, crowded with checkered tablecloths and candles of a rainbow of colors. The young waiter in tight black trousers showed us to a table in the corner of the room, and my eyes devoured the scene: young women with beaded blouses and long streaming hair, their dates in tailored brown shirts and clean white bucks; on the other side, two collegiate looking men, smoking long cigarettes and looking fondly at each other.

"You're *flushed*," said my brother.

"Well . . ."

"Different from Big D."

I tried to sound blasé. "Yes, I'd say."

We ordered antipasto and fettucini in a cream sauce. "It's spaghetti, but better," Jerome explained.

In those surroundings it was hard to concentrate on food. My brother was aware of my fascination. "While you're here, you can take the train to Grand Central by yourself one day, if you want to," he said, smiling.

"Yes," I quickly agreed.

"I'll drive you to the station in Stamford when I go to work. Then you can come back the same way, or I'll come and meet you in the city in the evening."

I lingered over the fettucini, delaying the moment when we'd leave a scene that took place so casually but for me was so dramatic.

We followed a roundabout path back to his car. Jerome pointed out the jigsaw intersection of streets in Greenwich Village and how they challenge the neat grids of the rest of Manhattan. Later, during that spring vacation, I did venture into the city alone, for my first look at Radio City and Broadway theater.

Before the trip had ended, a small seed was planted: New York would be my eventual address.

▶▶▶

Within the next year, I finished college, went back to Dallas for a few months, and got drafted into the army. Jerome had met Paula Cohen, a teacher who was living in Manhattan, and they had become engaged. Somehow, seeing my brother the year before in Stamford as the carefree single guy, I had envisioned bachelorhood as his permanent state. It was the same fantasy that I would have later about Uncle Morris, perhaps even less realistic, as Jerome always had one girl friend or another. "The best thing about getting engaged?" he joked. "You don't have to go looking for a date for Saturday night."

He asked me to be the best man in their wedding. It was to be held in a traditional lower Fifth Avenue hotel at noon on a Sunday in mid-July. For the trip, I secured a weekend pass from basic training in Georgia, flew to New York on a Friday night, then back to the army late Sunday afternoon. It was an exciting trip, frustrating for its brevity.

It was difficult as well. My parents were there from Dallas, happy and proud, my mother standing as tall as her five feet allowed. Florence, by then a mother of three, came from Denver, looking pretty and chic. The night before the wedding, Jerome and I shared a room in a hotel on Central Park South, and he was ready to go the next morning while I was still getting dressed. Our outfits were similar pastel summer jackets with trousers of a complimentary color. "Come on!" he said to me, with a rare edge of impatience.

In the mind of one of Paula's friends who attended the wedding, I appeared more nervous than the groom. "I wondered," she said later, "what the younger brother was so nervous about." I could tell her. It was anger I was suppressing and not even recognizing, misplaced anger from the feeling of betrayal that hit me when Florence was married ten years earlier. Jerome and I both being male, perhaps the upset was even greater this time. Stammering, I made my way through a toast to the bride and groom.

Three years later, in 1957, I did move to New York, and until I found a job and an apartment in Manhattan, Paula and my brother welcomed me to stay with them and newborn Elissa in Stamford. They had moved to a split-level house that backed on a lovely lake, and in the years that followed, I spent many weekends with the three of them, ice skating on the pond in winter. In September 1958, Paula gave birth to Marcia, their second daughter, and I traveled early one morning on the train from New York to accompany my brother when he went to the schul in Stamford to name her.

Less than a year after moving to New York—settled in a job and an apartment—I began to feel crippled by my homosexual desires. On my salary as trainee in an advertising agency, I couldn't afford even a reduced fee for psychotherapy, but I knew I wanted and needed it. What I didn't want was to bring up the subject to my parents, so one day driving from the station to his house, I approached my brother. "I really would like to get some therapy," I said, nervously. "It's because of . . . homosexual feelings."

I looked to see if I could find a reaction. There wasn't any. "Do you think . . . you'd be willing to loan me some money for a while?" I added.

"Of course," Jerome said immediately, and he did so. Somehow, what he didn't do was to remember the reason for my wanting help. After so many heart-to-heart discussions with him in earlier years, I waited for the topic of my homosexuality to be mentioned again. But, as if it hadn't been spoken, it never was.

As I approached my late twenties, my father began to complain about my unmarried status not only to me but to my brother. "Why isn't Stanley getting married like you did?" Dad asked on a visit to Stamford to see his granddaughters.

Jerome rolled out the list of accomplishments. "But look at all that Stanley has done," he said (as I happened to eavesdrop). "He won those awards in high school . . . finished college at twenty . . . went in the army and survived being stuck in Korea for a couple of years. Then he came to New York and got a good job and an apartment . . . ."

I smiled. Coming from my brother, I knew that Dad would take note of the review of my successes. Later, though, I realized that there was one accomplishment omitted from the list, the one that prompted Dad's original complaint. Jerome was married and I wasn't, and that was the achievement that my father mostly—maybe, only—cared about.

▶▶▶

Jerome's pioneer work in human engineering was so important that the profession still gives an award in his name today. It was in the middle of that career and a busy family life that my brother suddenly took sick with a fatal disease.

People, they say, die much as they lived, and that proved true for him. During the nine months of his illness, as he became progressively weaker, he struggled to present an optimistic face and to believe, at least to profess, that he would be well again soon. He dictated cheerful letters to Paula that she sent to members of the family and friends. Even long after he had stopped working, he asked whether I needed more money for therapy. "Oh, no," I said. "I'm fine."

Earlier, I had private phone conversations with doctors who had examined him at Yale New Haven Hospital. They told me that the prognosis was bad. But Jerome never talked of dying, so neither did I nor anyone else.

One night, in the hospital in Stamford, I suggested that Mother and Paula leave early and said that I would stay. The cancer must have reached Jerome's bones, because his arm and elbows ached. For a couple of hours, then, while we talked, I stood by the side of his bed and rubbed a warming jelly into those joints. It was one of the last times we were alone.

We reminisced about the days on Stanhope, good times, but times when we both were realizing that our futures lay elsewhere. I reminded him of my first happy trip east, of our dinner on Bleecker Street. Of how much benefit I'd gotten from the therapy that he supported. Of how much I loved his children, offering unstated assurance that I would keep watch on them. Quiet talk. Brother talk. The next day, he told the others how much he had enjoyed our evening together. We had talked of many things—but not of death.

Finally it became clear that Jerome was soon going to die, and I went to Stamford one weekend and met his friend Bob. We attended to selecting a casket so that it wouldn't have to be done at the last minute. After Jerome's death,

Bob carried out the Jewish tradition of sitting all night watching over the corpse, so that impure forces would be driven away.

▶▶▶

Like others who die young (and who may have some unconscious sense of their destiny), Jerome telescoped into the years he was given what others need longer, if ever, to achieve. Perhaps, in some mysterious way, his work on earth was finished; friends have suggested that to me. Nonetheless, the early death of my brother was a catastrophe in our family.

My mother's faith and acceptance helped her survive the years afterwards. For my father, there was courage but no acceptance. His car accident shortly after Jerome died was a clear outcome of my brother's death, and when I asked a physician cousin in Dallas whether he thought my father understood the connection, he surprised me by saying, "Yes."

The only solace my father could imagine from the loss of his son was to see an infant named in Jerome's memory. It was a loving idea, implanted perhaps from Jewish culture early on. For years, Dad asked one or another young relative whether they wouldn't name an expected baby for Jerome. None did, until Jerome's own daughter, Marcia, gave birth to a boy in November 1992. When she and her husband Andy named their first child Jeremy, my brother was remembered, through his own grandson. My father's wish was granted, and I believe he must rest better.

Jerome died not only young but before he and I had reached a solid plateau. For as long as he was alive, we played the roles we had always played, he the mentor there to listen, me the admiring younger brother.

Genuine as those feelings of admiration were, they couldn't have been of admiration only. I think again of the time when my father came to the office where I was working in New York and tried to sell insurance to my colleagues. Had I had the courage, I would have stopped him. Instead, I just got angry and deeply embarrassed. A couple of days later, he did the same at Jerome's office in Connecticut, and I asked my brother whether that hadn't bothered him. "No," Jerome said, calmly, "if it's important for Dad to do it, I don't mind."

I didn't understand how my father's behavior couldn't have irritated him.

Why didn't he object to something so inappropriate? Why didn't he stop it? In his case, it wasn't for lack of courage.

That thought came back after Jerome died. Why was he not disturbed by how my father acted in his office? And why, years before, wasn't he annoyed by a jerky little brother at camp? Why did he always build me up to his friends before I met them? Why, when he had dated non-Jewish girls, did he make it clear that, of course, he would never marry one?

Could anyone have lived so perfect a life? Weren't there any imperfections?

If he was so perfect, why did he die?

Unlike the older brother who never smoked but contracted cancer, I was the younger one who smoked for decades and thus far escaped the disease. Unlike the older brother who adhered to tradition, got married and fathered children, I was the younger one who stayed single and slept around with other men.

I would like to think that the questions I've asked were forgivable in that younger brother who felt he was on the brink of hearing someone at any moment say that the wrong son died.

▶▶▶

Now, more than three decades after Jerome's death, I speculate on how things would have been different if he were still here. I would not have played as central a role in the growing up of his daughters. In those first years after he died, I spent many weekends with them and Paula in Stamford, times they remember better than I. Introducing them to the statue of Alice in Wonderland in Central Park would have been his treat, not mine. So would have been the opportunity to attend their graduations, offer a toast at both their weddings, celebrate the births of their children.

And very often I wonder how he and I would get along, if Jerome were alive today. I'm more than twice the age I was when he died, so I would long ago have dropped my role of innocent younger brother. We both would have grown through some knocks, survived the deaths of our parents, experienced the harshness of aging. My new self would make certain that Jerome did not forget about my homosexuality. Since the older hero would have revealed feet with some clay, the little brother would be less uncritically admiring.

But, at the heart of it, would that matter? Would we two guys from Texas, long since having answered the imperative to be gone from our starting post, still be able to share any of that "quiet adventurousness" that Jerome recognized so long ago? I wish I knew. I'd like to think so, for no matter how we might have changed, that's a connection I miss.

Dad, Jerome and Mother, 1952

My parents at Lake Louise, 1947

Mother at Cape Cod, 1978

Dorothy and Morris, c. 1962

Florence, c. 1927

Florence, c. 1948

Tom in Mt. Vernon, 1990

Hebrew School of Dallas High School Graduation, 1941 -
Jerome at center, Jacob Levin to his right
Photo: courtesy of the Dallas Jewish Historical Society

Jerome in U.S. Air Force, 1943

Jerome and Stanley, 1954

Marcia, Elissa and Jerome in Stamford, 1959

Part Three

Around Town

18

A New Neighborhood

For my parents, the new world meant a trip across the Atlantic. For me, it meant a move to Stanhope in University Park in 1940, when I was almost eight. My crossing wasn't as long or dramatic as theirs, yet there were parallels. Both involved shedding a former life in search of a better one; both were part of a mass migration of Jews to unknown territory. Both even symbolized steps into freedom, as the move to Stanhope got me happily away from my parents' bedroom.

Once in America, my grandmother, Lena Shapiro, received loving letters from her sisters who remained behind in Russia. The letters we got from those who stayed behind in South Dallas were short on love. They were more messages of dislike from Jewish kids in the old neighborhood to whom we seemed like the ones gone to the ball while they stayed home. The only fight I can ever remember being a part of took place at the old Jewish Community Center between some South Dallas boy and myself when we were twelve. The topic mirrored the Civil War, North vs. South. I don't think he was into the event any more than I, so we played at it a while and then went our separate ways, him south, me north.

I used to bemoan the rivalry between South and North Dallas Jews and petition for inter-neighborhood love and harmony. Secretly, I relished the notion that I had transferred to the preferred side of town. Excepting events at the Community Center or attendance at Sunday school or high holiday services (plus those trips to the Pig Stand), or visits with elderly parents and grandparents who had refused to budge, we who had left avoided the old part of town. My mother had no desire to go back to the old country; I had no wish to go back to South Dallas.

I shouldn't have been so critical about Mother's inability to remember anything of her first years in Russia, because I don't remember much more than that of my first seven years on Grand Avenue. Our house had a small, uncovered front porch with a creaky rocker and a little back yard with a sandbox and the swing in front of which my brother and sister immortalized me with the woman's pocketbook.

In the bedroom which, for lack of space, I shared with my parents. I remember my little bed being placed near some windows and perpendicular to theirs. There must have been plenty that deserved forgetting there, and I have. Even my visits to Forest Avenue to see Grandpa Max or Aunt Fannie are recaptured more from photographs than from memory.

I well remember Marietha, the black (we called her Negro) lady who took care of me when Mother wasn't around (maybe even when she was) and who sent me crying when she said it would be too far for her to travel, once we moved away. She was young then, thirty or so, a buxom, sweet and warm woman who managed to cloak me with more security than some in the family with more primary responsibility. Marietha walked me that first day to John Henry Brown Elementary School, of which I have but one recollection, the time in the first grade when I needed to urinate. I waved my hand in the air and asked permission to go to the bathroom. The teacher, whose name I've managed to forget, denied my request, so the urge soon got relieved in my pants. I tried my best to hide the stain as I walked out of the class in misery. It was a moment so unforgettable that years later, when I became a teacher, I never questioned a student's need if he or she requested to use the bathroom.

▶▶▶

In 1940, our new neighborhood of University Park was in its infancy, with some streets and sidewalks not yet paved. Though it lacked the predominantly Jewish character of Park Row or Forest Avenue, and though synagogues and temples didn't move until later, there were enough Jews settling in to make any newly arriving family feel at home.

The 4400 block of Stanhope on whose corner we built our house was a stretch of some fifteen one-story brick homes, unostentatious but pleasant and individual with modest front lawns. Near us, on Larchmont and Windsor, were grander two-story dwellings with deep yards and curving driveways. Normandy, where Fannie and Arthur and Arthur's brother moved, was a street of two-story duplexes a couple of blocks away.

My new school, Bradfield, where Tommy and I met in the third grade, was on Mockingbird Lane, a trip of only six blocks. I'd walk there along Armstrong Parkway, a winding street that ran to the side of our house. On the other side of Mockingbird, University Park ended and Highland Park, the ritzier neighborhood, began. It was where Uncle Ben and Aunt Sara bought their new house. Together, Highland and University Park did and do still comprise the Park Cities, a suburban enclave with its own police and fire departments and school system. Dallas proper used to stretch only to the south of the Park Cities. Today, it and a bunch of prosperous towns stretch for many miles farther north.

Around the corner from Bradfield is the Highland Park Shopping Village, some thirty one- and two-story shops designed in a happy Spanish style and laid out around an oval of a couple of blocks enclosed by a decorative stone wall. The Village was where we went for Saturday afternoon movies or to catch the bus to Sunday school at the old Shearith Israel. It was also the place for groceries or drugs or a haircut as well as a summertime "Fiesta," a couple of nights of outdoor games and rides for the neighborhood.

My parents weren't privileged to have a preview of their move to America, but I got an advance look at Stanhope when, each Sunday for a year, we'd pile in the old Dodge and travel across town to watch our house being built from the foundation up. My dad had chosen a corner lot, and the house would sit four or five feet above the level of the sidewalk. Beyond having to take care of a front and back yard (and that slope), we inherited responsibility for the parkway that ran along the side of the house.

For me, watching the house take shape and anticipating our move into it and a new neighborhood was as exciting as gearing up for a trip to the moon.

And I wasn't disappointed. I developed a great affection for the place that was home for the next nine years that, for me, included elementary, junior and senior high schools. They were years when I began to hide sexual feelings but also took nervous, happy beginning steps in a move away from family.

Though my parents wisely sold the Stanhope house after Jerome's death, I felt a kind of resentment that some other family would tarnish the rooms that I had lived in. The intervening years when I had not been there made no difference. Even now, when I visit Dallas, I find myself driving around Stanhope and, unlike the period in South Dallas that I was eager to forget, enjoying the recollection of secure days in that neighborhood.

The jolt comes from seeing that our house's current owners have tried to make it look fancier than it was intended. Beyond costly landscaping that hides the clean lines, they've glassed in the screened porch and back terrace. The house has lost its open, welcoming look; with so much enclosure of former open spaces, the outdoors serves only for brief passage between air-conditioned rooms and cars.

The house sits comfortably, but not terribly far, back from the front and side streets, with a tall roof and an attic that could have been finished by us for another room but never was. A spacious living room, used intermittently, with a never-used fireplace, is to the left of a small entrance foyer. To the right is a dining room that did not get employed as such, since the next room over is a spacious, bright breakfast room with a large picture window (the one through which the rock was thrown and which Uncle Morris hurriedly got fixed), and that or the kitchen became our dining room. A round mahogany table with a couple of drop leafs and chubby legs that my parents had had since their wedding looked as if it had been designed for the breakfast room.

The "dining room," which sat empty for years, became a den when Uncle Morris presented my parents with a big television set. My father liked to pull a chair up near that set and laugh at the theatrics of hulks playing at wrestling on the screen. Next to the breakfast room is a good-sized kitchen, twelve feet square, with a window on the side and a door to the outside. It's where Mother prepared blintzes and chocolate cakes and where by helping set Friday night dinner tables I tried unsuccessfully to bribe her into recalling the days in Russia. It's where we listened to Jack Benny on the radio on Sunday nights and where Uncle Morris in his olive drab shorts did dishes during his days as resident on Stanhope.

A long hallway separates all those rooms from the back of the house, three bedrooms with two baths, one of which connected my parents' room with the bedroom next to it. To the side of my parent's room is a screened porch (where Tommy and I sat) that faces Armstrong. Both the screened (now enclosed) porch and the middle bedroom have doors that open to the outside and a large, then open (now enclosed) concrete terrace, where I used to see my mother convene with the heavens at night.

Behind the house is the garage that held our Dodge and Uncle Morris' Oldsmobile, and a driveway that slopes down to Armstrong over a modest grade. In the style of those days, atop the garage was built a small apartment, better said, an unfinished-looking room, with a tiny bathroom. That awful ten-foot square residence, we called the "servants' quarters." By the early 1940s, full-time servants were getting smart and expecting tolerable wages, and their numbers started to shrink. Before long, the "servants' quarters" simply got rented for a couple of bucks a week to whichever black persons happened to need cheap lodging in the neighborhood.

The room then became impermanent home to a succession of occupants who often drank and hollered. I thought it would be a neat place for a playroom, but my dad liked the small added income, despite whatever headaches went with it. If the "servants' quarters" happened to be unoccupied, I'd go up and treat myself to some earthy smells of drink and fun that had been left behind.

The lot next to our house remained empty for some years. That suited me fine, because in the bedroom facing that side there was a window through which I could observe life at the Gs, the family that lived in the house one lot over. The Gs were reputed to be heirs to oil money, but their house was smaller than ours and utterly plain, perhaps a reflection of their disorganized emotional state. Mrs. G, a tall, beautiful (gentile) woman, was a valued customer at the Village liquor store, and she and her husband and their friends partied long and loud. Mrs. G was rarely seen outside before noon, and often then in a long, silk negligee.

Unknown to my parents, I closed the bedroom door and spent nights with binoculars trained on the Gs' house, waiting for some outburst or screaming exit into their driveway. In this quest I was disappointed only occasionally.

The Gs had two sons, the older one a year or so younger than me and inappropriately named Goodie, since he always seemed to be ignored by his parents and in trouble. Sometimes Goodie and I would meet and play in the empty lot between our houses after school. That was where my passivity and politeness faded out and my latent need to rule erupted. The game of choice evolved into "King of the Mountain," and I elected myself to play the title role. My determination to reign at the top of that "mountain" surprised me as much as it did him.

I didn't socialize with Goodie otherwise, and before long we got too big for our empty lot game. I never let on that I knew of his parents' night-time frolicking. Later, I regretted that I hadn't been nicer to him, because I realized that he was not only not good, he wasn't lucky in finding himself born into that family.

▶▶▶

Before we packed up for the move to Stanhope, I had met a couple of Jewish kids who lived either on our block or one over and who became my new friends. They were riding around on their bikes as my parents and I did Sunday surveys of our new house.

"Hey, who are you?" said this kid who came around to take the measure of me and the house.

"Stanley."

"*I'm* Stanley!" he pronounced. I judged that he didn't like to comb his hair or put his shirt inside his trousers. He wore a cap with funny things dangling off of it and leaned on his bike as if it was the bike's duty to prop him up.

"Well, me too," I said.

"Your dad looked over our house before he made the plans," he advised.

"What plans?"

"For your house! He's gonna make it bigger."

"How many people in your family?" I asked.

"Me and my sister."

"You don't have a mother and father?"

"I didn't say them."

"I have a sister and a brother," I informed the other Stanley. "That's why we need more room."

In fact, our house was nearly a copy of Stanley's, with his located on the same corner one short block away, on Shenandoah. Once we had moved in on Stanhope, he was a frequent visitor, opting to use the kitchen door as his avenue of entry. I theorized that he liked that route for its proximity to the refrigerator (then still called an icebox). "Don't you ever eat at home?" I asked him one day.

"Sure," he said, opening the box to see what was available. "My home, and your home."

My other best-friend-to-be was named Mark, and he too always seemed to be on hand when we made our visits to the new house.

"You moving here?" he asked one Sunday.

"Yeah," I advised, eagerly.

"When you're moving?"

"July or August, I think. So I can start school in September."

"You're not already in school?" he asked.

What a dope, I thought. "Of course! I'll be in the third grade!"

"Third grade?" Mark echoed, sounding a touch surprised. "What are you, a kind of book guy?"

"No, no!"

"You can help me, anyway. School's not where I'm good."

"We'll see," I said, starting to add up the pluses and minuses.

"I live down that way, the next to last house."

Mark, I soon learned, was an only child. He was dark complexioned and handsome in a Semitic sort of way, though I never knew whether he was really Jewish since he was an adopted kid, the only one I'd met. Mr. and Mrs. Fine, his parents, were much older and deeply conservative, and they might have fared better with a quiet, studious daughter. Instead, they adopted Mark when he was a baby and drew a son who was the first kid on the block to insist on a bicycle and who then liked to ride it without holding on to the handlebars, screeching to a stop inches from someone quietly walking down the sidewalk. Later on, his mother would compare him, not favorably, to me.

He and I became friends in the tried tradition of the attraction of opposites.

19

Edging Up on the Teens

And so my life in the new world began. If I complained to my brother, it was like imitating my father—the complaint was over something inconsequential. I certainly did not object to Mother's ongoing campaign to emancipate me by leaving me alone when she and my father went out at night. Alone, as far as I was concerned, was happiness.

I'm grateful to have lucked out on a good school system that filled in some gaps, because the Jewish love of wisdom and humility seemed to miss our house. Even school, however, didn't prevent my inhabiting a world of both blindness and arrogance. I never wondered why there were no black kids in my class, or why I never saw any sitting in the same section of a movie theater as I sat. I didn't puzzle over why blacks did just menial jobs. I noticed but never questioned why there were one public drinking fountain for whites, another for "Negroes." None of those disparities ever was explained or even mentioned. It's embarrassing today to think that the one living in that stupefying ignorance was me.

I also watched my father as he endeavored to rent out the tiny room above our garage for the dollar or two a week that it brought. I never considered how subjugated those black renters must have felt not having money to live somewhere better, nor what anger they must have harbored toward me and my kind. If they drank and "made a racket," as my father would say, they had reason.

I knew a family whose maid was served only on paper plates. And one day I saw my friend Billy's mother put a wrestler's lock on the arm of an old black woman who worked in their house, forcing her to do something she didn't want to do. I knew that was wrong but didn't say anything. The look of anguish on the woman's face is fresh in my mind a half century later.

It'll be no surprise to learn that when I went north to college and for the first time shared a dormitory and classes with black kids, I was amazed to find that most of them were not only as smart but smarter than me, not only as well dressed but far better dressed than me.

The other part of my ignorance concerned crime, or even fear of crime. It was so distant that if my father hadn't insisted on our locking the doors, I would hardly have thought that it existed. We might as well have left the door unlocked, as some families did.

As for anti-Semitism, its worst effect on me would have been to bar my entrance into the Dallas Country Club, which I never applied for anyway. If classmates at school were anti-Semitic, the well-bred Highland Parkers of that era were polite enough to keep it to themselves.

Still, in even that innocent world, tragedy intrudes at times. My first brush with it happened in the fifth grade when our class in Bradfield School had just finished making a film about the history of writing. Some of us were assigned to play the role of monks, to illustrate the use of the feather pen. My friend Lloyd Fisher and I were part of that group. It wasn't a week later that my mother got a call from another mother. Lloyd had been riding his bicycle in the afternoon along Mockingbird Lane, just by our school, when a car sideswiped him, knocked him to the ground and crushed his skull. Ashen faced, Mother came to tell me that Lloyd was dead.

How could that be? I had just seen him in school that day! We had joked about g etting dressed up as monks, two Jewish boys. The news wasn't at all like hearing that Grandpa Max had died. Lloyd was my friend, olive complexioned, with a narrow face and a soft voice. He wore glasses, like me. He was my *friend !*

How, I asked my mother, could it be that Lloyd was dead?

She didn't have an answer.

▶▶▶

To Mark and Stanley, I added Larry, a boy a year older than me, who completed a quartet of friends that lasted through the next decade. We organized back yard carnivals behind Stanley's house and sent the proceeds to the Red Cross. Then, in April 1944, when I was eleven-and-a-half and the war in Europe and the Pacific was still going on, I decided that we ought to elevate our efforts for the nation by producing a theater evening and charging admission. "I'll write a play," I volunteered, "we'll put it on and donate the money we make."

The three others hardly had time to agree before I was at work on a mystery called "The Secret of the Press." It involved some shady characters (or my concept of such, since I'd never met any) who were caught in a newspaper scandal that led to someone getting bumped off. It was filled with long dialogues, changes of scene and asides to the audience.

Our theater had to be the garage behind my house, less than an ideal venue for the many entrances and exits I had included, but the only one we could afford. We borrowed dark, unfriendly looking garments appropriate for a mystery. Mark's mother donated a bed sheet for the curtain. We memorized our parts (with me serving as director) and advertised the event around the neighborhood with home-made signs tacked to telephone poles.

A respectably sized audience made up of parents, a few friends and some curious neighbors paid the quarter entrance fee and gathered in our garage for an eight o'clock Saturday evening performance. To my distress, Stanley forgot a couple of his lines (including, he reminds me, one that was key to the whole play). The bed sheet didn't slide the way it was meant to, either, but none of that deterred enthusiastic applause from our public. With no illusions about attempting a long run, we mailed the box office receipts for the sole performance—$7.50—to the Red Cross. The *Dallas Morning News* found out about it and took note of the achievement with a brief mention two days later. In April 1994, the same newspaper recalled the event in their "Fifty Years Ago" column.

▶▶▶

By then, the teens were hovering around the bend. That word comes into use right after twelve, just like manhood for a Jewish boy. My six years of Hebrew school were about to culminate in a bar mitzvah, an occasion that introduces a twelve-year-old to important Jewish traditions.

In the fifth century of the common era, for instance, Ezra the Scribe discovered that many Jews had forgotten the Torah, (a word taken from the Hebrew "L'horoth," meaning to teach). To insure that this wouldn't continue, with the help of the Great Council, Ezra instituted the weekly reading of a section of the Torah and the Prophets on Saturdays and Jewish holidays. It's a practice upheld still today.

For a young boy, Jewish manhood may be scheduled for the thirteenth birthday, but it doesn't really get going until his bar mitzvah Saturday when he mounts the pulpit with somber stride. Wearing yarmulke (cap) and tallith (prayer shawl), he participates in the tradition. He delivers blessings to thank God for giving Jews the Torah and recites a haftorah, or reading from the Prophets. Doing so in a soprano voice is forgivable, as long as the errors are few.

The date for my bar mitzvah was chosen in the established way, the Saturday closest to my thirteenth birthday on the Jewish calendar. Putting my play-writing career on hold, I undertook study of the haftorah that corresponded to that date.

It would be hard for the average and even above-average kid to manage the task alone. I was assigned a coach, Mr. Aronoff, a teacher in the old South Dallas Hebrew school. Though the big day wouldn't take place until the end of October, I started in early spring to take the bus to Park Row a couple of afternoons a week for sessions with Mr. Aronoff. I liked "Mr. A.," a 5'8" fifty-ish gentleman of black jacket that was too small, a gray and grizzly beard and head of hair, and a kindly smile. Going back across town—to the Hebrew school, not the synagogue—was strange. Had I not still been so young, it would have seemed like returning to a former life.

The haftorah is formidable, ten minutes or so, in Hebrew of course, to be recited before a congregation less intimate than the audience that had gathered in our garage for "The Secret of the Press."

Hebrew, like Yiddish, is known to be a rich and beautiful language, but with its own alphabet that bears no resemblance to English, it's a challenge. Difficult when printed with vowel marks, it's many times more so without them—as it appears in the Torah and Prophets.

One afternoon, when I could foresee feeling equal to the haftorah, Mr. A. greeted me with an especially mournful look. "Shlomey," he said, coming to the door and inviting me politely into a chair, "I have to tell you something."

"You do?" I asked, unnecessarily. His expression and the tone of his voice suggested that the news was not likely to be good. Then, too, the suspiciously familiar Shlomey instead of Shlomo.

"You've done a very nice job, Shlomey . . . ."

"Thank you, sir," I said, figuring that that was not the news.

He paused, then he coughed. "We assigned you the wrong haftorah," he blurted out.

I almost slid off the chair. The wrong haftorah? After all these weeks of. . . ? How could that be?

"I can't tell you how sorry I am, Shlomey," he added, nearly in tears.

You're sorry? I thought.

"Whoever converted the date of your birthday . . . well, they came up with the wrong day in October. We just discovered it. We need to move your bar mitzvah up a week."

I was speechless and probably looked it.

"You don't want to be bar mitzvahed on the wrong day!"

"It might be okay with me" passed through my mind, though I didn't dare to give that voice.

Mr. Aronoff promised to double up on the lessons—more trips to South Dallas!—because when the news sunk in, I realized that the new haftorah, unaided by the old one, would have to be learned with great speed. The corrected date for my bar mitzvah was only six weeks away.

Various alternatives went through my head. Let me, for instance, have the bar mitzvah on the new day, with the haftorah I had already practiced. No more than two people in the synagogue would know the difference.

Finally, of course—and given little choice—I did the moral thing and learned the new reading. On the fateful morning, I resisted the temptation to announce that if the congregation wanted me to, I could save them the trouble of coming back the following Saturday and read them the Prophets passage from that week, too.

With Tommy's memory of long-ago events, he says that before he and his mother entered Shearith Israel for the ceremony, he remembers hearing the chanting that seemed as foreign to him as jungle tom-toms. Relieved to see my father stationed at the door, he was handed a yarmulke but also an unexpectedly stern look. "Obviously," says Tom, "I had no understanding of the seriousness of the occasion," a fact I'm surprised to hear since I must certainly have complained about the doubling up of haftorahs.

Besides the new haftorah, there was one more obstacle to overcome. It concerned manner of dress. If a bar mitzvah symbolized manhood, I assumed that the attire should be a tie and jacket, so that's what I requested. It was a moment when my sister stepped in, though she had been married and living away in Denver for the past year. Offering unsolicited advice, Florence stated that the uniform for her little brother's bar mitzvah ought to be an open-necked shirt, and no tie. Her reasons, I don't recall—perhaps to keep him not a man, but still a child, who knows?

I protested, but not enough, and in an open-necked shirt, Shlomo (for "peace") Ely mounted the Shearith Israel pulpit on October 20, 1945, to do honor to my parents and Mr. Aronoff and, with considerable trepidation, open the door into manhood. The hard-bound copy of the Holy Scriptures that the synagogue presented to me that day sits still in my bookshelves.

But I must have been too nervous to remember any more of the day than the fact that I lost out on the choice of uniform—and immediately after that Saturday, I exercised my newly-won status to assign Hebrew school to a part of my past.

20

Early Scar

Before long I was fourteen, old enough to be Wade's babysitter and to develop the nervous stomach that would hit me without fail every September as a new school year approached.

"Why are you so jittery?" Mother asked me. "Is it new situations? But then, the situation isn't new, is it?"

"No," I would agree, cautiously. "It isn't."

"You already know the teachers—and the kids. You do well in school!"

I didn't know why. I knew, though, that when August was about to finish its allotment on the calendar, physical pains, real pains, would head toward my stomach. The principal one who took note of them was me.

With the manhood that bar mitzvah had proffered, I thought my habitual fearfulness, rational or not, would diminish. But it remained even more constant than the nervous stomach. Sexuality, a major new player, was also beginning to require attention.

Both sensations, fear and sex, reigned when I rode on the back of the motorbike that Mark had gotten. My friend of the opposite nature down the block had asked his parents for a motorbike early, at fifteen, before anyone else even considered such an idea. Characteristically, they gave in and bought him one for his birthday.

"It's a beauty," I said, the first day that he got the bike and I went over for an inspection. The metal shone, the leather was warmly fragrant and soft to the touch. The motorbike looked eager to go. "Your folks let you drive it?"

"Wadda ya think?" he asked. "Here it is! You wanna ride?"

"Yes, sure," I said, not at all sure. I got on behind Mark, and we circled the block. That was my first experience on a motorbike and of wrapping my arms around the waist of my friend in front. Holding on to him, plus the sensation of movement in the open air, took my breath away. "A motorbike?" my mother asked, when I reported the event. "What will that kid do next?"

"What's wrong with it?" I wanted to know.

"He's very young."

"He's fifteen!"

"You should just be careful when you go out with him."

The advice hardly seemed necessary, since being careful was what I usually did too much. In fact, it sounded in contradiction to her effort to make me independent.

"I don't know why those people give in to everything their son asks for," I heard her tell my father later on.

A part of me sympathized with her; the other part waited for another chance for a bike ride—a step into the daring and risky that I would never initiate myself. Whenever an invitation did come, my mother repeated her warning to be careful.

On an early November night, Mark called and asked if I wanted to take a short spin. "Sure," I said. "Homework's done."

My father had left for a meeting at his lodge. Mother looked disapproving as I threw on a new leather jacket and exited the kitchen door. "Be careful," she said, automatically. "Remember, it's a school night."

I nearly ran the distance between my house and Mark's. The road was slick as we set off, and the motorbike slid for a second at the foot of his driveway. "Watch it," I cautioned.

Mark turned and grinned from the driver's seat. "Relax back there, pal. With me you're never in trouble."

I wrapped my arms tightly around his waist. "With you," I said, "I'm usually in trouble."

We drove around Normandy, over to Douglas and Preston Road. It was drizzling, and I could barely see the leaves that had fallen to the ground.

"Maybe you ought to slow down," I offered from behind. "It's pretty dark here."

To make an uphill grade, Mark accelerated the bike. Passing over a pile of damp leaves, the motorbike skidded and swerved. "Hold on!" he yelled. The machine whirred and slid, and it fell to the side. Both of us were underneath it.

Mark groaned, pushed the bike away and extended his hand. "Are you okay?" he asked.

"I'm not sure. How can you see anything here?" I held on to my friend's hand and pulled myself up, but I could feel my arm hurt. "Damn," I said. "I guess I ripped my sleeve. I think my arm is cut."

We entered the glow of a street light. "You got the worst of this deal," Mark said. "Your jacket's covered with red."

I looked down and could see some blood. And I remembered Mother's warning. "I don't want to go home all bloody," I blurted out suddenly.

"You can come to my house," Mark offered. "My mother'll fix you up."

We started walking the motorbike toward Stanhope, a route I had done nearly blindfolded, though never so nervously. We didn't speak. A crazy jumble of surprise and pain swept through my head. A part of me wanted to cry.

"So, what do you want to do?" Mark asked finally, as we neared the turn onto our street.

My arm was still bleeding. "All right," I said, "I guess I'll go to your house. No, maybe I'd better go home. No, I can't! Not looking like this!" We passed my house, continued down the block, and went up the driveway of the Fines' home.

"Oh, my God, what happened?" asked Mrs. Fine, who looked amazed to see me any way except neat and combed, arrived to help Mark with some homework.

"We had a little accident," her son answered. "Stanley's cut."

Mrs. Fine looked at my arm. "It's bleeding," she said, nervously. "It has to be washed. Do you want me to wash it? Come on, I will." Then, quickly, she added, "But we must call your parents!"

"Yeah," I said, "I know. But wait . . . wait a little."

I was shaking as I took off my shirt, and I couldn't help but laugh. It was Mark who always courted danger, and it was me—the cautious one—who had gotten hurt.

The arm stopped bleeding, and Mark loaned me a shirt. We went into their kitchen, and Mrs. Fine poured me a warm drink. Finally I stopped shaking. Then I knew I had to go home. "Thanks for your help," I said.

"Do you want Mark to walk with you?" his mother asked.

"Oh, no. No. I'm okay."

"I'll call you tomorrow," said Mark, as I walked out their front door. And, after a moment, "I'm sorry."

The motorbike sat momentarily silent, forlorn and dirty, as I passed it in the driveway. I ran the palm of my hand over the part of the metal that still glistened. It was a half sensual caress. The rest of the way, I walked slowly through the drizzle.

Mrs. Fine had called my house, and Mother was waiting at the kitchen door. "I know what you're gonna tell me," I said.

"What's that?" she asked.

"'Why did you have to go out on that bike tonight'"?

"Oh, no! I'm just relieved you're not hurt any worse. From Mrs. Fine's call, I wasn't sure. But, you see," she added, peeling off my jacket, "the bleeding's stopped."

"I see," I said.

My mother's hand shook a little as she touched me. Her face spelled distress. "You're cold. Go and take a warm shower, then I'll put a dressing on the cut."

I silently went into the bathroom, undressed and examined myself in the mirror. My head and my arm hurt, but there was no more blood. My fingernails were filled with dirt. Somehow I felt like someone else, unsure of where he belonged.

Behind the curtain I let my shoulders drop as the warm water splashed over my head and down my chest. Closing my eyes, I tried to push away the image of lying underneath the motorbike, of the metal on top of me. I let the water cover me a long time. I touched my penis and felt it grow hard.

A large towel made a fine drape. I wrapped it around me and went into the bedroom. Mother was already there. "Listen," she said nervously as she started to wrap gauze around the arm, "thank God it's not serious. That's the main thing."

"Yes," I said.

She exhaled a long sigh. In a tone of near-misery, she went on. "But, why . . . why did you to go the *Fines'* house? Why didn't you come here? *This* is your home!"

I hesitated, embarrassed and not knowing how to answer. It occurred to me to explain that they were Jews, too! "I don't know. I was afraid you'd be angry. Or Dad. The new jacket, and shirt and all. I don't know. Maybe I was just afraid."

"I really wish they'd never given him that bike!" Mother snapped. "But if anything like this happens again, please—don't go somewhere else. You don't have to worry about a jacket or a shirt. And you don't have to go anywhere else. We're your family, not them! It's here you should be."

I looked up and saw her hurt expression. Should I have missed her statement, she said it once again. "*We're* your family. You don't have to go anywhere else!"

Too tired to answer, I nodded, threw off the towel, and wrapped myself in a blanket.

Mother turned off the bedroom light. "Good night, son," she said, and left quietly.

My eyes closed, I wondered whether a scar above my elbow would remain the souvenir of a night when I dared to dare, to take an early stand against my mother, to enjoy holding tightly to my friend. The road, the mud-covered bike, all blurred in a shadowy rush through my mind, and I fell into dreams. Instantly, I was passing a young woman and climbing on the rear of a motorbike, holding to the tight muscles of a young man's stomach. We laughed as we sped up a hill.

For a moment I awoke, stretched out fully under the covers. Looking out the window, I saw that the clouds had parted and the moon shone over Stanhope.

And later, in sleep, I came in the bed sheets.

21

Scotties Do Not Build Snowmen in Living Rooms

The mascot for Highland Park High is a Scottie dog, so their teams are called Scots. I can't remember more than two kids in that school whose family had anything to do with Scotland, but that's how it was. We were Scotties, some of us Jewish Scotties.

The Jewish Scotties whom I met in school or on bus rides to Shearith Israel Sunday school began to form a crowd that would gather at around age fourteen and fifteen in one another's home, delivered by parents or reached by foot. For a few hours we'd slow dance to records of Perry Como or Frank Sinatra. The more sure-footed jitterbugged to the rhythms of Glenn Miller. Refreshments consisted of Coca-Cola and cookies.

My parents and their friends expressed alarm at the fast life on which they saw their early teen-age children embarking. It hardly seemed fast to us, and it certainly doesn't seem so compared to the lives of many teen-agers today. What we failed to appreciate was the contrast between our lives and the lives of our parents at our ages. Many of them not only weren't dancing, they had left school and were working to support their parents.

What did suit our parents was that our get-togethers took place in some- one's living room, so they knew of our whereabouts. In the beginning, it fell to the girls to be hostesses to those affairs—boys were too busy playing baseball. Later on, boys joined in as occasional hosts. My choice of a time for inviting kids over was when my parents were away on trips, usually to insurance con- ventions. Mother and Dad trusted that I would take good care of things.

They went off to Kansas City one January, and I scheduled a party for a

Saturday night. It turned into one of the few days of the year when it snowed in our part of the Lone Star State. Many Texas drivers try not to let snow curb their cowboy instincts, causing smart people to stay off the roads. Friends who depended on parents to drive them canceled. Some of us lived near each other, however, so eight or ten neighborhood kids showed up. The snow added a festive note.

The day Mother and Dad returned from their convention, Mother received a phone call from Sadie Greenberg, a neighbor down the block and across the street on Stanhope whom she knew casually. "How are you, Becky?" Mrs. Greenberg wanted to know.

"Fine, Sadie," said my mother. "Nice of you to call."

"You had a good trip, Becky?"

"We had a wonderful time in Kansas City. I saw some people I knew when I lived there, as a very young girl."

"That's nice," said Mrs. Greenberg. "It snowed in Kansas City?"

"A little. They don't notice it much."

"You know, it snowed here . . . when you were gone."

"Yes, I heard."

"You know your son Stanley had a party at your house?"

"Yes. I'd rather the kids be here than out somewhere."

"You know the party took place the night of the snow?"

"I think so. I'm especially glad they weren't out then!"

"You know there was enough snow to build a snowman?"

"That must have been fun."

"And you know the snowman they built was in your living room!"

I happened to be doing homework nearby, while this conversation unfolded. I saw my mother's expression alter.

"Thanks, Sadie," said my mother. "I'll speak to you later."

She hung up the phone. "Know who that was?" Mother asked.

"Mrs. Greenberg. I recognize her high pitch way over here."

"Was Tommy Greenberg at the party you had while we were gone?"

"Sure. They're just across the street from the Fines."

"How was the weather?"

"A little snow. It was beautiful. Sorry you missed it."

"Enough snow to build a snowman?"

"Umm, yeah."

"Where was the snow?"

"*Where?* In the yard! On the sidewalk!"

"In the living room?"

My mind added one fact to another and got the sum. "That's what that trouble-making woman told you, eh?"

"That's . . . what she heard."

"A couple of kids dragged in some snow on their shoes. We tried to wipe it up. There was no snowman."

"No need to doubt you, is there?" Mother asked, rhetorically.

My silence gave her an answer. "And wait till I see Tommy Greenberg in school," I said.

▶▶▶

Football occupying the throne that it does in Texas, the heroes of Highland Park High were football players who were never Jewish but frequently handsome and usually aloof. It was they and their cheerleader girl friends who were chosen for the "Favorites" section of the yearbook. Some of the football guys lived near me, and I would timidly say hello if I couldn't avoid passing any of them hanging around in one's front yard.

Highland Park takes football so seriously that it eventually built a college-size stadium for its team. Even the old stadium was lit to accommodate evening games, and there wasn't a Friday night of football season that it was less than full. Kids who had passed their driving tests drove around the neighborhood honking, with crepe paper streaming from the roofs of their cars. Since everyone else went to those games, I went too, but for me they served more as social than as athletic events.

To graduate from high school, one was required to have taken gym classes, but for boys untalented at or intimidated by sports, there was an alternative. That was ROTC, a high school army training program. I wasn't planning a career in the army any more than on the athletic field. I figured, though, that rifle practice and marching out on a parade field once a week would be less embarrassing than revealing my hopelessness at sports. So I avoided gym by signing up for ROTC.

At the beginning of the school year, they issued us ill fitting, somewhat tattered olive drab uniforms and brass buttons that would go on the jacket. Those I polished to a shine at home with a chamois cloth. Boots were part of the ensemble; I polished them to more or less of a shine with shoe wax. On Friday afternoons, once we had some training, we marched onto the parade grounds—also, the football field—to the cadence of the school band. Given that other cadets were also avoiding gym and most of us weren't taking the military idea as seriously as we might, we didn't make an impressive picture. Still, we got through.

My success at marching was modest and didn't extend to the rifle range. There was indoor rifle practice a couple of times a week, and it was remarkable that I never hit anyone. The bullets that exited my rifle arrived a long way from the desired destination. It wasn't because I was wearing glasses—other guys were, too. It wasn't that the rifle was too heavy, or that I hadn't cleaned it. It wasn't that my hand was unsteady. I didn't know what it was! Week after week, though, I fired bullets that seemed aimed more at a flying bird than at a target directly in front of me.

Our instructor was Captain McCall. His expression would turn to open chagrin when he saw me arrive for my turn on the rifle range. Seeming helpless to correct my errors, he would stand by me, patient at first, impatient before long.

"Stanley," my friend Jay said to me one day when I described to him my problem, "what hand do you write with?"

"What hand? My left hand."

"What hand do you throw a ball with?"

"Neither, very much," I said. "If I do, it's with the left hand."

"What eye do you see better with?"

"My left eye. Much better."

"What eye do you aim the rifle with?"

"My right eye, of course. We all do."

"Stanley," he said, "try aiming with your *left* eye next time!"

Naturally, Jay was right. I hit the target the very next time, and before long, the right part of the target.

Captain McCall noticed the results but not my change of positions, and I didn't bother to explain it. "I see you've made a significant improvement, Corporal Ely," he said to me one day.

"Yes, *sir*," I said, in a high school military voice.

"You've been coming in after school and practicing?"

"Yes, sir, that's right," I said. As long as I was lying, I could take it a little further. "This is important to me!"

Captain McCall looked as if he were trying to decide whether I was serious or not, since he accused a lot of us of nonchalance about ROTC. "Perhaps we'll make a soldier out of you yet, Corporal," he boomed.

"That's what I hope, sir."

▶▶▶

By many graduates, Highland Park is probably remembered for its football successes (or who knows, even its ROTC program). By me, it's remembered because of its congenial atmosphere and its teachers who believed in hard work and eschewed the shortcuts that would have made their own jobs easier. Those teachers didn't call what they did volunteer effort, but it wasn't far removed. Our social studies teacher, Mrs. Holliday, resigned to go to work as a saleslady in a downtown department store. "I have to earn a living," she told our class, bluntly.

I joined the staff of *The Bagpipe*—what else would you call the newspaper in a high school that's stuck with Scottish stuff? Simultaneously, I fell for Miss Gunn, the sponsor of the paper and our journalism teacher. Jeanne Gunn was a woman of about thirty, with short, thick hair that danced as she moved, a full figure, a broad open smile and a deep laugh. She taught me a lot about journalism, and let me go with her and a few others to the printer's on Thursday nights to put *The Bagpipe* to bed.

It wasn't an important job, but it seemed so to me. Miss Gunn or some kid with driving privileges would pick me up right after dinner, we'd go to a quiet end of downtown, climb upstairs to the printer's shop, fragrant with ink, and spend the next three or four hours resolving what to do with this article that ran too long or that photo that looked too dark. I paid special attention to my column on the ROTC to be sure there were no errors. When the paper arrived at school in the morning, I felt almost equal to the players on the football field.

In the spring, Miss Gunn chose me and three others to travel to Austin for a journalism contest for high school students. There I won an award for headline writing. Those moments, more than my bar mitzvah, felt like my entrance into adulthood.

At the end of my junior year, Miss Gunn announced that she would be changing her name during the summer, since she was going to be married. True to her word, she returned as Mrs. Rousseau in the fall. Just before I graduated, Mrs. Rousseau awarded me a "Gold H" for meritorious service on *The Bagpipe*. But in the yearbook, where I expected a florid statement of praise and love, she simply wrote, "Good luck, Stanley." We had a year-end picnic for the newspaper staff where I met Mr. Rousseau, a man who seemed to me to fall short of the qualifications needed to make Miss Gunn change her name.

Today, nearly half a century later, Highland Park High is considered as much like a private as a public school, with far fewer Jewish students. Long-standing residents, I've heard, are intimidated by the academic competition from recently arrived Asian students, forcing their children to engage more with books and less with football.

In my day, the school gave us wonderful preparation for what was to come. When I enrolled in college, I met kids who had never written an essay in a high school English class; I had written more than I wanted to remember. "*Another* essay this week?" we'd moan every Monday. It never occurred to us, of course, that every time the twenty-five of us wrote papers, our teacher, Miss Watson, had to correct them, a task she did with particular care. We didn't know that discipline and writing practice would serve us well later on, but she did.

In junior high school, we also had to begin studying a foreign language. I opted for Spanish the moment word got to me that French was hard and Latin was impossible. Miss Schulkey, a tall, lanky, somewhat bucktoothed lady, started us in the ninth grade learning time and days of the week. Miss Coleman picked up with the two past tenses when I transferred to high school.

Miss Coleman was a portly bachelor lady, less sexy than Miss Gunn but just as likable. Materials for teaching foreign languages weren't nearly as good then as they are today, but Miss Coleman kept me interested in Spanish for the next three years. I ended up majoring in the language in college, and much later becoming a foreign language teacher myself.

With firsthand knowledge of how unappreciated teachers feel, I decided, on a much later visit to Dallas, that I should go back to Highland Park and tell Miss Coleman about my career. I figured she'd be happy to know that she had set one of her former pupils on to her profession. But I was too late. Calling the school to speak to her, I learned that she had retired the year before. Calling her home, I was told that she had died only a month earlier.

I felt terribly sad that I'd waited too long, that Miss Coleman passed away before I acknowledged to her how much that school and she in particular had done for me.

22

A Lady of the Night and Others

Mr. and Mrs. Fine, Mark's parents, occasionally went out of town for a vacation, leaving him on his own. He'd lay in some beer and invite Larry or the other Stanley and me over to spend the night. On an especially hot July evening as I was pushing sixteen, Larry and I came to the Fines' to stay over with Mark. We managed to down half a case of Texas' Pearl Beer.

Around midnight, when all three of us were in our undershorts and a good bit sloshed, Mark said: "You know, I have the number of a girl—a whore. I can call her. She'll get a cab and come here."

"*Here?*" I asked, not believing that even Mark could arrange anything like that.

"Sure," he said. "Here!"

"Well," I stated, "you sure don't have that kind of money."

"Wanna bet? Here it is: a hundred dollars!" Mark pulled out a roll of $10 bills.

"Where the hell did you get that kind of dough?" Larry asked.

"Whadda you care? You guys are game? We can all have a turn."

There was a pause. Larry looked interested. "You know this girl?" I asked.

"How would I know her? Tommy Greenberg gave me her number."

Larry and I were both considering the idea, I think from different perspectives.

"So, you guys game or not?" Mark repeated.

"Sure!" said Larry. "*I* am."

"I guess so," I added. "But that's a lot of money to throw away so fast."

"Don't worry, sonny," Mark declared, with a smile. "It's my treat."

It was hot, and we were half in bed. Mark took out a slip of paper that he had carefully folded and started dialing a number. Larry stretched out on the bed next to mine, and I could see that he had an erection. He was a blond fellow whom no one ever thought was Jewish. Occasionally I spent the night at his house, and I liked it because we would share a big double bed in his bedroom, occasionally lightly touching. Tonight, of course, was different.

"It's Stanhope, near Armstrong," Mark said into the phone, trying to sound older.

He hung up. I started toward another bedroom. "I don't think that girl's going to come here," I said defiantly. "I'm going to sleep."

"You'll see," Mark said.

I went into the other room, closed the door and slid under a sheet. I closed my eyes. What am I doing here? I thought. Suppose the girl does come, and that nosy Mrs. Greenberg across the street hears a cab pull up at one o'clock. Suppose Mark's folks find out later on. Or my folks. . . .

Sleep held back. I turned on my stomach and remembered the first time in the shower when I soaped up and got an erection, then an orgasm. What an amazing discovery, I thought. I wondered if anyone else knew about it? Maybe I'd write a story and make a lot of money. I'd call it, "How to Have Fun in the Shower."

Then I repeated the soap routine with each subsequent shower, and, increasingly, without the shower. At fourteen I joined in when my pals jerked off together. It was exciting to look at their bodies. Getting an erection was easy, but after a few minutes I grew less bold. I had to go off by myself when it was the moment to come.

I heard the doorbell ring. From the other room came a light female voice, with Mark answering in a forced baritone. Then it turned quiet. "Lord," I thought, "they're really gonna have sex!" After that, it would be my turn.

Well, who would know? It couldn't be safer. Here I was in a trusted friend's house, with him and another friend nearby. I moved my hand down to feel my penis, but I already knew it was hard. Why not go ahead?

What seemed like a half hour passed with no sounds. Then Mark threw open the bedroom door and walked in nude, his frame outlined from behind by a light from the hall. In the shadows, I could see that he had an erection. "Hey, pal," he said, "why're you hiding in here?"

"Not hiding," I answered.

"Come on, then. It's your turn. Larry and I have had her. She's hot. And she likes young guys—inexperienced guys."

"Okay," I hesitated.

"You *want* to, don't you?"

"Yes," I said. "In a minute."

"Then, come on. She's already asked me to call her a cab. She's not gonna stay all night!"

Mark walked out of the room, and I gripped the sheet. "I don't think I can do it," I said nearly aloud, my throat tightening. I felt the same wish as when I had jerked off with my friends, but I couldn't let go then—or now.

After a while, Mark's voice came from the hallway. "I guess my friend's asleep, honey," he said. "And there's your cab. Here's the dough. Thanks for coming!"

Even in the warm night, I felt a chill and pulled the sheet around me. The girl left without my ever seeing her body. My only glimpses were of the bodies of my friends, naked and erect, sweaty.

Eventually I fell into a troubled sleep and dreamed of falling. I awoke from a streak that was shooting up through my stomach.

Before Mark and Larry had awakened in the morning, I was dressed and on the way home. After the motorbike accident, Mother was skeptical any time I spent the night at Mark's. She said I looked tired and asked if anything was wrong.

"What should be wrong?" I answered, angrily. "We just stayed up late playing cards." I thought for a moment. "I lost."

The memory of that night stayed with me as an unmet challenge. The temptation, the fear, even the regret—and the image of my friends' bodies—all lodged in my head.

I worried whether Mark would think less of me for not having joined in, whether he knew I had stared at their erections. I didn't tell anyone else about that night. Mark never mentioned it again.

▶▶▶

That episode might have put a brake on dating, but it didn't. I went out with girls as frequently, if not as earnestly, as did other guys. A duality developed in which I was dating girls while also beginning to seek out the muscle magazines to hide in my drawer and use for jerking off. It's impossible to explain how I didn't admit to or even see the contradiction, but I didn't. If you had asked me if I was homosexual, I would have exploded with denial.

So, I dated girls. By sixteen, with licenses to drive, my crowd shed the need for parental chauffeuring and started having parties other than at home. The Jewish girls (and I guess non-Jewish, too) were feted with a dance upon their sixteenth birthdays. Those parties were held at one or another of the halls for rent in Dallas, some as far away as White Rock Lake, where Mr. Bagby and Aunt Fannie had had their (for him unproductive) picnic.

A printed invitation would arrive in the mail: "You are invited to a Sweet Sixteen Dance honoring _____, on Saturday, March ___ at 7:30 p.m. at Lee Hall. Dress: Semi-formal." (The latter excused you from needing to rent a tux.) Who a boy escorted to the party wasn't decided by him, since the invitation concluded: "Your date is Miss X." That meant that if you planned to go—and you did—you'd have Miss X as your date and dance at least some dances with her. You'd arrange transportation and arrive at her door with a modest corsage (a gardenia or carnations would do).

The dates I was assigned usually rotated between two or three girls. The relationships never became serious, the deficiency being mine more than theirs. Those girls eventually forgot me and married doctors, lawyers, businessmen. They probably looked back, as I did, on the innocent fun of the sweet sixteen dances.

For less innocence, we headed out of town. Larry, older and bolder than me, had started to date a girl in Houston, and he'd go there for parties and occasionally invite me along. The Houston my mother knew when she first saw

America had gone through an immense transformation. Houston Jewish kids of my age seemed to be uniformly rich—not merely comfortable, like the ones I knew in Dallas, but wealthy. Their addresses led you to enormous houses, and at sixteen they drove their own cars. Houston became known as the fast town, and Houston girls as fast girls. That's why Larry liked it.

I was more attracted to my friend than to any of the girls, and that's why I went. But those trips produced uncomfortable moments—necking sessions late at night—which everyone anticipated but me. Midnight would arrive with a date sitting next to me, or perhaps on my lap, my hands remaining innocent. "Stanley," Larry would whisper while the girl excused herself to go to the bathroom, "she's waiting for you to start. She wants to pet!" Since my advances progressed little, the girl must have written me off as a slow-moving Dallas dud, an assessment with which, embarrassed, I wouldn't have argued.

If Dallas wasn't known as a fast town, it did have a reputation for being hospitable, and summers always brought cousins or friends from Tulsa or New Orleans to visit. That gave rise to evening get-togethers or swimming parties. A couple of Jewish country clubs had opened far north, handsome compounds built to rival the Dallas Country Club where Jews were not welcomed. I'd be invited to swim at the club by kids whose parents were members, excursions on a snobbish level that I quietly relished.

By the time I was ready to graduate from high school, our gang was a tightly-knit, unmalicious, self-centered crowd. For most of us, the connection to Judaism had been reduced to attendance at High Holiday services with our parents.

Some of us (though not I) were given cars as graduation gifts, solid evidence of the success our immigrant parents had achieved in the new world of America and Texas. Non-Jews weren't exempt from ostentation; plenty of wealthy Highland Park gentiles regaled their kids with convertibles, too.

Highland Park High graduation exercises, which were so elaborate that they had to be moved to an auditorium at SMU, resembled a debutante ball. "The dresses those girls wore!" my mother would exclaim, of formal white gowns bearing Neiman-Marcus labels. "Like wedding dresses they were!"

Reunions with that crowd, when I came home from college, were warm and wonderful. I thought of them with affection and still do. But as I told Tommy on the screened porch two or three years before graduation, I knew that my future had to be molded a distant somewhere else.

For reasons more than an escape from Uncle Morris in the bedroom, I had to travel.

Mother, Stanley, Florence and Jerome, c. 1942

Florence, Aunt Pearl, Stanley and
Mother, 1948

Part Four

Author! Author!

23

Some Stay Home,
I Go Away

Americans may be ever on the move from one part of the country to another, but you wouldn't know it if you took your sample from Highland Park High graduates. From its alumni association directory, I've learned that not only have the majority of graduates not left Texas, many haven't even departed the neighborhoods where they grew up. So that my peers could give their children the benefit of also being Scotties, their parents simply passed houses down to them.

In the second or third generation of family ownership, many of the houses were upgraded with a new bedroom, a swimming pool, central air conditioning or all of those. Large signs in support of conservative candidates for city council or mayor or governor got heavy exposure in the front yards.

Highland and University Park today have a settled and elegant look, a look of indifference to whatever disruption may have popped up in the world in the last five decades. Azaleas and tulips flourish in the lawns and parkways. Still predominantly white, the school system is more an anomaly than ever. Cars remain full-size, and the high school is surrounded by them, many owned by students. If there's a clue that life in the Park Cities falls short of perfect, it's the elaborate lighting installed around large homes to discourage night-time intruders.

As for the "Village" where we used to go to catch the bus to Sunday school, it has long since ceased to host outdoor summer "Fiestas." Even the hardware store no longer has a place there. The "Village" now consists of designer boutiques, valet parking and police who cruise through to make sure you have a reason to be present.

I know about the latter because not long ago I drove slowly through the "Village" around midnight on a sentimental jag, and I was stopped by a Highland Park policeman who flashed me over to the side. "Everything's closed here, as you see," he stated in a deep voice. "Did you want something?"

"Actually, officer," I said in a reborn southern voice, "I was just reminiscing about the place. I grew up a few blocks away, a long time ago. I live in New York now."

"Reminiscing?" he asked slowly.

"Oh yes! We used to come to the movies here on Saturday afternoons. I got haircuts here, too."

His expression told me that he was unconvinced. I was commanded to follow him for a visit to the precinct station.

On the way, I kept laughing at the absurdity of the scene, but I soon saw that no one else noticed the humor. At the precinct, several higher ups came around and asked the same question. "Reminiscing?"

I offered the same answer, with an added compliment. "I believe you men deserve commendation for doing such an impressive job. Keeping the "Village" safe, I mean. It must be very reassuring to the folks who live around here."

"Yeah," stated an officer, "it is." He paused for emphasis. "And we like our visitors to do their . . . reminiscing . . . during the daytime."

"I quite understand, officer," I said.

▶▶▶

The Park Cities have lost most of their Jewish residents. Many Jews of my generation and their offspring have moved elsewhere, mostly to suburbs further north. This has all happened in the years since I left. The reason I hear is that "we just didn't feel we belonged there any longer." Maybe the unspoken anti-Semitism ceased to be unspoken.

Highland Park High, therefore, is mostly non-Jewish today. The valedictorians have to be picked from some other group, maybe from among the recently arrived Asians. An old friend reported that she went back to a Highland Park reunion recently, decked out in all the many diamonds she owned. "I just love being Jewish," she reported telling the gentile crowd in a loud voice that comes to her effortlessly. "It's so wonderful!"

▶▶▶

The first order of business as high school ended was to choose a college, and nearly every Jewish friend of mine stayed within the state, at SMU in Dallas or the University of Texas in Austin. Some went north to the University of Oklahoma in Norman. An adventurous few traveled to New Orleans, to Tulane or (for snob appeal) Sophie Newcombe. One or two even got as far as North Carolina to go to Duke. Beyond that, no one wanted to venture.

I had decided that I wanted to go away to study journalism, and not near-by. Or, perhaps to go not nearby, to study journalism. It became a contest between Northwestern University and the University of Missouri. Because it sounded snappier and was farther away, I opted for Northwestern, in Evanston, the first town along Lake Michigan north of Chicago.

In those days, being accepted required no battery of preliminary tests— mostly, just a letter, a transcript and a few kind words from someone like Miss Coleman, my Spanish teacher. For reasons lost in the unconscious, I went into liberal arts and never got around to enrolling in the Northwestern University School of Journalism.

Though my parents acceded to my plea to go away, they said I should stay home for the first year of college. That was because my double promotion back in elementary school had me finished with high school at sixteen, an age that they thought too young to go so far from home. I didn't like the idea but I knew they were right, so we worked out an agreement in which I would spend my college freshman year at SMU, living on Stanhope. Then, I could pack up for the move to Chicago.

The year at SMU went by as slowly as stationary clouds. Tommy enrolled there, too, and we shared a few classes. In preparation for the world up north, I tried learning to play bridge. And I joined the staff of the college magazine and wrote an article with fulsome praise about a student who was stuck in a hospital at Christmas. Even sick in bed, he was courageous and very handsome. It was getting harder for me to keep those crushes down. I did manage, though.

The following summer I worked, mostly as a driver, at my Uncle Herbert's auto repair garage. My mother's comment in a letter to Rose was, "Stanley needs roughing."

At SMU I also got my first close-up look at fraternities and sororities. During their days there, Florence had joined the one Jewish sorority and Jerome the one Jewish fraternity. Neither group owned an elaborate Georgian or Victorian house like some of the non-Jewish Greek societies. They didn't have houses at all, since most of the Jewish students at SMU were local kids who lived at home.

Democracy, or better said, non-selectivity was at work at the SMU Jewish fraternity and sorority. Eligibility didn't depend on looks or athletic prowess or social standing or anything except an urge to join and the few dollars needed for membership. I had no interest in the fraternity because I learned that it had no branch at Northwestern. I figured, though, that fraternities operated everywhere in as casual a manner as the Jewish one at SMU. That was a miscalculation.

Researching the picture at Northwestern, I found out that it had a powerful fraternity system, in part because the university depended on fraternities and sororities to help provide student housing. There were two Jewish fraternities, neither one with a name familiar from those I knew from Texas. But one somehow sounded more prestigious than the other, so I mentally assigned myself to it. In the unlikely event that a bid to join wasn't forthcoming, I didn't rule out a willingness to join the other.

During the summer before I went away, I talked about it with the cousin of a friend who was in Dallas visiting from Kansas City. "Stanley," she said, "don't expect those northern fraternities to be like the ones here. They're not."

"They're not?" I asked.

"Especially where you're going. That's a school known for having rich Chicago Jewish kids. They can be rough."

What, rough? I thought fraternities were friendly and polite. "What do you mean?" I asked.

"Snobs! Unfeeling. Not easygoing like the kids here."

Her advice was not to be disappointed if my wish to join didn't correspond with a wish from them to have me. I thanked my friend's cousin for her warning, and then dimissed it.

Mother and I went shopping for a footlocker and some warm clothes. With a hot iron, I pressed labels with my name into everything I was taking. Then I started to say goodbye to the old gang, a process I found exciting, since I was going where no one else ventured. The trip started to become real when the mail brought railroad tickets. One was for the overnight Santa Fe trip to Chicago, the other for the Chicago & Northwestern line that connected on to Evanston. It was September 1950.

Except Colorado, that first trip to Chicago was the first time I'd been anywhere outside Texas. I was going to a college sight unseen. But it took no more than a couple of fraternity parties to realize that I was indeed far from home. My Texas wardrobe, which didn't look shabby to me, was not up to the style of the V-neck cashmere sweaters and gray flannel slacks that 1950 fraternity boys adopted as daily attire. My newness to the scene must have seemed apparent in other ways as well. I had none of the polish or travel experiences of wealthy Jewish kids who had grown up in Chicago or other big northern cities. A boy arriving from Texas would provoke some interest, I thought. But he didn't.

So I went through Rush Week, visiting the two Jewish fraternities slightly out of uniform, a non-athlete, and without a father whose financial statement would classify me a don't-let-him-get-away candidate. As the week progressed, members of fraternity number one could hardly be bothered to notice that I was there.

Then I set my sights on choice number two. Mel, a fellow in that house who was just a year older than I, sensed my desperation as invitations to return for more parties began to be pared down. I came around to see him once without an invitation. He championed my cause to his "brothers" even to the last day of Rush Week, and came out looking crushed as he shook his head and told me that it was no go. "I really tried," he said, embarrassed by the exclusivity that his brothers relished.

If in my life there was a dramatic moment of moving on or turning back, it was then. I was a singularly young and inexperienced seventeen, crushed by not having been invited to join either of the fraternities I visited. My friend's cousin had warned me that it would be different from Texas, and I hadn't believed her. I wished then that I had.

Like the night at Mark's house when the prostitute arrived, I wondered what I was doing there? What craziness made me leave an environment I knew so well for this hostile land? And, worst of all, then to be rejected by Jews!

That Saturday night at the end of Rush Week, I walked alone down the long blocks of Sheridan Road that border the campus and parallel Lake Michigan. I was fighting tears of hurt and the urge to call home, admit that I had made an awful mistake and say that I was ready to come back to SMU.

I went into the Huddle, a college hangout in downtown Evanston, and ordered a hamburger. "You've waited so long for this," I lectured myself, looking around at some happy, handsome kids. "Don't chuck it yet."

I went back to the place I had been assigned to live for the first quarter of that school year. It was one of a group of quonset huts that the university had erected as temporary housing during the war and not yet torn down. A low-ceilinged, barracks-like set up with two bunk beds and four boys to a room, it offered no innate cheer.

My three roommates, all non-Jewish, were there, chattering. A couple of them had been through Rush Week, too, though of course to different fraternities from the ones I'd met. The experience was as unpleasant for them as for me, but they didn't take it as seriously. Unlike the Jewish fraternity boys, my roommates were intrigued to meet a Texan and urged me to give the school a try. They helped me decide to stay.

I didn't return to Texas until Christmas vacation and the confrontation with my father about smoking. In the meantime, classes began and other friendships, too. What comforted me as much as anything were two letters I received before September ended, from Florence and Jerome. I read them many times and, like Rose with my mother's letters, I have saved them.

Florence wrote: "I feel as if your fraternity experience in a couple of months' time will be too completely insignificant to matter. Besides, those little knocks are what make us bigger people. Fraternities may seem important when you first get to school, but when the novelty wears off, you can see them for the adolescent things they are. . . . When my kids are ready to go to school, if I can influence them in any way, they'll go where there are no fraternities or sororities. I made up my mind to that a long time ago." Jerome's letter read: "Remember how I've complained for years about the fraternity system? Now you can see why! There isn't any doubt in my mind that you're going to be just as happy in the long run—and that the experience in itself will make you a wiser and more understanding man. . . . It's going to take guts to stick it out and rearrange your plans. As a pledge, you would have had your friends selected for you. Now you've got to go out and make your own. I hope you're not too impatient in the matter. I really think that the people you meet there will be the most valuable part of your college career."

Those were as lovely letters as I ever received from my sister and brother. And they were both right.

▶▶▶

When the big footlocker arrived at the Evanston train station, I figured I was ready for whatever was coming between then and the following June. But my notion of what to expect from a Chicago winter was inexact. The first snow of the fall was a typical Chicago blast of all day wind and stacks of white. I took my trusted cowboy boots out of the trunk and wore them all morning and afternoon. By the time I got back to Music Hut #27 around five in the afternoon, the boots stuck to my feet and ankles and I couldn't get them off. "Don," I said to the cutest of my three roommates, who later joined Sigma Chi but never stopped saying hello to me when we met on campus, "help get me out of these things." He tugged and tugged, and I thought my foot might be coming off, too. But finally I was free. I wrote home and told them that Texas boots seemed not to work very well in snow.

▶▶▶

Spirits revive, of course, and mine did quickly after the fraternity episode. I loved the freedom to be on my own, the change of leaves in the fall such as I'd never seen in Texas—even the football games on brisk Saturday afternoons.

Something I hadn't considered before was that without joining a Jewish fraternity, I was in a place where for the first time I wasn't already identified as Jewish. It was a curious realization. I went to parties given by one or the other of the two Jewish sororities and even dated a girl in one for a while. But I also discovered that, if the urge hit, I could pretend not to be Jewish and get away with it. Now and then I did, especially when I was making talk in a class with a handsome gentile fraternity boy. Mostly, though, the game paled and I never played it long.

After a quarter in the Quonset huts, my name came up to move into Sargent Hall, a dormitory that had some earmarks of a fraternity without being one. It was a brand new building that held 150 boys in double rooms, nicer accommodations than many of the older "frat" houses. Many of those who moved to Sargent Hall turned out to be interesting fellows, not mere fraternity rejects. I became social chairman of Sargent the following year, when I was a junior.

It happened that there was another boy living in Sargent Hall who had come from my high school in Dallas. Herb was a dark complexioned, handsome fellow who at Highland Park had been remote and solitary but in college had spawned a smooth charm. I judged that he was on target with his ambition to become a Hollywood film writer. We greeted each other with feigned warmth if we met in the hallways of Sargent.

To my knowledge, Herb had never belonged to a synagogue or mingled with Jewish kids in Dallas, a pattern he continued at Northwestern. But coming from the same town, I knew something no one else on campus knew—that he was Jewish.

As time passed, a dozen or so of us in Sargent Hall became close pals, and someone decided that we were creating a "Tong," traditional Chinese gang. That premiere Tong perpetuated itself with new arrivals for some years. An amorphous collection, fellows in the Tong tended toward the possibly weird and preferably anarchistic, though an occasional All-American kind joined, too. We were Jewish and not Jewish, northern and southern. I was one of the founding Tong's least colorful members.

The Tong contained an inner circle and an outer circle, determined by a mysterious process or simply because one or the other was where someone wanted to be. Nobody ever got turned down, though when the majority of the fellows in Sargent heard about it, they stayed as far away as they could. (Herb was clearly non-Tongal.) Most of us had an interest in politics, the more serious of us in national affairs, the rest of us (like me) in campus doings. We didn't disguise our intention to wield political power within the cosmos of a college community.

At the beginning of my senior year, fellow members of the Tong proposed that I run for president of Sargent Hall. "Who else?" they asked. "Stan's the Man!"

The house by then had a good name on campus, and the idea certainly appealed to my "King of the Mountain" syndrome. The job might take time, but that didn't matter since my out-of-classroom activities rarely had been hampered by studying. Perhaps I also found it a chance to snub the fraternities that rejected me three years earlier. So, "Sure, I'll run," I said.

We were surprised when we found out that Herb, my fellow Dallasite, had the same idea and put himself forth as the other candidate. He hadn't manifested interest in the political world that we in the Tong inhabited every day. And being less well known than me, he didn't seem like a formidable opponent. The Tong, who in retrospect seemed to have had nothing better to do, took no chances, however. They made posters, plotted strategy and went around quietly gathering votes on my behalf.

One day it got back to us that Herb's supporters—the non-Tongal types—were engaged in a whispering campaign. "Do you want a Jew for house president?" they were asking around. While everyone in the Tong knew I was Jewish, others in Sargent may not have known. Herb had come up with a cunning strategy.

The Tong convened a midnight council meeting in my room. Cigarette smoke and tension filled the air. "We gotta find something to kick that guy's butt," said George, my campaign manager, in a deep and serious voice.

There was a troubled silence. "But what?"

I hesitated. "Well . . ." I started.

"Well, what?"

"I could tell you a secret about Herb that no one here knows."

"A secret! Yes! He sleeps with his sister?"

"He's Jewish, too."

"Jewish, too!" There was screaming and applause. "Oh, Ely, that's brilliant," they hollered. "That'll do it!"

The Tong quickly inaugurated a counter whispering campaign around the dormitory. "Did you know?" they asked, going discreetly from room to room, "that with the two guys who are running, you're gonna get a Jew for president no matter which one you vote for?"

On the night of our formal speeches, I was nervous, sweaty and sincere. Herb was cool and suave. The vote was taken the next day, and my wish to thumb my nose at the Jewish fraternities, plus at Herb, got granted.

Can I avoid sounding like sour grapes if I say that the two fraternities who rejected me did me a favor? Now, it seems so. If I had lived in one of their houses, I would never have shared a dormitory with black fellows whose acquaintance brought me into a world I'd never known. I would, as Jerome wrote in that letter, have had my friends built in and not had to go out and make them. But what interesting ones I would have missed—including four fellow Tong members who remained close friends forty years later.

During those years I occasionally bumped into Mel, the young man who had tried to argue my case to his fraternity brothers when I went through Rush Week. He always gave me a smile and a warm greeting. Mel stayed at school an extra year and was still there in the spring of my final year. He heard that I was serving as president of Sargent Hall. "Did okay here, after all, didn't you?" he asked me, grinning, as we passed each other by the lake.

"Yeah, Mel," I said, pleased. "Thanks to your brothers."

▶▶▶

What about socializing? Not being restricted by a Jewish fraternity, I dated Renee, a wonderful girl who did the right thing, went back to Minnesota, married a fellow Catholic and had a bunch of children.

I continued an affectionate, Platonic relationship with Pauline, my Dallas girlfriend who had gone off to the University of Texas. Shortly before I was ready to graduate, I invited her on a whim to come to Evanston for Sargent Hall's spring dance, and she did. She was so taken with the university that she transferred the next fall to its speech school, became friends with my Tongal pals and before long met a Chicago Jewish pre-med student whom she later married. Today she is a grandmother, and we are still friends.

Those were sweet, harmless romances, ideal for me who was not aiming for sex with the opposite gender. Even for those who were, sex was no easy achievement. The 1950s were the era of panty raids and curfews for college girls. Boys were allowed upstairs in a girls' dormitory or sorority house under extreme circumstances and then only if preceded by a loud chorus that announced, "Man on floor."

Opportunities for boy-girl intimacy were hard to create, a pain to many, a relief to me. In my senior year my roommate kept a "Make-Out Chart" on which he recorded his sexual successes, or near successes, after every date. The achievements he posted seemed suspiciously grand to me, but I didn't say so.

▶▶▶

Contact between guys may have been desired, too, but, at least as far as I knew, never went beyond desire. My sexual urge was taken care of through jerking off. It's a habit hard to practice in a dormitory, but it could be managed if you took a shower early or late enough at night. "You in there?" Gordon, my next door neighbor, would yell at me through the shower curtain.

"Yes, Gordon," I answered in a desultory tone, since he was disturbing my fantasy and hard on. "Go away."

"You've got your psych homework done, Stanley?"

"Yes, Gordon. Now leave me alone."

"Can I borrow it? I'm stuck for time."

"For God's sake, yes, Gordon. Now go away. There's not a moment to yourself in this place!"

In contrast to the dormitory was the trip home by train, once they had installed roommettes where one could close the door and enjoy privacy.

Undisturbed by dormitory mates, I could strip and engage in an unhurried session, enhanced by a floor-length mirror. It was a trip I began to eagerly anticipate.

Following one of those train rides home, at the end of my sophomore year, I got a summer job filling in for the vacationing secretary at Shearith Israel. My father arranged it, being the organizer of seat reservations for the High Holidays.

The synagogue was still in South Dallas, adjacent to a quiet city park. Since most of its congregants had moved north, the building was visited by few at any time and even less during the summer. I'd drive my father to town every morning and continue in the car to the synagogue.

For a couple of months, while both the rabbi and his secretary were away, I sat in her office, answered the phone and took reservations for High Holiday seats. It was so quiet that a couple of days would go by when I didn't see anyone except the Shamash (sexton), who was more or less on vacation himself and only came around to see that the place hadn't blown up. Occasionally I'd take a break and walk through the old sanctuary, the room from which I had fled with Aunt Fannie for barbecue sandwiches, scene of my bar mitzvah and confirmation. At a time when I was entering my junior year of college, those days already took on the feeling of a past childhood.

The secretary's office had an air conditioning unit that hummed quietly and generated an even more placid atmosphere. I'd read or write letters or call Stanley or Larry to pass the time. "Wadda you doin' there?" Larry asked.

"Nothin' much. It's awful quiet."

"Playin' with yourself, I'd bet."

"Larry!" I exclaimed. "This is the synagogue."

"Just checking." I thought I could hear him grin.

It was the synagogue, but Larry gave me an idea. I opened my zipper and allowed myself to play a bit. There was no thunder or lightning.

Next to the office was the men's room, the old-fashioned kind with the residual aroma of Lysol, tall wooden booths with frosted glass doors and metal hinges. I went in to piss and thought . . . well, no one's here. . . a quick few whacks and I'd most likely feel better. I checked the hall to be sure that no one was there and entered one of the booths to finish things off.

Like my father, I'm a creature of habit. The men's room break evolved into a daily routine. I began, in fact, to plan on it. Methodically, I'd rotate between booths and wipe up the floor so one part wouldn't look noticeably cleaner than the next.

"Jerkin' off again?" Larry asked on the phone one afternoon.

"Well . . . ."

"Stanley," he admonished, "don't you know what they say happens to guys who do it too much? It drops off. You'd certainly miss it!"

"That's where you're wrong, Larry," I replied. "Nothing happens when it's done in a holy place."

At the end of that summer, before I headed back to college, my father asked me how I had liked the synagogue job. "Fine," I answered. "It was fine."

My enthusiasm for even that distant connection with religion surprised him. "Really?" he asked.

"Sure. It was quiet. I'd walk in the park during lunch. Got a lot of reading done."

"You think you'd want to do it again next summer?" he asked, hesitantly. "Miss Schwartz said that you left things in good order . . . very tidy."

"Next summer?" I answered. "Well, why not? Absolutely, in fact!"

My father looked pleased, in an amazed kind of way.

24

Texas to Past Tense

The Tong organized a couple of chilly, late-spring picnics by the side of Lake Michigan and then I packed clothes and memories into that metal footlocker. With a room reserved at the Edgewater Beach Hotel, my mother arrived for my graduation by sleeper on the train from Texas. Regretfully, I bade goodbye to Sargent Hall and the ivy-covered college days. It was June 1953.

I took leave of college with a bachelor's degree but no plans. They would have been pointless, since it was around the end of the Korean war but not the end of the draft of fellows ripe for service like me.

Back in Texas to await the call, I worked in the office of my friend Pauline's father, a generous man who assigned me clerical chores while he lectured me sternly on avoiding a career around just such work. In March 1954, Tommy and I were summoned for the army physical that I've forgotten and he remembers. And in April I said a teary goodbye to family and boarded a plane for a ride to Fort Bliss at the other end of the state. Ahead lay my reduced status as U.S. Army private.

El Paso is the place you wouldn't choose for early summer basic training. Marching across the sand was what we did for many hours most days, going nowhere special. The luckiest draw turned out to be K.P. or even latrine duty, when you spent the day doing nothing more than keeping the latrine tidy.

Nobody knew the dangers of smoking, and we all smoked, usually half a cigarette at a time, at rests granted in the middle of a march. Privacy was more scarce even than in college, and the opportunity to practice my obsession with jerking off got severely frustrated. One Saturday, on a pass to visit friends of my family's who lived in El Paso, I excused myself and went into their bathroom just for the chance to masturbate in private. I stayed behind closed doors so long that the husband knocked to see if I was all right.

When the first eight weeks of basic training ended, we were given five days to go home and gather strength for the second eight. Thin to start, I had gotten so much thinner that my mother greeted me with horror. Most of that leave I spent sleeping.

Part two of basic training took place in Augusta, Georgia. (It was from there that I got the pass to fly to New York to attend Jerome's wedding.) Topographically, Augusta varies little from El Paso. The sand was everywhere, and it was summer and hot. I was assigned to study for a signal corps job, running a message center. The classes were geared to a mind that ran on slow, but I didn't care because they took time away from marches, less frequent but of no less ambition than the ones in El Paso.

At the end of the sixteen-week basic training came one's assignment for the rest of the two-year army stay—or what seemed like the rest of forever. One was assigned to Europe, which probably meant Germany, or to the Far East, which probably meant Korea. Very few of us would remain in the U.S. I prayed for Germany, weekend leaves to Paris and Rome skipping through my imagination. Seoul never entered the fantasy. My draw was Korea.

The army couldn't spare us long enough for a trip home, so those assigned to the Far East piled onto an army plane in Augusta for the trip to Tacoma, a stopover before boarding army ships to cross the Pacific. I was desolate. The injustice was compounded by the fact that my college friend Phil, drafted the same time as me, was on his way to Germany.

Washington was in its fall rainy season, which added to the gloom. On the one Sunday there, I took a bus tour to Mt. Rainier. The bus drove higher and higher, to altitudes that were already snow covered, then it let us out to wander for a couple of hours on our own. I continued to climb, up to a point to where the clouds had descended. Lost in a serene world of snow and clouds with tiny perforations that assured you of a sky still above, I was alone and finally reluctant to leave.

The Pacific was more immense than I had realized, and rougher. On an army ship with no stabilizers, I was seasick most all day of the five or six days on the water. Enlisted men were expected to perform some duty, so I volunteered to work in the nursery. It was ostensibly to watch over the children of dependents who were going to Japan, actually to be able to lie on the floor trying to avoid seasickness. We arrived in Yokahama and looked on enviously as the wives and children debarked for their stays in Japan. The rest of us continued to Pusan, on the southern coast of Korea.

On land, we boarded what was called a train but looked like a streetcar. For a day we chugged and bolted north, over hill after hill. I was going to my assignment in the 24th Infantry Division, presumably to practice my message center skills. That bore no guarantee, however. I figured that my bad luck in coming to Korea could be extended to an assignment that involved climbing those hills with a pack and a rifle.

Rumor said that you could swing a job inside if you knew how to use a typewriter. So when we arrived at the replacement depot, I announced to anyone who looked important that I was a formidable typist. I was lucky, for it landed me an assignment to division headquarters, to the operations section. There, I proceeded to sit in a bunker at a makeshift desk and rustic typewriter and produce battle plans devised by Colonel Long. "Men," he'd bellow, stomping in, "be prepared. We're going to the field at dawn tomorrow!" When he left, I'd look at my new friend George and the other guys and we'd shake our heads. "I wonder where he thought we already were?" George asked.

Service to our country was popular during World War II, but that was ten years earlier. Colleagues like George and Charlie were college graduates, draftees like me. Like the old days in high school ROTC, we were hard pressed to take the army business seriously. Our officers, however, were ambitious young majors and colonels who had graduated from the Army War School (sic) and who, I imagined, prayed at night for more battles so that they might become generals. They thought I was a treasure, because I could type *and* spell.

In those days there were no wives or children of American servicemen in Korea, because there was nowhere for them to live. Our own residence was a long Quonset hut with a curved ceiling, our tableware tin plates and cups, our dining room a makeshift mess hall, our baths primitive showers with low watt light bulbs. We heated water for shaving over oil burner stoves and were not allowed to wear civilian clothes. The one luxury granted us was Korean house-boys who picked up our fatigues and washed and ironed them at the cost of a dollar a week.

With no wives, the only women nearby were natives, and American soldiers officially were not permitted to have contact with them. But when the hormones got busy, some guys did, jumping the fence to have sex. Soon they started to develop cases of the clap. That gave me an excuse not to fol-low suit and to enjoy a world with no pressure to mix with women. I didn't realize it at the time, but that odd, exclusively male world must have helped change an unhappy situation into one that was tolerable and on some level even enjoyable.

I hadn't been in Korea more than a couple of months when news came that our division was to move to Japan. Suddenly, my fortune was changing. Indoor toilets and civilian clothes again!

Part of the division's advance party, I headed to Japan's southern-most island of Kyushu in a mild, early winter. A base in Fukuoka that had been a Japanese hospital compound in World War II became our home. Lodgings were heated buildings, tableware ceramic instead of tin. Thrilled with my unex-pected luck, I bought a few civilian togs and started to study Japanese.

But there really are no guarantees in the army. Someone had erred. In January, after only a couple of months in Japan, we learned that the division was not to move there but to a different part of Korea, to replace a Marine divi-sion. That proved a logistical horror, since some units of the division were already in Japan, some on the water, some not yet out of Korea. We drew up plans to turn it all around, a project of no small waste to taxpayers. My office dragged out its stay in Fukuoka as long as possible. We finally gave in and sailed back across the Korea Strait, regretfully leaving behind showers and indoor toilets.

Our new headquarters was not far from Seoul, but rural was rural, and it all looked alike. Civilian clothes were stored away and excepting a couple of short and wonderful visits to Tokyo, I remained in Korea for the next thirteen months.

Friendships formed. I developed a crush on George, the lanky, funny fellow from the South, and became jealous when he seemed more attached to Charlie than to me. We all exchanged inexpensive Christmas gifts from the PX and got drunk on bourbon or beer on weekends. I initiated a little thigh rubbing when everyone was tipsy at two or three in the morning. Is there anything more to say about that? No, nothing. It's something I regret.

My pals and I complained about loneliness on holidays or birthdays as we spent our nights writing letters or watching old American movies. On the couple of R&Rs to Tokyo, we ordered suits that could be made overnight, after which the guys ran off for rendezvous with geishas. I was as horny as they were but passed up the geishas and easy chances to meet a Japanese guy or even another American serviceman in a Tokyo bar, facts I also regret.

My mother sent home-made cookies, largely in fragments when they arrived after a month's trip; Jerome went to the Lower East Side of Manhattan and shipped a salami which survived better.

There were other contacts with home, largely long-traveling letters between the U.S. and Korea. Stanley, my friend starting from the early days on Stanhope, got married while I was in Korea, and I often wrote him and his wife Shirley. Early in 1997, in an experience paralleling that of my mother when her friend Rose sent back batches of her letters, Shirley sent me some thirty letters that I wrote them starting in 1955, from Korea. Interspersed with frequent complaints, I tell of how I celebrated the High Holidays that year:

"The division finally got a Jewish chaplain (that makes two in all of Korea). He arrived two weeks before Rosh Hashanah, with no plans made for services. He's young and sincere and homesick, and very mixed up. The difficulty in arranging where 300 men could stay overnight and eat Kosher food, etc., just about did this guy in. Finally, Rosh Hashanah got celebrated at our replacement company, the most barren spot in the world. We all gathered under two large tents with forty-watt bulbs and a sand floor."

People who know me have asked how I survived the Korean experience.

I, in fact, surprised myself—I even earned periodic promotions. A lot of the answer must have been the absence of a real war together with the presence of a totally male domain, the chance to drop all pretense of an interest in girls. It was a warm and unthreatening society.

Finally came January 21, 1956, the last day on the calendar I had been keeping. I said goodbye to Colonel Long and Major Baden, to George, Charlie, Fritz, and David, and took a train to Inchon, on the west coast of Korea. Waiting there was the *General Breckenridge*, thought to be one of the better troop ships but it seemed to me no more stabilized than the one coming over. I embarked on an even longer seasick trip back across the Pacific.

Fourteen days later, at dawn, I arrived in San Francisco for that memorable meeting with Aunt Pearl. I was discharged a few days later at Fort Ord, south of San Francisco. After a week in Mill Valley, I got back to Texas and found a letter of commendation from Colonel Long. It contained great compliments, exaggerated perhaps, but they made me feel that the two years in service had really not been wasted.

Suddenly, the life I had always known seemed unfamiliar. I was again in the universe of cars and girls, feeling for a while an odd nostalgia for the male world of Korea. Over the next several years, my army buddies and I exchanged letters and Christmas greetings. The others began to get married and send cards with photos of themselves together with wives, then children. George started to look more bald, less and less the slender fellow I had found so enticing. After a few years I failed to send him a card, and soon he did the same.

▶▶▶

Even if one wanted to study conversation, language classes in American universities in those days focused on grammar and literature. I therefore had managed to complete a major in Spanish and leave Northwestern with scarce knowledge of how the language sounded. (I harbored the suspicion that our professors also either didn't know or didn't care, or both.)

The army duty done, I enrolled in a summer Spanish program in Mexico City. Long before the Mexican capital had become smothered by smog and traffic, the city sparkled with summer freshness, and in July 1956 I embarked

219

on a happy six weeks as a student again.

A dark-haired lady set eyes on me the first day of school. Señora Maza had come to find boarders. I went with her and took a room in the home that she and her husband had filled with six beautiful children ages one to seven.

Each school day after breakfast with the Mazas, I'd take a long one-peso cab ride that traversed the Avenida Insurgentes out to the northern edge of the city. At the National University, I studied Spanish in morning classes and at noon swam in their outdoor Olympic-size pool. Predictably, at four or five in the afternoon, the clouds thickened and rain would fall for an hour or so, giving entry into a cool, dry evening.

Once in a while the Mazas chaperoned me and their other boarders to a restaurant undiscovered by tourists. Señor Maza's parents, who lived in an elegant fence-guarded house in Lomas, invited us for Sunday afternoon barbecue, with a flock of grandchildren running across their lawn and servings of sumptuous dishes, not to exclude the Mexican delicacy of dried blood.

The summer concluded with my contracting "Montezuma's revenge" after returning to Dallas, as well as with a respect for the care with which Mexicans treat their tongue and their culture. I found that I loved communicating in a different language, decided to study the language further and to investigate a career in foreign trade.

In September I headed to Phoenix for a year at the American Institute for Foreign Trade. Though it was still young, AIFT already had a reputation for its strong language programs and its placement service. It's located on the former Thunderbird Field, a World War II air force base, near the suburb of Glendale in what was then still desert. It was a shock to exit the plane—the only time I had ever come from Dallas to some place hotter!

A heterogeneous, heavy-drinking group of 250 students, both single and married, came together at Thunderbird, many, like me, with undergraduate degrees and military service done, using the GI Bill to pay tuition. Most of us arrived with a moderate desire to learn and a large desire to find a job, maybe in a corporation or bank's training program, with the prospect of overseas assignment.

I enrolled in mostly nonrigorous advanced Spanish and international advertising and marketing classes, and lived in a kind of two-room suite with three other bachelors. But the whole campus was laid out air-force style, in barrack-like rows of rooms, so no one was far from anyone else. With buildings facing one another across open lawns and the availability of inexpensive rum and tequila, there were parties (with faculty rarely missing) and Harry Belafonte music blaring through open quadrangles late into many nights. "Private parties" that weren't very private were the thing. Inhibitions dropped with a few swallows of tequila, and some of the married couples, it was heard, began to exchange partners.

The mid-1950s was an era when Jewish girls (probably non-Jewish, too) mostly remained virgins until marriage, and weddings took place early. Friends my age in Dallas were already getting married, and I served in two or three of their wedding parties. I stood my celibate ground—I'm not sure there were any other gay men at AIFT, anyway. But that November I turned twenty-four, and it was growing more difficult to continue postponing dealing with sexual feelings.

Many others at Thunderbird thrived on the hot, dry climate and claimed that Arizona was the place they hoped eventually to retire. But I found that being isolated in the desert while repressing my own feelings was leaving me tired, off balance and more anxious than I had ever been. The year at AIFT produced some interesting friends and a lot of progress in Spanish, but by the time the following June arrived, I was ready and very eager to leave Arizona.

25

I'll Take Manhattan

During the year at Thunderbird, I determined that I wanted to go into international advertising—and that required moving to New York. Which decision dictated the other, I didn't bother to think about. My parents were less than pleased and also less than surprised, since by then I had been away most of the preceding seven years. It hardly seemed a coincidence that my departure made 100 per cent—three out of three children—who forsook our Texas beginnings.

During the Christmas vacation from AIFT, I traveled to Connecticut to visit Jerome and Paula and newly-born Elissa and to begin meeting Manhattan ad agencies where I would apply for work the following summer.

In June of 1957, with a diploma from Thunderbird, I flew to New York to attend the wedding of a Tongal friend from Northwestern. For six weeks I lived in Stamford with Paula and Jerome while pursuing jobs at several international advertising agencies. Paula accompanied me to White Plains to shop for a couple of suits I could wear for work. I didn't bother sending out a press release, but that marked the unofficial end of the time I would call Texas home.

My motives for going into advertising were anything but sound. I liked the look of attractive ads; clever television commercials, like the ones for Piel's Beer, were appealing. There was a certain glamour attached, too, or so I thought. Whether advertising had any redeeming social value never crossed my mind.

Other young men were seeking the same places as me, and Young & Rubicam, the agency I had especially hounded and which came through with a job offer in August, could—and did—start me at a salary of $85 per week.

My first year was to be spent on a training program through different departments of the agency.

With a job in hand, I embarked on finding an apartment and instinctively went back to Greenwich Village, the neighborhood I first saw during the dinner with Jerome four years earlier. I wanted not just to be in the Village but, having foregone privacy in college and the army and at Thunderbird, by myself—without roommates.

A broker led me up the stairs to a fifth-floor apartment on Horatio Street, years before it turned into a trendy West Village address. The furnished studio could be rented for $78 per month, a very large sum. I hesitated. It was the best I'd seen for the price, however, and I took it, thrilled to sign a lease for the first time.

Along one wall the apartment had three casement windows that looked out on Horatio and opened wide the way for the five o'clock noises of morning trucks from the meatpacking district nearby. Jerome came in from Connecticut and helped me paint. I bought contact paper and covered some scratched wooden furniture, then said hello to the man who banged out a limited repertory on his piano and seemed to have four or five locks on the door of his apartment, the other one on my floor. I learned to ignore the truck noise and settled into life as a young bachelor in New York, meeting a friend or two and getting standing room tickets for the original productions of *My Fair Lady* and *Auntie Mame*.

Six months later, no longer distracted by the search for a job and an apartment, socializing almost entirely with old friends from Northwestern or Arizona, twenty-five-years old and unable to reach out to gay connections, I found myself in knots, bursting with sexual energy and afraid to find somewhere to put it. I would go around and visit with Nan, a lady draped in scarves, heavy jewelry and makeup who held court in a small jewelry store she ran nearby on Greenwich Avenue. "Stanley," she said, "you act too *old* for your age. You shouldn't be hanging around here with me; you should be out having fun with young people!"

Nan was right. I found myself tense at work and lonely at night.

Everything was colliding. Maybe, I thought as I took a membership in a gym, if I worked out and gained some weight, those homosexual desires would go away. They didn't. That was when I approached Jerome about borrowing money to go into therapy—and when he gave me his support. It was when I took perhaps the step that went farthest to save my life.

After a year of living alone, I also missed having company at home. Someone at work told me about three fellows who shared a duplex apartment on West 12th Street and were looking for a fourth, to help pay the rent. I went to pay them a visit.

Old but still elegant, their building was just off Fifth Avenue, only a mile or so from Horatio but far more fashionable, on a block filled with handsome brownstone buildings, near Washington Square. Though the downstairs of the apartment was grand and spacious with a double high ceiling and a front wall of tall windows, sleeping quarters upstairs were cramped—four people to use one bathroom and share a bedroom and a half. Still, I liked the look of the place and needed friends, and I moved to West 12th Street in the fall of 1958.

It was an era when the Village was still a carefree, inexpensive place to live. We were a quartet of guys in our mid-twenties, going every day to jobs in marketing and banking and advertising that were presumed to hold high potential. I'd leave in the morning, catch the Fifth Avenue bus uptown to 40th Street, and walk the short block to Madison Avenue, affecting nonchalance with take-out coffee from Chock Full O'Nuts and the day's *New York Times* folded under my arm. At lunch I'd stroll to Rogers Peet to view the sales and (discreetly) the salesmen.

On Saturdays, Gus and Skip and Dirk and I would take our shirts to the Chinese laundry on the corner of Sixth Avenue, for laundering at eighteen cents each. We'd go down to a delicatessen on Eighth Street and buy pastrami for Sunday night suppers and once in a while cook together, Gus preparing some Greek recipe and me making salad with an elaborate dressing. We shared the expense of a cleaning lady who kept calling each of us Mr. Watkins because our telephone exchange was "WA," for Watkins.

At first it was difficult for me to sleep in the odd and unprivate bedroom arrangement, but that faded in time. We melded together, bachelors of differing but somehow complementary personalities, not best friends but good roommates.

A few Friday nights I went to Sabbath services at a small temple in the Village, but I found them unfulfilling and mostly populated with couples who suggested I give their daughters a call. I also started to take piano lessons, something that I'd never done before. They were facilitated by the spinet piano that sat in our living room among several chairs and sofas that needed repair.

Accompanied by wide gestures, Gus would undertake weekly half hour phone conversations in Greek with his mother in Detroit. If he'd had a bad day, Dirk would enter, slam the door and curse in Dutch. I'd interrupt in order to practice my piano scales. Skip served as anchor, calm and smiling at the noise around him. We all filled in as brothers to Susan, the young artist who lived on the other half of our upstairs floor and rang our bell late into the night.

In therapy I finally was beginning to confront my homosexuality. However, my roommates and their straight friends together with my own provided me a still needed social safety net, as the Jewish crowd had in Dallas years before. The apartment's living and dining room were made for parties, and we'd assemble forty or fifty at a time. With a balcony off the living room, facing 12th Street, those evenings would spill over to the outside and somehow incorporate cars and pedestrians who waved as they passed by. It was during the tenure on 12th Street that a couple of my roommates met their future wives. To my recollection, however, no one had sex in the apartment.

In time, a couple of our group moved away. Finally, no longer able to afford the rent, the remaining roommate and I departed the Village and, at his suggestion, moved to a small apartment uptown. It's the neighborhood where I've remained ever since, most of those years by myself. Even now, however, the two and a half years on 12th Street are lodged in my scrapbook as an especially happy period, crowded with parties and people, young, hopeful and safe. I ended up buying some of the apartment's furniture, the spinet piano and the old pine dining table that still serves me, thirty-five years later.

I was alternating between dating and waiting. I went out with a couple of girls, one Jewish, one not, relationships that I thought of as serious but that never led to sex. The women understood me better than I did myself, for, seeing little future in me, their interest waned. There were a couple of ventures into the social milieu, debutante parties to which I was invited (where I probably passed for non-Jewish). And there was Clarisse, who had a reputation as an easy lay. One night I took her home after a date, we had a long French kiss and I pulled back, frightened to go any further. "Any other guy would have had me undressed by now!" she said, furious. It was true. I left, got a cab and headed directly from her house to the Everard Baths, the first of many visits to that place where I began nervously practicing the sex I'd been postponing.

If you opened your eyes, gay sex was anywhere. It was during that time that I met the fellow in Washington Square of whom I spoke to Tommy. Later, confused and angry, I went into a gay-owned clothing store and hung around until the owner invited me upstairs and offered a blow job. The pattern of quick sex got started.

The year's training program at Y&R ended when there was a vacancy that needed filling in the international division. They moved me up to a small private office and pronounced me an account executive. I was authorized a secretary, Maureen, a proper young graduate of Katherine Gibbs who adhered to their rule of coming to work with hat and gloves. I got to know the other account men, Marc and Bruce and especially Joe, a hulky, outspoken Yugoslav who seemed as steady as I was insecure. Joe was my age but already married and a father, and he would invite me to his apartment in Brooklyn where his Italian wife would bring forth dinners of seven courses.

At twenty-five, still green and unprepared, I was handed four or five low-budget international accounts to handle simultaneously, a task that would have challenged someone more seasoned than I. Along the way I attempted switching to copywriter, but to my dismay the copy project I handed in was deemed better on the marketing aspects than the copywriting. So I stayed as an account executive, uncomfortable as underling to a boss of ruddy complexion and ostentatiously masculine voice who frowned on my coming to work without a hat. "That's a dust collector," he bellowed at me one day. "Take it down!" What was gathering dust was a mobile for a baby's room made by my Beech-Nut baby food client that I had hung from the ceiling light in my office.

Aside from not being a young married, like Joe and Marc and Bruce, I lacked the bravura manner that eases one's way in the world of ad agencies. Joe and Marc seemed to benefit from a good dose of brashness and love of the insecure, qualities I lacked. I was trying, unsuccessfully, to survive on hard work and earnestness.

Clients liked me, but my own superiors did so less. This became glaringly clear when my boss started criticizing everything I did. That went on for two or three months, and it left me perplexed and troubled. "That's no good," he'd holler about work it had taken me a week to complete. "Bring something else to show me—tomorrow!"

Eventually, I understood. He was building reasons in his mind to let me go—because of budget cutbacks, he said. That occurred only a month before my third Christmas at Y&R, when I would have started to participate in their pension plan.

I asked whether I couldn't be kept on the payroll until the new year, and my boss suggested that I plead my case to the chairman of the agency. The chairman, a man who proclaimed that his office door was always open, liked to further his reputation as benevolent by giving annual birthday gifts and flags on July 4th to his couple of thousand employees. I finally got an appointment to enter his open door and explained my case. He said that unfortunately he was helpless.

Once the air was clear and he had discharged his assignment, my boss did an about face and turned eager to help me find another job. However, to a colleague, who repeated the story to me, he confided that he wished he had never hired me. Why? I don't know. Maybe he was bothered by the differentness he perceived in me. But the remark seemed reason enough for me never to return to Y&R, once I had left.

During our time as account executives, Joe and I often had lunch. I'd been feeling the need to "come out" to some straight friend, and since I knew him well, I thought he would be the person who would understand. "Joe, let's sit down, I want to tell you something," I finally said one day, screwing up my courage on a noon walk. "I think you should know . . . that I'm gay." He turned to me, thunderstruck, and said nothing.

We went back to work without speaking. Later that afternoon, looking still amazed, he stepped into my office with a note that he had written. He placed it on my desk. "It makes no difference," it said in great large letters. But it did.

After I left Y&R and called to make a lunch date, I noticed that Joe started suggesting that we make it a threesome. "Why don't we ask Bruce, too?" he'd say. It happened so many times that there was an unavoidable conclusion: Joe no longer wished to have lunch with me alone. Eventually I called less, the lunches became fewer, then stopped. And I didn't see him again.

What I thought I had—a valuable, solid friendship that would be bigger than our different lifestyles—I didn't have. For a long time I felt hurt and wondered if I had made a mistake in what I told him. Still, what was it I told him? The truth.

▶▶▶

Much as I didn't fit in with Y&R's management, I admired Van Reynolds, the boss of my next job at Dorothy Gray, an international drug and cosmetic firm. A cultured and aristocratic man, Reynolds already knew me, having been my client at Y&R. He was apparently not bothered by any difference he found in me and quickly offered me a place in their New York office.

I was to oversee marketing of their products in Latin America, and soon I traveled to visit distributors in Puerto Rico, Venezuela and the Central American republics. Because I was deep into analysis by that time, I passed up an offer to move and work in their Mexico City branch. It's a decision I've regretted, since I'd have had the experience of living for a time in another culture and a city I already knew.

During this time I was assigned as secretary a fifty-ish German woman who, I later suspected, no one else in the office wanted. Trudy was motherly but defiant if I corrected her misspellings in English. Maybe her boss, who by age if not inclination could have been her son, was looking for a way to find fault with her work.

One afternoon when things were slow and we sat sampling the cookies that Trudy made and frequently brought from home, I led her into talking about her past. Until then all I knew was that she had left a medium-size German city and come to the United States shortly after the end of World War II.

"What did you think about the concentration camps?" I asked, halfway between genuine curiosity and the possible chance to provoke.

"Camps? Nothing," Trudy stated, flatly.

I was naive, and her answer wasn't what I expected. "I thought you were in Germany all through the war," I said.

"That's right."

"Well then, you knew about the camps. I guess everyone did."

"No, nothing."

I put down a cookie, half eaten. "You knew nothing about what was happening to the Jews?"

"How would I?"

I considered what to ask next. "Didn't you . . . notice that Jews were disappearing from your town?"

"Disappearing? Umm, no."

I had to force my voice to remain low. "Didn't you even wonder what was happening to them? Where they had all gone?"

Trudy replaced the lid on the box of cookies looking irritated. She turned and started to leave my office. "Jews," she added. "No, nothing."

Though I worked well with Reynolds, I was frustrated by not being assigned to European markets, by the conservative nature of the company and the low salary, as well as the simple fact that selling moisturizing cream and lipstick to ladies abroad began to fall short of what I thought I wanted to do forever. Reynolds once asked me where I'd like to be ten years hence. I searched nervously for an answer, then said, "In a job like yours." Even I heard my lack of conviction, and I'm sure he did too.

Unfortunately, my tenure at Dorothy Gray coincided with the time that Jerome fell sick. His illness and the conflict it caused in me were profound, and shortly after his death I hurriedly accepted the offer of a change of jobs. Unlike the time at Y&R, when I had to leave, Reynolds tried to persuade me to stay. By then, I had moved to my own studio apartment on the Upper East Side, but it was a moment when I needed a new work address as well. With some ambivalence, I took leave of a comfortable Park Avenue address and transferred to work in a couple of rooms of a residential apartment building.

It was for the husband of a friend, a wealthy, free-wheeling man who was starting an export finance company. I neither knew nor cared anything about finance, but with the offer of more money and the simple urge to flee, those considerations were ignored. The job he hired me to do was purely clerical and impossibly unstimulating. I stuck with it, unhappy, and after a couple of years had to admit that I had made an awful mistake.

By then my mid-thirties were coming at me. I knew that I had to make a change, but one that would be bigger than to another advertising or marketing job. Knowing to what, however, wasn't easy, especially since by then I was suffering from a profound fear of flying. It was altogether the darkest time of my life.

On a lark, I registered with a neighborhood association and volunteered to tutor a high school student in Spanish at night. To my surprise, I enjoyed the experience, more than I had expected. It was a wonderful contrast to day-time work, and it put me in mind to consider full-time teaching. To test the waters, I enrolled at Hunter College nearby and started to take education and Spanish courses in the evening.

Soon I decided to make the break. I wrote the news to my parents, and from my father's response I knew that he understood what I was planning no better than he understood me altogether. In his view, that might have been the time to return to Texas and work with him in his insurance business (and maybe get married).

Going back to Texas, of course, I didn't consider. I was eager to be in a classroom, knowing even that a teacher's work meant less pay. By then I was desperate to escape a job that had become my equivalent of time enslaved in Egypt. It was a moment of pleasure when I resigned from the finance company, which by then had been sold to gentile and, I suspected, anti-Semitic owners.

I undertook a semester of student teaching in Spanish at New York City's High School of Music and Art, and at the end of that spring semester started to search for a full-time teaching position.

It was 1969, and I was thirty-six years old.

▶▶▶

For me, becoming a teacher simultaneously meant becoming a commuter. In searching for a job, I learned that private secondary schools in Manhattan paid only slightly more than volunteer work; I didn't consider New York City public high schools. That meant the suburbs, and the placement service at Hunter College put me on to an opening for a language teacher at the high school in New Rochelle, in Westchester County, some twenty miles north of Manhattan.

The department chairman who interviewed and later recommended hiring me was the first black graduate of Wesleyan University in Connecticut, coincidentally the alma mater years later of one of my nieces and two of my nephews. Charles Blake was the also the first person of a different color for whom this Jewish Texan would work, a fact never discussed between us but certainly not unnoticed by the politically wise Blake. He had an appreciation for quality, and we got along, and when other teachers who had never been in business complained about being over-supervised, I laughed. What they didn't know! If I experienced difficult moments with Blake, I reminded myself of the courage it must have taken for him to enroll years before at Wesleyan.

For a couple of years I borrowed the car of a friend and drove the forty minutes to New Rochelle. Later I bought my own and became chauffeur to a couple of other teachers also living in Manhattan who had no cars. If the early morning company was welcome, bearing the sole driving responsibility for the next two decades grew heavy.

New Rochelle is a community of some 80,000, mostly Jews, Italians and blacks. Though I was hardly a young teacher, the first couple of years in a classroom were still a blur, especially as they coincided with the end of the tumultuous sixties of student rebellions. At first I taught just grammar; later, conversation and literature classes as well. I took on the sponsorship of a

231

Spanish honor society and once each spring chaperoned a senior group to Manhattan's Metropolitan Museum for a tour of the work of Spanish artists. "You've been here before, I guess," I'd say to the kids who looked bug-eyed as the bus proceeded through Spanish Harlem with real signs in Spanish.

"You mean the museum?" I'd hear back. "Well, we did take a field trip when I was in fifth grade!"

I looked dumbly at the kid who likely as not had been to Europe, maybe more than once. "You know that you're only thirty minutes away from one of the great museums of the world! You could take the train." If it was an especially likable group, I might share the knowledge that I lived only a few blocks away, the kind of statement that always elicits from teenagers the startled look that says, "You do have some other life?"

By the end of the day at the Metropolitan, at least some students might have been convinced that a return visit would be worthwhile. If so, I chalked it up as a successful trip.

Many of those students were Jewish, and there were moments when it was tempting to further the bond between me and them by introducing the common Jewish factor. I never did, though.

Resisting the temptation to further the bond between me and a handsome male student proved at times more difficult. I invariably learned boys' names faster than girls' and wondered if they noticed. The student to whom I developed the deepest attachment I met in my first year of teaching. He wasn't the most handsome or athletic; he was slender and a bit shy, and I thought maybe he appealed because he seemed to be what I might have been at his age, if I had been better rounded. But he passed without distinction through high school, not seemingly much more developed by the end than at the beginning. After he graduated, I wrote occasional "just to keep in touch" notes to his home, but he didn't respond. I don't know whether the attention embarrassed him, or perhaps he never turned out to be the success that I was sure—and assured him—that he would be.

Did students like him "figure me out"? I always thought that sheltered suburban kids didn't know much about sex at all, but a couple of times I returned from a break to my classroom and found, "Mr. Ely is a fag," written in chalk on the board. I smiled, to tell the truth. Well bred, these kids, who respectfully included the "Mr." All in all, I was glad to be in a high school, not a university, where boys would have been more mature and the physical temptation stronger. When I looked around at those teaching in my school—male and female—whom I knew or thought to be gay, the old chestnut that homosexual teachers are a threat to young people was rendered absurd. Those were among the most energetic and creative of any on our faculty.

Time went by, measured by the September-to-June calendar. With courses at Hunter College at night, I finished my master's degree, and when Spanish became restricting, I started taking credit courses in French, leading up to teaching French as well. Loyal to life in the big city, I remained a New Rochelle teacher without being a resident. I'd locate wherever I had left my car the previous day, hope it would start on winter mornings and that I'd find parking on a Manhattan street near my apartment again in the afternoon.

Teaching five classes five days a week to even the best students takes a physical toll. I'd come home from school far more tired than from an office, and I relished the school holidays. But I was finding unmistakable satisfaction in doing work no longer with print or television advertisements or cosmetics or finance but rather with young people. If there was any sadness, it was the inevitable sending seventeen- or eighteen-year-olds on, knowing that some may remember you kindly in another decade or more, but that in except the rarest of cases, you're destined not to see the finished man or woman.

With the façade of dating girls finally dropped, my thirties became a time of relationships with men whose appeal frequently faded shortly after leaving bed and getting dressed. Even those relationships had to compete with evenings at the baths. In my forties, as those friends of mine still unattached seemed to pursue partners more seriously, my random sexual encounters flourished. Some extra sense fortunately kept me off drugs, but summer vacations to California in the 1970s became mostly prolonged orgies.

Sounding annoyed, a friend of mine said to me, later, "There were years of Saturday nights when we knew we couldn't invite you to anything!" Those nights, sometimes stretching until the sun started to rise, gave freedom for my fantasies to be realized, verified my ability to attract other men, filled voids that reoccurred shortly after the night ended. I accepted being alone in exchange for the steady chance to pursue sex. Even the allure of places like Studio 54 didn't work for me; I went for the straight avenues to sexual encounters.

Breaks in the school year—Christmas, summer and even spring vacations—were usually spent in Dallas, reached at times by days of driving. Though I watched my father grow older and more senile, my one-sided war with him continued. In the late 1970s, after he had been gone a couple of years, there was no one left to fight the war against. Then I went beyond just disposing of the beard and cigarettes that he disliked. I enrolled in a course for "fearful flyers" and succeeded in climbing back on an airplane after a boycott of over fifteen years.

By that time, I had finished a decade in New Rochelle. Willing to fly again, I started to split the summers between a visit to my mother in Dallas and trips to California or Europe, some to study French in Paris. I began to teach French, too.

Years increasingly blurred together, and by the time Mother died in 1987, I was approaching two decades as a teacher. In another couple of years I'd be at an age at which I could leave and begin to collect a modest pension. I knew too many teachers who stayed in their jobs much too long, well past burnout. I became eager to leave while the years locked in my memory were good ones and I had energy to do other things.

Consulting friends wise in finance, I determined that the pension, together with the inheritance from my mother, would allow me to quit full time work. In the spring of 1989 I surprised folks in New Rochelle by telling them that I would resign in June. I even threw away a full year of unused sick leave. With parties offered by students and faculty, I said a satisfied goodbye. Now, nearly nine years later, I keep some contact with young people by working periodically as a substitute teacher in a Manhattan high school for gifted students.

When I hear others belittle teaching or teachers, I look back on my thirty-two years of full-time work in New York. With experience in several different areas, I feel qualified to say that, some shirkers notwithstanding, teaching remains among the noble professions. For me, though it was the last thing I considered years earlier, it was where I stayed the longest and was the most successful. I was glad for the experience and the perspective gotten from business but grateful that that was not my last stop. I laugh to remember that from coming to New York for something glamorous and commercial, I ended up in one of the least glamorous, least commercial professions.

Even now long gone, my parents are seldom far from my mind. I can see my mother endorsing my decision to leave a full-time job for the chance to write and do volunteer work. My father is different. He and his brothers were brought up on work, believed in it, found it essential for not only the money but the respectability that it brought them. That was never true for me. Thanks, in fact, to my father's support, my first experience with real work didn't come until I had moved to New York at twenty-four.

Still, I'm torn between what I wanted to do and did and what would have pleased my father. If he didn't understand my becoming a teacher, he would have understood still less my leaving it at age fifty-six. "Fifty-six years old!" I can imagine him saying. "That's just a baby!"

I remind myself that the course he followed was the one that filled important needs for him. The one I followed did that for me.

Dad, Mother and Stanley, 1951

Mother and Stanley at
Northwestern graduation, June 1953

Stanley, 1950

Stanley in U.S. Army, 1954

Part Five

Pick Up Sticks

26

Ben & Sara,
Bye and Bye

I grieved when my grandfather died. A part of me ceased to exist; he took it with him. We begin life whole, the sum of many people: fathers, mothers, grandfathers, brothers, cousins. And then as they die, one by one, each death lessens the whole and we shrink, we shrivel, whittled down until all that remains from the subtraction is our self.

T. N. Murari, *Taj*

Aunt Sara, the lady with the clean kitchen, was so much the right wife for Uncle Ben that he didn't want to leave her alone and die before she did. And he didn't. They passed away within three months of each other, she first. That was in the winter and spring of 1990. Ben Ely was eighty-six, Sara a couple of years younger.

Now all the Elys of that generation are gone—my parents, not only my father's siblings, but all their spouses—Big Becky, Aunt Bessie, every one of them. On that side I'm left with Marilyn, whom I rarely see, and a few other cousins whom I never see.

To me, Uncle Ben's passing marked the last of a tough breed of self-made Jewish Texans, many transported young from middle or eastern Europe. After his death, his business, like that started by other young, aggressive Texas Jews, was sold to people outside the family. Earlier, though, as the years passed and the Ely Company flourished, he and Aunt Sara seemed to ride on a sense of power. In a moment of unmasked pride, some might say arrogance, she said to

241

me, "Look where we started from, Stanley. And look where we've ended up—on top!"

When the daughter of a friend of theirs was having difficulty becoming pregnant, my aunt and uncle were on a trip to Italy and arranged for an audience with the pope. The purpose was to ask him to bless the young woman so that she would conceive a child. He did so—and she had a baby!

Trips like that also gave them the chance to acquire possessions that money and travel can buy. From a visit to Japan they brought back two of the most beautiful woodblock prints I have seen. Every time I visited them after that, I'd go to admire the prints from up close.

"Before we went to Japan," Aunt Sara explained, "we found out who their best living artist was—and that's who we went to see. That's where these are from."

To celebrate their golden wedding anniversary, they arranged a formal dinner dance at the Jewish country club in Dallas, and the event established two traditions in their society. Rather than blatantly announcing that they were giving themselves a party, the invitations listed their children and grandchildren as hosts. It also said, "No gifts," which I figured kindly excused guests from trying to come up with anything they didn't already have. Instead, many of their friends and relatives made donations to Jewish charities in their names, a habit commonly practiced now. I was not in town for the party, but my mother attended and reported that under Aunt Sara's supervision it was, hardly any surprise, perfection.

After Jerry and Marilyn moved away and were married, my aunt and uncle sold the house where we once had Thanksgiving dinners. They supplanted it with a series of condominium apartments, north of the Park Cities, where wealthy Jews were starting to reassemble. Each of their apartments was more elegant than the one before, and none was moved into "as is." Aunt Sara liked to add a new bathroom, or custom built closets, or a redesigned kitchen before they took occupancy.

Luxury apartments in Dallas typically are two-story affairs, well landscaped with an adjacent swimming pool. But a couple of decades ago, a Dallas builder got the idea of a New York-style luxury high rise condominium with secured garage. That became Aunt Sara and Uncle Ben's final address.

Before reaching their apartment, it was necessary to pass the inspection of a concierge and proceed through a formal lobby with polished marble floors, uncomfortable furniture and immense flower arrangements. With that done, you entered a music-playing elevator for the ride up. On a high floor, their apartment contained a magnificent living room, a spacious dining area, an enormous bedroom, a small den, a couple of redone bathrooms, a lovely terrace with a view several miles farther north, and a small kitchen where, naturally, nothing was seen on counter or tabletop.

By that time, Aunt Sara's collection of Imari and Lalique was complete and extensive. Each piece seemed to have been made for its spot in their living room. Like the kitchen, one might question whether the room ever was used. Cushions were always puffed up and plants shone as if they had been polished and arrived from the florist that afternoon. Even picture lights had their own sockets installed behind the pictures, so the wires and sockets wouldn't show. That's a setting easy to misconstrue. At times it seemed like a varnished painting, but those beautiful objects and their meticulous placement had meaning for Aunt Sara. That extended even to the books that were carefully arranged along built-in shelves. If you assumed that their covers had never been opened, you'd have been wrong. Aunt Sara had read everything in their library.

My parents' apartment, though far more modest, was a couple of minutes from theirs, and once my father had passed away, Aunt Sara and Uncle Ben often invited Mother out to dinner. If I happened to be in town, I'd be invited, too. We went to their country club or a seafood restaurant, always a place where they were known. We'd eat well, and Uncle Ben would leave a large tip. "I've spent a lot of money in my life," he remarked, "and I plan to spend a lot more."

"Being on top" isn't a permanent location, and both my aunt and uncle eventually suffered severe setbacks. Uncle Ben had a couple of strokes that left his speech halting and his reasoning and memory damaged. Jerry had to drive him to the office. "I'm not what I used to be," Uncle Ben once told me, sadly.

A sentence that started with perfect sense ended with nonsense. He would call me first by my name, then by my mother's name. A "she" would turn into "he" and "he" into "she." Nonetheless, if we went out to dinner, I saw him correctly verify the addition on the bill.

Aunt Sara was reported to be seen on the street, talking to herself. Then she took ill and went through cancer surgery, surprising everyone by surviving. "This life is not fun anymore," she confessed to me once, after they both were mostly apartment-bound. I offered to take her out for a drive, but she refused, because she feared that Uncle Ben would miss her. Even then, she wasn't so removed from the world that she didn't again inquire, "Don't you think you'd be happier if you were married, Stanley?" That idea was as close as anything she and my father had in common.

Coming from someone else, Uncle Ben's remark about having spent a lot of money and planning to spend a lot more, might have seemed insufferable. From him, it was a statement of satisfaction with himself, expressed in grand Texas style. No small amount of the money he spoke of was donated to organizations that work for the betterment of the Dallas Jewish community. His and my aunt's names are on several plaques around the city. Then, he did one thing more. Uncle Ben solicited donations for organizations from other wealthy Jewish men, the kind he knew and knew how to talk to. He sought and got large sums and fulfilled the Jewish notion that it's a still greater mitzvah (gift) to ask for money than to give it.

I like to think that Uncle Ben gallantly waited for Aunt Sara to die, before he could. That may be my fantasy, since his comprehension was limited and he was never told what happened to her. Uncle Morris, who respected Uncle Ben's success, said that 500 Cadillacs lined up at his funeral. One pallbearer was the first young employee that Ben and Sam and I.G. hired to work in the Ely Company six decades earlier.

I'm glad that in time I got past being intimidated by my aunt and uncle. The good that Uncle Ben did for Dallas Jewry spoke louder than even his panache. But I don't think my father ever saw him that way; though brothers, he and Uncle Ben may as well have come from different worlds.

I remember my aunt for her unquestionable love and understanding of things beautiful. Uncle Ben, I remember for words I often heard from him. "Do it right and tell the truth," he said. "If you tell the truth, you never have to try to remember what story it was that you told."

27

After Normandy—
Quietly Angry

When Aunt Fannie sold her half of the duplex on Normandy and took willing leave of Arthur's brother Harry and his wife Minnie, she settled into a modern one-bedroom apartment on Town & Country Lane, a mile north. It was the opposite of what she left behind: more plants but less furnishings, little silver, no loud family downstairs, no sick family upstairs. A little carport where she could park her Chevrolet. Her own name on the door. "I like to look out and watch people passing by, to see some life outside," she explained. "So I searched for somewhere facing the street."

Living by herself, Fannie struck up even more acquaintances with each trip to the bank or the grocery. She still hovered over Wade, making calls to help him find a job as a sportscaster, though she knew nothing whatever about that profession.

She also still loved traveling and would set out on a moment's notice for a trip, usually to visit Aunt Pearl, her sister in Mill Valley. "Sara, I have tickets for the San Francisco Ballet tomorrow," Pearl would call and say. "Can you make it?"

"Sure I can," Fannie would reply. "I'd call the airline," she told me, "take out my little bag and get on the plane. Pearl would meet me, and we'd go straight to the delicatessen across from the theater for a quick meal of matzo ball soup and blintzes."

By the time of this conversation, Pearl had passed away. But that didn't end my curiosity about her. "What did you think of Pearl living all by herself, up in those hills?" I asked.

"It was the most beautiful place I'd ever seen," Fannie said. "But I felt for Pearl. That wonderful setting didn't keep her from being a lonely person. She never had a husband, though goodness knows, that's no guarantee of happiness.

"There were times when she said cutting things to me, but I never said anything back, because we had so many good times together. We'd drive down to Monterey or Carmel and, you know, when we were young, we'd get in a car and go all the way from Dallas to Colorado by ourselves. I would never have had the courage to do that alone. But Pearl wasn't afraid of anything." The exception, according to Fannie, was men—perhaps because Pearl was just inexperienced. "Once when we were still in our early twenties, we stopped at a resort in Colorado, and that night a fellow asked me to dance. I said, 'Well, I have a sister with me, and I can't leave her.'

"He said, 'Oh, don't worry, I have a pal here.'

"Then he brought over a very nice looking young man, and the man said to Pearl, 'Can you dance?'

"She said, 'If you push me, I can.'"

I laughed hearing the sort of thing that sounded so typical of Pearl. "You two had plenty of nerve, young girls traveling by yourselves in those days."

"Yes," said my aunt, "and your mother didn't think much of it. One time we had a flat tire when we were somewhere on a deserted highway in New Mexico in the middle of the summer. An old Negro man came along, and we asked him if he could fix the tire. He seemed like a nice man.

"He said, sure, he could. As he was doing it, I started talking to him. 'What are you doing way out here?' I asked him.

"'Well,' he said, 'they let us out of jail once in a while, and we work on the roads.'

"I blinked and asked him what he did to get in jail."

"'They say I killed my wife, but I really didn't. I swear to you!'

"I scooted over to Pearl and whispered to her that the man was in jail for killing his wife. 'Well,' she said, 'let him fix the tire and we'll pay him five dollars and go.'"

"So you did?"

"Uh, huh. And we never told your mother about it."

"Good decision. You miss Pearl a lot today, don't you?" I asked.

"I always felt a connection to her that I never had with anybody else. I hope she's in heaven, making up for all she didn't have on earth. There were times when I was visiting her in Mill Valley and she was sure her friends liked me better than they did her."

"Did they?"

"Well, they shouldn't have. I wasn't nearly as smart as she was."

When a trip for Aunt Fannie wasn't real, she imagined it in her dreams. "Every night, I'd go to sleep and right away be off on a plane to California, or France, or wherever," she said. "The moment I fell asleep. To places I'd never been. Oh, how I loved to travel!"

▶▶▶

Into her seventies and even her eighties, still laughing like a southern belle and with skin that her friends envied, Aunt Fannie had a gentlemen or two calling for a date. The problem, according to her, was that they were the wrong ones. "I don't want to go out with old men, and end up having to take care of them," she stated. "I did that with Arthur. I want to go out with a young fellow—and go dancing."

It didn't work out that way. The ones drawn to her were the older men who sniffed her talent as a caretaker. Invitations came for dinners instead of dancing.

One caller was David Bern, a widower who decades before had been a neighbor of Fannie and Arthur's in South Dallas. Half deaf with a scant head of hair and in need of a cane, Dave at seventy-five was still a genial man with a broad smile and a lot of friends. His wife had died and left him in a low-slung house in the newer neighborhood of Preston Hollow, north of University Park. With no wife, no business, an only, unmarried son Jerry and no grandchildren, Dave hadn't much to do. Soon Fannie found herself getting regular calls from him. She tried to speak loudly enough that he could understand her.

"Becky," my aunt said one day, "guess what? Dave Bern wants to marry me!"

From the old days, my mother also knew Dave and Liala, his deceased wife. Reviewing the picture, she concluded that a match between her sister and Bern sounded not only better than Fannie being alone but maybe a step up over her marriage with Arthur. Characteristically, Mother sent forth a warning. "Where does he want to live? In his house?"

"I think so," said my aunt.

"You know what that place is like. See if you can get him to get rid of the things that Liala collected and sell the house and move to a nice apartment. If you don't, you'll never get away from her."

Aunt Fannie decided she would postpone the subject of moving until she and Dave were married, which they soon were. It was 1969, nine years after Arthur died. My mother gave them an elegant reception at home, with all the friends they had known since the early days in Dallas. "Your mother's party was the nicest moment of that marriage," Fannie told me.

It wasn't long before my aunt agreed with Mother about her new address. It was crammed with things that Dave's wife had bought and collected and never thrown out. "But Dave loved that house," Fannie said, "so I thought, well, if it means so much to him, I should try to like it, too."

Occasionally they'd go to my parents' for games of gin rummy. Other times a friend across the street would invite Dave to come and play cards in the evening, not bothering to include Fannie. She stayed home alone. "It reminded me of the days when Arthur went upstairs to Harry's," she said, angrily.

Finally, she did raise the issue of moving. "But we're so comfortable here," said Dave, perplexed. "If there's something you want, just tell me; I'll get it for you."

"Dave didn't understand," Fannie said. "It wasn't a question of not being comfortable, we just were never more than a breath away from Liala. What I wanted was less, not more. But I couldn't bring myself to tell him that."

Dave's son Jerry accused Fannie of marrying his father for his money. As if my aunt were ever so practical. "Jerry was wrong," Fannie stated. "If I had wanted to, I could have lived in that house the rest of my life and taken a lot of his inheritance. But I didn't want anything from his father—and I didn't get anything."

After a couple of years, Fannie confessed that the marriage was hard, and she missed having a place with her own name. "You know how much I like being with people," she told my mother, "but . . . well, I think I have to ask Dave for a divorce."

"Divorce?" my mother exclaimed, sending back a word virtually unknown among Jews of that time. "He's one of the most eligible Jewish men in this town! A lot of widows will gladly take your place." Fannie knew that was true. She told me later that many of them were jealous of her. Many thought she had married into millions.

"I know he's kind and he'd give me anything I want," Fannie said to Mother. "Anything except a different place to live. You warned me about that before we were married!"

After three years of marriage, Fannie asked Dave for a divorce. Though he found it difficult to understand why, he agreed. Initially, his son Jerry was relieved. Soon thereafter, Dave remarried again, to a widow also known from days past. His third wife voiced no objection to Dave's house or the furnishings, in fact started multiplying them with more items of her choice.

"Maybe then Jerry realized that I wasn't so bad for his father," Fannie said, wryly.

That marriage lasted even less than his marriage with my aunt, because Dave's new wife died, unable to make good on her plan to outlive him and enjoy an ample inheritance. By then old and frail, Dave had no choice but to give up the house he loved and move to Golden Acres, Mother's last home—and eventually, Fannie's, too. Since she was no longer a threat, Jerry would pick Fannie up and drive her to visit his father. "Dave and I became better friends after we were divorced," she recalled. "From his wheelchair, he said he still loved me—even after another marriage. I think that was because I was the only one he could understand. He was so deaf he never knew what anyone was saying!"

After Dave died, my aunt said that divorcing him was the biggest mistake she ever made. "He was the only one who saw me as anything more than a pretty helper. Aside from leaving that house, there was nothing he wouldn't have done for me. I should have been satisfied with that."

▶▶▶

Finished with college at the University of Oklahoma, Wade moved to Annapolis to take a job as a local sportscaster. He had not been a star athlete or an athlete at all, but he had a vast knowledge of sports and a willingness to work hard. One year he was named sportscaster of the year in Maryland, but the job led nowhere.

While in Annapolis, Wade fell in love with Alice, a pretty, blond, strong-willed girl from a close-knit Baptist family in West Virginia. He told his mother that he planned to get married.

"Wade," she asked, "have you met her family?"

"Yes," he said, "but what does that matter? I'm not marrying her family."

"I remembered Harry and all the Feldman's, Arthur's family," Fannie said. "'That's what you think!' I told Wade."

Alice had been raised by her grandmother, an especially devout Baptist, and Fannie tried to do her a favor by helping her down the aisle at Wade and Alice's wedding. Fannie said that the grandmother nearly hit her to get her away. "Wade and Alice don't dare to leave out a bottle of wine if the mother or grandmother are around," she added. "I don't know how they ever agreed to let Alice marry him."

Maybe, I suggested, Alice did it without her family's agreement.

"Or maybe they thought all of us Jews are rich," said my aunt. "Little did they know how un-rich I was!"

Wade and Alice had a daughter and then a son, and since Wade didn't care or didn't say if he did, there was no question about the religion in which they would be raised. Finally, Wade and his family moved to Texas, where there was more opportunity for work. His children enrolled in schools and became converted Texans. Fannie gave them whatever money she had.

By then my aunt was living in another small, sunny apartment. Like my mother, she finally had to give up her car, the old Chevrolet she would have fixed year after year. Like my mother, she started to depend on friends to pick her up for card games. And like my mother's friends, hers began not to show up. "If I could only get out in the car," she'd say, angrily, "I'd find another job. Or go back and volunteer at the hospital. That's what I'd like to do!" I tried to remember what volunteer work she had done, but there hardly was any.

In 1993, past ninety, Fannie suffered a severe heart attack. I was on a trip to France and called Uncle Morris several times, expecting to hear that he had just returned from her funeral. She surprised everyone and lived on.

But the doctor ordered her to no longer be alone, and reluctantly she moved in with Wade and Alice, who had rented a large house in one of the burgeoning suburbs north of Dallas. Though they gave her the largest bedroom and bath, and Morris supplied her with an immense television set, she was angry at having been forced to give up her apartment and said so.

The person left to placate her was Alice. By then Fannie and her daughter-in-law seemed to have become close friends, because if I went by, I saw Alice patiently playing cards with her in the afternoon. For a couple of years Alice even postponed a trip to see her family in West Virginia.

But she paid a price for being assigned the role of caretaker of a frail, unhappy mother-in-law: she soon suffered a stroke. Uncle Morris interceded and they (all except Fannie) decided that it was time that Aunt Fannie move to Golden Acres.

▸▸▸

And there, in my mother's footsteps, she went. Having saved only a diamond ring, Fannie couldn't afford a large room or suite. She ended up in a small studio where the view was not of an active street, which she liked, but of the brick wall of another section of the building. A visitor found her drapes mostly closed.

I had encouraged my aunt to go to Golden Acres long before, figuring that friendly as she was and starting out there with a few people she knew, she'd quickly meet everyone else and have them all as friends. I was wrong.

When Fannie moved in, she was assigned to a small room with another woman until single rooms for both of them became free. Mrs. H., her roommate, required an oxygen tank always be nearby. She supplemented that with a bed pan for her convenience at night.

"Well, of course, I felt sorry for her," said my aunt, though she was even older than Mrs. H. "So, I started to watch out for her, to be sure she was okay. She was company for me."

Not surprisingly, Mrs. H. got to like my aunt, and so did her daughter. When single rooms became available and it came time to move, Mrs. H.'s daughter begged my aunt to move with her mother into a large double room. "I figured maybe I should do that," says Fannie, "since otherwise she'd be alone. I was about to say yes, when Louis, one of the residents here, heard about the plan and took me aside."

"What are you doing?" he asked Fannie.

"Well," she said, "I thought I'd move into a large double with Mrs. H. You know, she doesn't have anyone around to watch out for her."

"With all the nurses here?"

"Well . . . ."

"What about her daughter?"

"Her daughter doesn't come much."

The man looked at my aunt and paused. "Don't you have a son?" he asked.

"Yes."

"Where is he?"

"Ohh, he works long hours!" Fannie explained.

"Don't you have a couple of grandchildren here in Dallas?"

"Umm."

"Where are they?"

"Well, you know, they have their own lives. The boy just graduated from Texas A&M and got a good job. He's traveling a lot. The girl's about to get married."

"In that case," concluded Louis, "since you don't see much of your son or your grandchildren, you have to look out for yourself, don't you? You can't depend on them."

It was a comment my aunt didn't expect.

"That's what we *all* have to do here, Fannie," the man said, sternly. "Look out for ourselves. Not depend on children, or anyone else. That's what Mrs. H. will have to do. Meanwhile, you look out for you!"

Soon after that, Mrs. H. moved into a room alone, and my aunt moved into another.

Fannie said that Mrs. H. and her daughter were never friendly to her after that. "I'm still not sure I did the right thing," she added.

It was a warm October day, and my aunt and I were seated on an outside porch of Golden Acres as she related to me the story of Mrs. H. I hadn't been to the home since my mother died eight years earlier. Uncle Morris' original assessment held: Jews do know how to take care of their elders. The place stretched over several acres, with additional rooms, a lot of well-tended new shrubs and trees and a large, new sun porch facing the yard. The floors glowed with the reflection of whoever walked on them. Unlike many senior residences, the only aroma was of flowers. A good looking staff of nurses and custodians came and went through the building.

Familiar names, including some Elys, filled plaques as donors of rooms. The place gave the unmistakable impression of being if not joyful, orderly. And from the sign that greeted visitors in the parking lot, you knew that it was a home for the Jewish elderly.

In her middle nineties, my aunt finally looked old; the impeccable skin was still rosy but deeply wrinkled. The young girl's laugh had faded, and she was sad. "I think you made just the right decision," I said, taking her hand. "Why should *you* be the one who takes care of her?"

The sweetness that all my life I had associated with Aunt Fannie vanished, and she gave me a hard look. "Stanley, I have to do what's good for me," she stated, "and that includes trying not to be lonely. It's lonesome here! Wade doesn't come, Morris comes to make sure I'm alive, and stays five minutes. The grandkids never come. When Wade's daughter got engaged, she didn't even bring her fiancé to say hello or ask a blessing from me. They're getting married in a church, of course. It's miles from here, and I don't think they care if I'm there or not."

254

"But . . . " I started to say.

"See all these people here?" she exploded. "They may be friendly, but they're not friends. If I still had my car, I could get away once in awhile. But I can only get out when someone takes me—like you did today."

She had that faraway look that I saw in my mother, very old. But lacking the essential difference: acceptance. "It's a shame that Mother isn't still here to give you company," I offered, looking for something to say.

"Yes, but you know, I'm not sure whether your mother really loved me. Before Becky died, she marked pictures and things for everyone else, but not a thing for me. If you hadn't brought me that pair of fine lamps, I wouldn't have had anything of hers."

"Maybe," I suggested, "that's because everyone else rushed in to take something. You're the only one who didn't!"

The early dinner hour at Golden Acres was approaching, and I started to walk my aunt slowly back inside. "I know it wouldn't be your choice to be here," I said, "but you've had such a long, full life. I wish those memories gave you more consolation now."

"I wish so, too. Maybe the next life will be the good one. I *have* had a long life, but I'm not like my friend who was helped by the memory of her marriage. Thinking back on the past doesn't make me happy."

Fannie stopped and looked directly at me. Her thin body trembled a bit. "Don't let anyone tell you that getting old is fine, Stanley. I see myself in the mirror and think that I used to look pretty good. No more. I take no pride in getting to this age. I think I'm still young! Remembering the fun times I had when I was thirty—do they do me any good now? No. I want them still! When I see those handsome people on television, I think how lucky they are. They won't know the whole story until they've reached my age."

Another resident passed and she gave him her southern smile. "Good afternoon, Louis," she said, with a little bow of the head. And to me, softly, "That's the man who saved me from Mrs. H."

It was time to go. I bent over to kiss my aunt goodbye. "Please come back soon," said this woman I've known all my life, whom I suddenly saw retreating from the star role where I always placed her. She clung to my hand with her own cool, thin hand. "Thanks for listening," she said.

"But you're my family," I insisted, "one of the few who's left. And you've always listened to me. I don't need a thank you."

"It's you, dear, who's listened to me," she said, chuckling and briefly smiling that familiar smile, then taking her hand away.

As she pushed her walker, I watched her move toward the dining room for five o'clock supper. I turned toward the car, wondering whether that was the last time I would see my aunt.

It seemed so much like telling my mother goodbye all over again.

Back where I stayed at Uncle Morris', he asked how I found his sister. Because he assumed so much responsibility for her, I answered hesitantly. "Fannie seems a little . . . lonely at Golden Acres. I always thought she'd fit in fine there."

Morris turned to me with an unexpectedly firm glance. "Don't you know that Fan has been lonely all her life, Stanley?" he said in the tone of a statement more than a question. "Jealous of others, too!"

"No!" I said. "Lonely? With all that she's . . . well, no, I didn't know."

"She's doing as well as anyone can expect for somebody ninety-five," he added, turning to go upstairs, calling the conversation closed. "She's well taken care of."

Of course he was right. And that she was well taken care of was thanks more to him than anyone else. Then, what *should* one expect from someone ninety-five?

But, no, I didn't know any of that. Jealous? Lonely? As well as I've known her, how could I not have seen that?

Did it matter? Fannie was one who was nearly as present as my mother in the years I was growing up. Later on, she listened to me, loved to see me when I came to Dallas to visit, even seemed to come alive when I'd take her out and we'd talk. She was the one who maybe felt for my loneliness. The one from whom I learned the little I know about the Shapiros' lives in Russia.

256

▶▶▶

That visit did turn out to be my last with Aunt Fannie, because she died in March 1996, close to what was probably her ninety-seventh birthday. I was startled when Uncle Morris called me with the news. Fannie had lived so long that I seemed to have assigned immortality to her.

Morris reminded me of how, when Florence was first married and moved to Denver, a stranger came up and said that Florence reminded her of someone the lady knew from Dallas. It was Fannie Shapiro. "They were both such beautiful women," stated Morris.

As usual, it fell to my uncle to take charge of what needed to be taken charge of—arranging my aunt's funeral and her burial next to Uncle Arthur in the old Shearith Israel Cemetery. With Alice's help, he cleared out Fannie's belongings at Golden Acres.

Morris' visits there may have been, as she said, hurried, but his practicality didn't exclude sentiment. "This," he said to me after she died, "was the time of day when I'd call and tell Fan what programs were coming on television that evening."

For me, it's simply been hard to imagine Dallas without her. I think of her smile and the long talks we had during every trip that I made there, back even to the rides on the Forest Avenue streetcar many decades earlier. No one else took the special role Aunt Fannie played in my life. No one else could have.

28

They've Made Texas a Better Place to Live

Immigrants from places like Russia and Romania like to have fat children. If they do, they're stamped as successful. One look at those chubby offspring, and you know they had a good dad who worked hard and made money in the new world to do a lot of feeding.

I never cooperated in helping my folks cop that rating. At birth I weighed eight pounds and several nice ounces, but that was my only moment verging on fat. Afterwards, I didn't even exceed skinny, and everyone worried about it. Mother used to give the food-filled spoon a circular ride in the air before it landed near my mouth. Marietha sang upbeat spirituals as she offered me Cream of Wheat. But none of that worked, and the Romanian style eggplant didn't, either.

Food offered little appeal until I went away and allowed myself to discover in it the pleasure that everyone else knew about long before. My resistance to eating was a kid's unhappy power play.

University dormitory food isn't appetizing, however, and weight didn't get automatically added on in college, especially with the interference of cigarettes. Between my sophomore and junior years at Northwestern, our family doctor, who happened to be Aunt Sara's brother, dictated that I undertake a regime of concentrated peanut oil blended together with other foolproof fattening liquids. With the menu went an admonition that if I didn't gain some pounds, he'd consider putting me in the hospital. That was the summer I worked as the secretary's replacement at Shearith Israel, so along with walks through the park and forays into the men's room, I'd put a bottle of the brew in the synagogue's refrigerator every morning and force some of it down a couple of times during the day. Dr. Joe excused me from a hospital stay.

My father's idea that salt was good and pepper bad never seemed convincing to me. But the notion that fat was good and thin was bad had successfully penetrated my belief system. The first time I went for a medical check-up after moving to New York, I entered the new doctor's examining room with my head hung. "I know I'm awfully thin," I mumbled, apologetically.

"Thin?" he repeated, taking a close look. "Not too much. Anyway, that's healthier than fat."

Healthier than fat? Where did this man get his training? Would that hold true in Texas? Had Dr. Joe heard about it? I was twenty-four, and that nice doctor's statement came as a wonderful bolt of news.

▶▶▶

The facts about fat and thin *have* apparently reached Texas, since when I go back there now, I see a lot of tall, good-looking urban cowboys and cowgirls jogging along the streets after work.

Whether the news has gotten to my old friends, I'm not sure. Trips to Dallas are mostly to see family, and aside from them I call only my old friend Pauline and make an overnight trip to Mt. Vernon to see Tom.

When I do catch up with one or two of the old crowd, I indulge in the silly exercise of pondering how it is that they could have gotten so much older when I haven't. That's an exaggeration, of course, but not altogether untrue. I haven't had the responsibilities of raising children. Neither, however, am I consoled while getting older from the pleasure they're reaping from having grandchildren.

Turning the corner into the later years, I discover that I hate aging as much as Aunt Fannie or Cousin Ann or Florence did. An obsession to stay young—to look young—to take on as formidable an opponent as Nature—seems to permeate our family, as card playing did. Unlike cards, in which I did not participate, this narcissistic trait has roped me in. It tends to make me glamorize past times more than they deserve.

If I don't seek out the fellows I first met when we were about to move from South Dallas to Stanhope, it's not for dislike or because the memories are bad. Just the opposite, in fact. Their lives and mine have unfolded in such different directions since then, and for so many years, that it would be impossible to recapture that erstwhile closeness. Their friendship and approval meant a lot to me in the University Park and early college years, and I like remembering them—and myself—as we were then.

▶▶▶

I find myself with a twinge of envy for those Jews who, like my mother, find solace in the prayers and congress with fellow Jews, traditions that have sustained our people through so many centuries of trials. Better Jews than I, they understand why the Torah is the only thing that our people ever have crowned.

My old Dallas friends are late-twentieth-century Jews, living now in air-conditioned, comfortable homes. They attend services and hold weddings at Conservative Shearith Israel or Reform Temple Emanu-El or, to my surprise, one of four Orthodox synagogues that have been erected and still flourish in fashionable North Dallas. (Orthodox Jewish women can even participate in the ritual cleansing of a mikvah in the middle of a wealthy residential neighborhood.)

Where our parents became leaders of the synagogue or a local Hadassah in their day, my friends have undertaken those roles today. And they've done a good job, perpetuating the traditional concept of Jew helping Jew. If new immigrants reach Dallas from Europe or the Middle East, facilities are in place to ease their arrivals, including classes to help them learn English. Jewish schools and study groups for every age thrive. Golden Acres, supported by private donations, is recognized and emulated as one of the best senior homes in the country.

A lot of those services take capital, and a lot of Dallas Jews open their purses to furnish it. Like Uncle Ben, my generation may show off with costly affairs at the country club, but they donate generously for the well-being of their community as well.

Those facts help one forgive the Jewish family so rich and fearful of robbery that they bought an old police car and leave it parked outside their home, or the one that hid their Christmas tree in the back of their house, so Jewish neighbors wouldn't see it.

▶▶▶

Though the old concentrated Jewish neighborhoods of South Dallas have long since faded, Jews still mingle with Jews. But they remain largely unseen, except by each other.

So say a gentile couple, friends of mine who moved to Dallas from New York City in 1994. According to them, the estimated 38,000 Jews who lived in the greater Dallas area in 1996 formed an unobvious minority of the total two million or so who inhabited the same area. "Jews in Texas seem a lot more low key than the ones in New York," claim my gentile friends. "They stand out a lot less. There aren't any obviously Jewish neighborhoods."

Are there other differences between Jews in Texas and those in the rest of America? Yes. It's the dual citizenship. My father had it. So did Uncle Ben. And Uncle Morris. Not just to Judaism do Texas Jews pledge allegiance; it's to Texas, too. In 1980, the Texas Jewish Historical Society was founded "to preserve and disseminate the history of the Texas Jewish experience." In 1996 that organization had 750 family members. If the Texas Rangers are playing a late season baseball game that happens to coincide with Yom Kippur, you shouldn't be surprised to discover a discreet pocket radio accompanying the prayer book into services.

The unique combination of qualities that Jews bring to Texas—the drive and tendency to showiness and, on an equal plane, the sense of community service and loyalty—has made it a better place to live.

Aunt Sara and Uncle Ben, c. 1970

Stanley in Santa Fe, 1991

Epilogue

29

Is There a Happy Ending?

"One shouldn't get married, indeed one shouldn't. It's a bore."
Andrei Prozorov, "*Three Sisters*," Act II
Anton Chekhov

If I'd taken note of Andrei's statement forty years or so ago, I'd have thought that there was a frustrated and unhappy man, and wrong as well—even if he was a sort of hero of the literature I loved. What else should a guy do, a fellow of good Russian background—which could mean me as well as him? Get married.

But for me to prove Andrei wrong—and do what I had been indoctrinated to believe Jewish boys ought to do—would mean eradicating those increasing and very troubling desires for men. My dating with girls may have been frequent but never wholly sincere. So I went into therapy soon after moving to New York.

The plan my analyst laid out was unlike that of others I've heard of. She never included conversion to heterosexuality as an objective for me. A person has a right to do whatever it is that makes him happy, she believed and frequently stated. "Sometimes people undertake therapy not to change but to enjoy whatever they already are," she said. "If so, that's fine."

I rebelled at what I heard. "Well, that's not for me!" I countered. "I'm here to change!"

"Okay," she said, gently. "Let's see."

Months went by and with them the slow, reluctant recognition of how

I'd kidded myself. There was a summer in the late fifties when I shared a house with several other guys in one of the straight communities on Fire Island. One evening, with our dates, we took a beach taxi to Cherry Grove, then the main gay area on the island. In the bar, the handsomest collection of men I'd ever seen were dancing with each other, an image that left me changed and shaken. So, my pronouncement to the therapist was as dishonest as the times I played the sweet conciliator while busting to be "King of the Mountain," a deceit that must have been apparent and especially grating to Florence and Jerome.

Some people may rejoice in an overnight epiphany of their homosexuality, but not me, not even after the night in Cherry Grove. To dare enjoying being gay has been a long process, maybe, for completion, a lifetime. In doing so, I had the support of a wise and compassionate therapist.

In time, the institution of marriage also took on a different hue that made me think that Andrei Prozorov might not have been wrong. That was in part because my mother, unlike my father, didn't pressure me toward the altar—and, I suspected, not just because she came to accept my homosexuality. Like Andrei, perhaps she found that her own marriage didn't bring the lasting joy or companionship that story books promise. She seemed to sense that possibility even before she met my father. "Sometimes it is rather hard to make life like you would like it to be," she wrote as a teenager to Rose, her friend in Houston.

Oddly enough, she believed that I could. "Stanley," she used to say, "if something is important enough to you, you usually figure out how to get it." If her theory bore any truth, independence has been more necessary to me than a relationship, since I've remained the most stubbornly unattached bachelor.

Once past denying my orientation, sex with men turned me into a dependent who cried out for constant attention. But it didn't lead to love. Came the days when I complained about the ease of finding a partner for sex but frustration in finding one for more than sex. "Those men are there, too," I heard the therapist say. "You just don't want to see them."

I guessed that she was right because I knew men, including a few on the plain side of dreary, who were never without a suitor. Let one depart and by the end of the month a replacement was knocking at the door, hair combed, bouquet in hand.

That's certainly not been my story. If in recent years I've not been pursued romantically by a suitable gentleman, it's possibly due to radar from me signaling that I'm not much of a candidate for more than sex, one-sided at that. Yet, I've clung to my freedom even while lamenting the absence of a mate. "Stanley," a friend pointed out, "maybe it isn't the marriage you want, maybe just the honeymoon."

Lately, though, I've become more eager to know whether Andrei was right, at least if his remark is applied to marriage within the same sex. In what may be nearly old age folly, I've joined a couple of gay dating services and placed personal ads in gay newspapers.

They've produced strange intersections. I've met dozens of people, some good, some bad, some truthful, a few deceitful, some who really might prefer going to bed with women, some who (like me) chop a few or quite a few years off their age, some with whom you spent nearly the most wonderful evening of your life (possibly including sex) and then never see again, some of 250 pounds who describe themselves as slender, some whom you like who don't like you and who like you but whom you don't like, leading to the not-infrequent thought of "why did I ever get started with this and I'd rather just stay home and play with my cat."

Yet, for now, I keep dating. That's because in the dark of night, I'm still not sure if Andrei was right.

▶▶▶

While going forward, I sometimes feel as if I'm simultaneously pedaling backward. On a couple of recent trips to Chicago, I paid sentimental visits to Evanston to indulge in reverie and amble around the campus at Northwestern. Long decades after living there, those buildings and walks and green lawns stay in my memory as the scene of sheltered and carefree years, the time when I started to leave geographical and social boundaries behind.

It looks so different today. There's a costly landfill that extends the campus well out over what used to be water. Sargent Hall, which in my day stood at the very banks of Lake Michigan and where I felt the winter wind and cold whipping through the hallways, now sits a couple of football field lengths back from the lake. The building's shiny newness has long since been tarnished from decades of use by college boys and girls residing therein.

But Sargent was the home of the Tong and for me the birthplace of great friendships, thus an important destination on my latest visit to the school. In the lobby I struck up a conversation with a current resident, an attractive young man shepherding his books and bicycle inside.

"You know, I lived here when Sargent was brand new," I said, smiling and nearly apologetic.

Silence. The young man looked at me with the kind of amazement that breaks out when one comes upon a medieval manuscript. "Brand new!" I saw pushing itself into his mind. "Wow!" was what he said.

▶▶▶

I was recently reminded of those early days when (on yet another blind date) I met a man of about age fifty who moved to New York five years ago. "I still don't feel as if I belong here," he said, wistfully. "I work hard and rarely have time to meet anyone."

"You're at a disadvantage," it suddenly occurred to me to say, thinking back to my own experiences: the dinner with Jerome and that first look at Greenwich Village, the excitement of moving east, securing a job and renting my first apartment on Horatio Street. "The time to move to New York isn't when you're forty-five, it's when you're twenty-five," I stated. "The time to come here is when everything is new—and everyone is new and looking for friends."

"That's right," the man agreed. "I became a grown-up somewhere else. I don't even feel as if I've brought all of me here."

He struck a note that I understood. New York is where I've mostly become me, and I leave part of it behind when I go to visit in Dallas. It isn't that anyone there tells me to, but it happens. Some of the full three dimensions of me stays back, and at those moments there's a signal that Manhattn is where I belong.

"Yes," I said to the man, sympathetically, "by the time you're forty-five, you're pretty well set, but so is everyone else, and it's harder to make friends. They've mostly already been made."

He smiled in polite agreement, and it occurred to me that even then I was belying my statement. What else was I doing, talking to him, if not setting out to find a new friend? Maybe the guy decided I was nuts, since I haven't heard from him.

▶▶▶

It's early 1998, and a couple of months ago I splurged and threw myself a nice sixty-fifth birthday party. It was pretty nasty, how fast that birthday came, but I was up to it, more or less. So many thoughts raced around my head—how commonly, for instance, gay men of my age weep at having grown up in a time of such conformity. We had no gay liberation. "Young guys enjoy so much freedom these days," say my peers, wistfully. I've said it myself.

The truth is that I grew up in exactly the age that suited me. I needed those teenage parties with the faux living room snowman as much as the denial and sex with men I didn't allow myself, that I've been making up for ever since. Sex life got postponed, allowed to enter with the slowest of steps. There was no other way.

If the same me were young in today's freer world, I think I might be even more torn than I was when I was young.

Still, it's a mixed blessing for someone who was always the youngest to suddenly hit a birthday that grants him half-price subway fares. Happy for the savings but disturbed at why they're there, I find myself looking unkindly at others no older than me. That doesn't make me feel good, and it's not the only shortcoming I see when I look in the mirror. Here I am, the frequent peacemaker with a still frequent appetite for conflict, the tidy housekeeper with a decided taste for trashiness.

Until I discover a better solution, I'm left trying to embrace those contradictions.

Getting ready for that birthday party, I also chuckled to realize that so much of what has happened to me occurred in such unplanned ways, all the more so given my obsession for being organized. Past the age of about sixteen, when I obstinately started talking my way into going off to college, so many turns in my life have arrived by accident.

Perhaps Jerome's prediction that we would succeed as "quiet adventurers" has proven true.

▶▶▶

Free of full-time work, HIV-negative by dumb luck, the person that became me is long since settled in an apartment with my own choice of art work and mixture of Oriental and American furniture, a place visitors often call comfortable. Occasionally teaching, frequently exercising, trying to cement relationships with friends and nieces and nephews, my days hurry by. In December 1997 I put to sleep Kid, my Burmese cat. It was the sad end to a seventeen-year relationship.

The hard, courageous work of making life freer for gay men was done by others over the past three decades. As for me, I'm finally a gay man for more than sex. An active supporter and worker for a prominent lesbian and gay health clinic in Manhattan, I try to carry on the Jewish tradition of service— to my community. And my straight friends and relatives no longer get protection from my denial and shame.

On a visit to Dallas in the fall of 1996, I stopped by the local AIDS Resource Center where a program I head is sending books as gifts for HIV-positive clients. One of the center's executives told me that it receives no funding from the City of Dallas. And though the Dallas Public Library maintains a lesbian and gay archive, it's turned over for housing to the local Gay & Lesbian Center. "They can say they gather the material," observed the executive, "but that it doesn't dirty their own building."

No, I thought. Can that attitude still pervade my home town? If Dallas wants to fit into its niche as one of the ten largest U.S. cities, its mentality has to catch up to its size. Texans are good at knowledge of history. It's time for them to note that the 1950s are history.

For me, too.

▶▶▶

I seem fixed these days on visits to burial grounds, with speeches delivered to those who are gone.

Reaching the Shearith Israel Cemetery every time I'm in Dallas, I seek out the familiar plot under a cluster of live oak trees where I know I'll find the handsome white stone that marks my parents' graves.

The Kaddish done in rusty Hebrew, I lay some flowers on my father's side of the grave. I apologize for not having acknowledged his good—his simple decency and loyalty to family—along with his pettiness. Some interpret the Passover holiday as an exaltation of the freedom that God desires for man. I remind myself that all the things my father didn't teach or do for me had surely to do with the fact that freedom of most every kind was rarely his.

He may be surprised to hear me thank him for providing a home with, I see now, a significant absence of corruption and greed. Those points elevate our family high on the charts.

All this has to be conveyed, of course, in a one-sided conversation whose chances of being heard are far from certain. But I'd like to think that he hears me. If so, he'll also get a plea to release me from the need to imitate and please him, a wish misplaced, of course, since I know that's my job, not his.

With my mother, I request another early evening walk in the neighborhood around her apartment. Those were quiet, intimate times when the façades were gone, when understanding was the agenda. I might question why she did so little to help reconcile my father and me; on the other hand, I'd reminisce about when she bade me goodbye and, at seventeen, I packed that footlocker and left her and my dad for the initial, scary train trip to college so far north.

Mother probably already knew—and later I also realized—that that was the essential crossing of the ocean for me. Maybe her refusal to look back to Russia helped her to understand my need to go away to school and eventually to assign Texas—and who I was in Texas—to my past.

It pleases me to let her know that she is remembered through Elissa's daughter, named Rebecca, born in January 1997. Rebecca makes the fourth great-grandchild whom I know my mother would love to sing to and play with.

When I leave a flower or two on Aunt Pearl's grave in Dallas, I thank her for her example of forging a life away from Texas. I let her know that I realize now the price of loneliness she surely paid in exchange for the independence she valued.

If I were to go to Denver, I might pass by John's grave, but I'd take time to tell Florence how profoundly I regret not having had the courage, while she was well, to talk with her about our fractured relationship. I'd try to lead her into an understanding of the homosexuality in me and especially in her son Arden. "It's okay!" I'd insist. "It's okay! Narrow-mindedness is unworthy of any of us.."

Once in a while I visit Jerome's grave on Long Island, set in the plot of Paula's family, far from our Texas roots. "It would have been easier for me if you had simply said that you weren't perfect," I suggest to my brother, years too late.

Still, when I think how many are gone—Mom, Dad, Florence, Pearl, all the Ely brothers and sisters and even their spouses, recently dear Aunt Fannie— I realize that Jerome was by far the most cheated. He went long before any of those others and much too young. It amazes me that I've lived more of my life since his death than before. "Forgive me my ambivalence toward you," I say at last to my brother, the first one to see me as an individual. "Just leave me with your love."

My niece Elissa and I both have a quirky affection for burial grounds. I like going because in those places I bring all of me and experience not just peace but clarity of feelings. It's easy for me to talk and cry at a cemetery, and I do so.

But there's something odd about my visits to Jerome's grave or the Shearith Israel Cemetery in old and deserted South Dallas: over the years each trip has been slightly different. Goodbye, I've discovered, rarely is goodbye. I say one "Rest in Peace" after another, but each comes out in a somewhat different key, with different feeling. Isn't that strange, I think? That the adieus never seem to finish and rarely seem to repeat?

Perhaps that gives hope for a kind of immortality.

▶▶▶